PEACE & PARSNIPS

VEGAN COOKING FOR EVERYONE

LEE WATSON

Photography by Alistair Richardson

MICHAEL JOSEPH
an imprint of
PENGUIN BOOKS

MICHAEL JOSEPH

UK | USA | Canada | Ireland | Australia
India | New Zealand | South Africa

Michael Joseph is part of the Penguin
Random House group of companies
whose addresses can be found at
global.penguinrandomhouse.com.

Penguin
Random House
UK

First published 2015
001

http://beachhousekitchen.com

Set in Addison West Flat, Glypha, Lulo,
Revers and Funkdori

Colour reproduction by Altaimage, London
Printed and bound in Italy by Printer Trento Srl

A CIP catalogue record for this book is
available from the British Library

ISBN: 978–0–718–17951–9

www.greenpenguin.co.uk

MIX
Paper from
responsible sources
FSC® C018179

Penguin Random House is committed to a
sustainable future for our business, our readers
and our planet. This book is made from Forest
Stewardship Council® certified paper.

CONTENTS

For Sweet Jane
and my little family
(Carol, John, Laura and Paul)
and my big family (all of you). xxx

WELCOME TO THE
BEACH HOUSE

Introduction

Vegan cooking is all about creativity; it's full of surprises, new techniques and ways of using ingredients. Anybody can have a go at being vegan. I know that anybody can do it because I have – me, the mightiest nose-to-tail carnivore of them all, and look at me now. After leaving meat off my plate for the last five years, I've never felt more energetic, happy and healthy. Since then, I've made it my mission to travel the globe looking for new dishes, scouring food markets and hanging out with locals, and learning that vegan cooking is a global craze and always has been. Many of the recipes that I've collected here have been brought back to my home in Wales and served up at the Beach House Kitchen, where I do most of my cooking and write a blog at http://beachhousekitchen.com. The way we eat reflects so much about who we are, and vegan food puts a huge emphasis on amazing fresh produce, food bursting with vitality and a generally more peaceful approach to life.

There's so much more to vegan cooking than tofu and rubber-like nut cutlets. I'm going to show you, with minimal fuss, and plenty of accessible ingredients, how to make food that would satisfy both a fully-fledged vegan and someone new to the idea who is dipping their toe in the water. I'll be bringing the wonders of veganism into your kitchen, showing you new ways of preparing some of your favourite dishes. It will teach you to be resourceful – stews can be stuffed into roasted vegetables, soups can be made into sauces, smoothies can be thickened up and eaten as desserts; this kind of flexibility is the hallmark of a happy cook. There are recipes here designed to be rustled up in a hurry and others for more fancy occasions. The truth is, making delicious, varied, nourishing vegan food is easier than you thought.

More and more people are realizing that the way we are producing food, especially meat, is unsustainable. Veganism is the best way to protect our environment and the welfare of animals; even by cutting back on meat and dairy just once a week (or once a year!) you are making a very positive statement.

A vegan diet can fulfil your nutritional requirements, pack your belly with goodness and consistently boggle your mind with new culinary angles and diversity. You'll end up saving money, you'll feel healthier, you'll have energy, you'll feel satisfied and you may just save the world, one meal at a time! Why not feel good all the time? A vegan diet is a big stepping-stone to a brighter, lighter way of being.

The recipes in this book are mere guidelines – I am terrible at following rules. No matter how closely you try to follow a recipe, the dish will often alter and you will produce something unique, to be proud of and savoured.

Peace and parsnips,

Lee x

Eating from the soil, shoot or branch

'Nothing will benefit human health and increase the chances for survival of life on Earth as much as the evolution to a vegetarian diet.' Albert Einstein

For me, organic and seasonal eating are the most natural ways of acquiring the sustenance we need to live the lives we want to lead. All energy comes directly from the sun – without it, we'd struggle! Plants transform that energy into something we can live on, which is one of the coolest, if not the coolest, things about nature. I break it down like this: organic = perfectly natural, chemical free; seasonal = perfectly natural, vastly superior nutritional content. Both make a lot of sense.

I believe that we feel instinctively and know ourselves what foods do us good. Some people can eat loads of meat, dairy, gluten, etc. without any obvious issue, but eating high levels of these foods will affect us at some point in the long run. Sometimes these negative effects are subtle and do not always show immediately.

We are all unique, and therefore need to find a diet that suits us. Veganism takes experimentation, an open mind and a greater sensitivity towards sourcing and combining ingredients. I see choosing to eat plant-based food as the best experiment possible for your body! No dairy, no saturated fats, lower levels of gluten (which is almost indigestible); most food allergies are readily catered for, without a need to think twice about recipes.

Eating food that grows directly from the earth, fed by the sun, dangling from trees, does not seem like a bad way to approach food. Nature gives us ample plant-based foods to nibble on; in fact, nature has given us the perfect way to fuel ourselves with optimum, pure, high-grade wonder-fuel: this way is veganism. Our furry friends would agree.

Dynamic ways of consuming vegan produce to boost your system

Raw power!

Research has shown that living plants contain unique health-giving properties, special energy that is destroyed when foods are cooked or processed. Raw foods (meaning the food hasn't been heated above 46°C) are used by many doctors to restore the health of patients. Even eating a diet based on 50 per cent raw foods will have a huge effect; 75 per cent raw and you are flying! We still don't understand the exact relationship of the subtle energies contained in our bodies and those contained in 'living' foods but the positive effects they have are irrefutable. They encourage detoxification, improve cellular metabolism, heighten enzyme activity and generally restore and nurture the body.

Raw power = a more energetic, slimmer and healthier way of being.

Fermented food

Fermented foods are becoming ever more popular and their health benefits widely acclaimed. Fermentation is the process whereby ingredients such as cabbage and cucumbers are left to sit and steep until their sugars and carbs become bacteria-boosting agents that lift the immune system. We already consume plenty of fermented food: leavened bread, beer, wine, cider, yoghurt and, increasingly in the UK, sauerkraut and kimchi.

Seasonality

Spring

Fruit:

Gooseberries, apricots, mangoes (alphonso), blood oranges, rhubarb (forced)

Vegetables:

Asparagus, wild garlic, nettles, broccoli, peas, artichokes, spring onions, leeks, morels, rocket, purple sprouting broccoli, Jersey royals, chicory, celery, cauliflower, salad leaves

Herbs:

Chives, tarragon, oregano, bay, rosemary, chervil, flat-leaf parsley, thyme, dill, marjoram, coriander, basil

Foraging/Other:

Elderflowers (cordial), Viola odorata, wild garlic, hawthorn flowers and leaves (tea), nettles (soup, tea, etc.), burdock, dandelion leaves, morels, St George's mushrooms, seaweeds (May–June: sea lettuce, dabble locks, gutweed, kelp, pop weed, dulse, Irish moss)

Summer

Fruit:

Strawberries, crabapples, blackcurrants, raspberries, cherries, plums, peaches, blackberries, rhubarb, gooseberries, melons, grapes, pears, elderflowers, apricots, figs, damsons, redcurrants, nectarines, blueberries

Vegetables:

Chard, peppers, courgettes, runner beans, radishes, cucumbers, beetroots, rocket, aubergines, chillies, calabrese, chanterelles, asparagus, potatoes, sweetcorn, spring onions, tomatoes, samphire, peas, fennel, borlotti beans, broad beans, salad leaves, shallots, sweetcorn

Herbs:

Dill, oregano, rosemary, coriander, tarragon, mint, sage, marjoram, basil, bay, chervil, thyme, flat-leaf parsley, summer savory

Foraging/Other:

Borage, calendula, wild marjoram (oregano), courgette flowers, dandelion leaves, lavender, nasturtiums, blackberries, sorrel, sea kale, cranberries, blackcurrants, wild strawberries, sweet cicely, coriander, chamomile

Autumn

Fruit:

Blueberries, apples, plums, blackberries, cranberries, clementines, grapes, quinces, figs, pears, nectarines

Vegetables:

Swede, beetroots, aubergines, butternut squash/squashes, leeks, peppers, tomatoes, wild edamame, endives, mushrooms, courgettes, French beans, kohlrabi, rocket, spuds, onions, turnips, celery, Jerusalem artichokes, parsnips, kale, radishes, tomatillos, pumpkins, celeriac, carrots, fennel, cavolo nero (black kale), Brussels sprouts, cabbage (red, Savoy and white), sweet potatoes, lettuces/salad leaves, marrows, onions, pak choi

Herbs:

Basil, marjoram, mint, chives, oregano, rosemary, sage, flat-leaf parsley, thyme, bay

Foraging/Other:

Chestnuts, cobnuts, elderberries (chutney), blackberries, wet walnuts, chamomile, rosehip (cordial), sloe berries (for flavouring, gin mainly!), juniper berries (gin again, mainly), salsify, barberries (dressings), wild cherry (best for flavouring brandy), rowan berries (jam), hawthorn (tea), poppy (seeds), horseradish, heather, bilberries, redcurrants, dandelion roots (dried and roasted for coffee sub), chanterelles, ceps

Winter

Fruit:

Blood oranges, pomegranates, clementines, quinces, cranberries

Vegetables:

Butternut squash, cavolo nero (black kale), cauliflower, spuds, Brussels sprouts, leeks, celeriac, cabbage (red, Savoy and Hispi), watercress, spinach, kale, broccoli, turnips, parsnips, onions, Jerusalem artichokes, chicory, swede, salsify

Herbs:

Rosemary, bay, sage

Foraging/Other:

Sweet chestnuts, hazelnuts, walnuts, Viola odorata, chanterelles, oyster mushrooms, field mushrooms, ceps

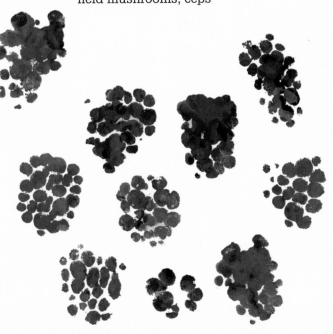

A very meaty problem

'If anyone wants to save the planet, all they have to do is just stop eating meat. That's the single most important thing you could do. It's staggering when you think about it. Vegetarianism takes care of so many things in one shot: ecology, famine, cruelty.' Paul McCartney

My 'veganity' didn't just sprout from my love for nutritious and super-tasty food, it was also an ethical decision: I decided that the way the large-scale meat and dairy industries were treating the animals in their care was just not acceptable. Animals were suffering to put cheese in my sandwich, and that was enough to turn me off dairy for good.

The meat industry is now a larger contributor to climate change than the entire transport industry. Going vegetarian is one big step in the right direction, but going vegan is a giant leap of positive intent. Veganism moves us forward in the way that we co-exist with our planet. The more people who choose to eat vegan meals more regularly, the greater opportunity we have to stem the tide of pollution and disruption to nature and the greater hope we offer to future generations.

Eating meat is tough on the digestive system. It requires digestive juices high in hydrochloric acid to break it down. The stomachs of omnivores (humans) and herbivores produce a twentieth of the acid produced by carnivores. The body is not naturally disposed to eating large quantities of meat.

This sounds quite gross, but meat decays and becomes toxic when dead and it rots within our bodies, releasing putrefaction poisons. This is the process that our body goes through every time we eat meat. Carnivores are designed with a much shorter digestive tract than humans – they basically expel their dinner much quicker than we do. Like humans, non-flesh-eating animals have a digestive tract twelve times the length of their bodies; carnivores have a digestive tract only three times the length of theirs. Carnivores also eat their meat raw, and humans prefer it cooked. Cooking meat (and vegetables for that matter) decreases the natural enzymes that help true carnivores digest their meat. This leads to the pancreas being put under pressure to produce more digestive enzymes, so that it eventually becomes weak and overworked.

Meat has a toxic effect when we digest it, which the liver must try to cope with. Generally the livers of meat-eaters are forced to work much harder to extract poisons from the blood than those of vegans. This is just one considerable example of the increase in the likelihood of disease and potential organ failure that regular big-time meat-eaters face.

Carnivores are also experts at digesting huge amounts of animal fat and cholesterol without a great number of adverse effects. We all know the dangers of furry arteries, strokes and the like; these conditions are a direct result of eating too much saturated animal fat. Cut that out and you'll have a healthy ticker. Putting it into numbers, vegetarians, on average, have 14 per cent lower cholesterol than meat-eaters, which equates to half the risk of serious heart disease.

That was morbid, but important for me to get off my chest. I care about the health of my family, my friends … in fact all of us. I hope this has put part of the ethical, non-meat approach into some form of context. A no-meat or low-meat diet equals a hugely better world for all of us. Choosing to leave meat off our plates has huge implications. Also, health-wise, vegan vs. meat can only have one undisputed champion.

Jane with our neighbour Dawn's chicken Pinky. Perky is just out of shot!

Food Myths

1. **MYTH:** Vegans struggle nutritionally and are generally skinny, weaklings.

FACTS: *There are vegan body-builders, big beefy folk who pump iron (if you're into that). There are also millions of vegans around the world living very healthy lives. With a little nutritional information (all contained in this book, I may add), a vegan diet can provide the body with all it needs and probably more! People who take the plunge and give a plant diet a go generally feel lighter, imbued with greater energy levels, with shinier hair and skin, sparkling eyes and . . . you get the picture. They feel pretty damn good.*

2. **MYTH:** Fats make you fat.

FACTS: *Almost complete nonsense. Fats (with the exception of some saturated fats and the alien hydrogenated fats) are essential for the maintenance of a healthy body, especially relating to the nervous system and brain, which are, of course, very sensitive and best looked after.*

Sugars are generally what pile the pounds on. You have to eat high levels of fats, many handfuls of cashews, before the body begins to think of storing these fats as bottom bulge.

3. **MYTH:** Meat is the best source of protein/vegans don't get enough protein.

FACTS: *Plants are packed with protein and a balanced plant-based diet provides all the proteins needed to conduct a healthy and happy lifestyle. They're guilt-free, ethically clear and easily digestible. The body thrives on plants, the body buckles and stutters on meat.*

Here are the facts, produced by men and women in white coats: ➡

Studies have shown that people who eat a plant-based diet have a lower BMI (Body Mass Index), lower cholesterol and lower blood pressure. Plant proteins are lean, so you will be ingesting considerably lower levels of saturated fats.

Quinoa and soya provide what is called 'complete' protein, which means that all our amino acid needs are catered for. Eating a balanced veggie diet will always fill in the protein blanks left by 'incomplete' proteins.

Most of us actually eat too much protein, and this excess cannot be broken down properly by the body and is turned into toxins. It has been said recently that eating too much protein is as bad as smoking, especially if those proteins come from animal sources. In middle age especially, it is better for our health to eat a lower-protein diet.

So the question is not how do we get more protein into our diet, but how do we eat a reasonable amount that will not harm our health? We need much less protein than we have been led to believe.

4. **MYTH:** Milk is the best source of calcium.

FACTS: *Milk is not the elixir of life we thought it was. We need milk for a while – as a baby it's essential. After that, we can drop the bottle and pick up the leaf or berry with no detriment to our health (see page 45 for more info on dairy nutrition).*

Good sources – there are plenty of very rich sources of calcium, even richer than the mighty milk! Kales, rocket . . . green leafy veg in general, sesame and tahini, white beans, bok choi, molasses, oranges, okra, broccoli, sugar snap peas, almonds, wholewheat grains, pulses, dried figs and other dried fruits, seaweed, tofu (calcium set).

5. **MYTH:** Orange juice is the best source of vitamin C. ➡

FACTS: *Here is a list of fruit and veg that contain higher levels of vitamin C than oranges: Papaya, peppers, broccoli, Brussels sprouts, pineapple, strawberries (most berries, in fact).*

Other great sources are: kiwi, tomatoes, cauliflower, cabbage, grapefruit, parsley, spring greens, spinach, sweet potatoes.

6. MYTH: We have incisors and we know how to use them.

FACTS: *When was the last time you saw a human fell a wildebeest on the hoof? Our incisors are only wee, and all physiological evidence would suggest we are omnivores at best. Our teeth are generally quite flat, better for grazing than for tearing at legs of meat.*

7. MYTH: Eggs are essential for vitamin B12, thiamine, niacin, riboflavin and the other B vitamins.

FACTS: *Egg yolks do contain some quite special things, but these can be found from other sources, even in glorious Marmite! The Bs are quite a complex bunch, generally helping our body's cell and nerve functions and metabolism. They include thiamine, riboflavin, niacin, folate (think foliage), B12, B6, biotin and pantothenic acid. A well-balanced diet will cover all these more than adequately: including plenty of green leafy vegetables, nuts, wholegrain cereals, fresh and dried fruit, rice, potatoes, capers, most spices, black pepper, bananas, asparagus and lentils.*

Vitamin B12 is a little tricky in a vegan diet, as it is normally contained only in animal products. Many tofus and whole grain cereals are fortified with B12, and our faithful friend, nutritional yeast flakes, contains B12. You will also find it in mushrooms such as chanterelles and ceps, and in some seaweeds like nori; spirulina is also a source. Some people even say that if you leave A little soil on your veggies, you obtain B12. This approach probably isn't for everyone.

➡

The evidence relating to the B12s is still quite contentious due to the way they are measured, and the many different scientific bodies around the work doing research all have their own opinions We need only a very small amount of vitamin B12 to be very healthy, but if you are thinking about becoming a full-time vegan, it's worth reading up on.

8. MYTH: Things just aren't creamy without cream.

FACTS: *Nonsense really. Tofu and soaked nuts/seeds, when blended, can give a very acceptable 'creaminess' to dishes that can even fool some non-vegans into thinking cows are involved. Nut milks are also a brilliant way of adding richness to a vegan dish.*

9. MYTH: Where do vegans get vitamin D and iron from?

FACTS: *Vitamin D is mainly found in animal-based foods, but there are plenty of sources outside the animal world. The plant world is blessed with many excellent sources of iron. Iron is best absorbed when combined with vitamin C. Worth bearing in mind!*

Non-animal sources for Vitamin D – The sun! Mushrooms (especially those grown outdoors; shiitake are best), fortified foods (cereals, soya drinks), and you may even look at venturing into supplements (if you don't like the sun and mushrooms). Check that vitamin D supplements come from lichen and not from animal sources.

Mushrooms can even be charged with sunlight after they're picked. Put them on a sunny window ledge for a day and this will boost their vitamin D content. In winter time in Britain, you may like to get your Speedos on and take a sun bath. Watch out for excess UV, but generally, blue and broad spectrum lights will give a real vitamin D boost.

Iron – pulses, wholemeal grains, sprouted beans and pulses, date syrup, molasses, green leafy vegetables, nuts, dried fruits.

The Vegan Larder

A vegan's larder is not that different from a non-vegan's larder, and most of these recipes are flexible and do-able, without difficult-to-find ingredients. You will almost certainly have the majority of these knocking about in your kitchen to start with.

I know that not all local shops stock all the ingredients in my recipes. 'Do you stock seitan?' will normally raise a few eyebrows down at the corner shop (I live halfway up a mountain in North Wales). However, with the advent of online food shopping, combined with a visit to your local health food shop and 'Asian' food stockist, none of these ingredients should be too tricky to unearth. Buying grains, seeds and pulses is always best done in bulk, if you have the space to store them. The outlay may seem like a lot at first, but when you break it down, it works out loads cheaper. I keep mine in large plastic containers or liberated (and well cleaned) plastic bins. Several co-operatives (like Suma) offer a delivery service for bulk orders, and it works well when a group of friends get together to order once every so often. These co-operatives may also offer some of the more difficult to source vegan ingredients and you can kill two peanuts with a potato.

Some 'speciality' ingredients are superfluous to a balanced vegan diet. If you have a decent selection of veggies, fruits, pulses and nuts, you are well on your way to vegan-hood.

I tend to gather odds and ends when I see them at local markets or in shops. My larder grows organically from little gems picked up on travels, such as spices or herbs from a certain region, and most have some sentimental value. Some people bring back silk scarves and jangling trinkets from holiday, I return laden with spice mixes and cocoa beans. This kind of providence can only add to the magic and enjoyment of cooking and eating, bringing together so many disparate and wonderful ingredients, transforming them into something completely new, harmonious and unique.

I am not going to go through the entire range of items for the 'ideal larder', as there is no such thing, but if you start with a core selection of spices and dried herbs you can branch out steadily. Each new recipe tried will normally add one or two new additions to your larder gang.

HUA HIN ON SEA

SANCERRE
GRAND VIN

Human Mandala

DENOMINACION ESPECIFICA

LENTEJA DE
LA ARMUÑA

LENTEJA DE LA ARMUÑA
CATEGORIA EXTRA
Peso Neto: 1 kg.

LEGUMBRES
MONTES

Grains

Grains are a cheap and plentiful way of filling ourselves up, and always have been ever since humans started wandering around the earth. However, there is much more to grains than just stodge, particularly if their natural nutritional properties are maintained and not processed away.

Buying whole grains is essential – anything polished should be avoided like a nutritional plague, as when grains are processed they lose much of their good bits, from vitamins to fibre.

Grains should be kept in big jars or containers, away from sunlight, and never left in torn plastic bags, exposed to harsh larder elements (air and occasional damp spells are no good for grains). Grains keep for an age if stored properly – we even have some leftover grains in clay pots from the Harapan civilization in northern India, circa 3500–4000 years BC! They knew how to look after their larders.

Most grains need a good rinsing before cooking and some will appreciate a little soak before cooking, but this does change the quantity of water needed and the cooking time, so soak with caution. All grains need slightly different cooking times and water quantities for best results, although covering them with roughly 2cm of water, bringing to the boil, popping a lid on, then simmering for half an hour was a general rule of thumb that I used throughout my student years. It never let me down, apart from one memorable voyage into black rice!

I like to use gluten- and wheat-free grains regularly, normally buckwheat and millet.

Barley – Whole barley is best. Pearl barley has been refined and has lost lots of its integrity and nutritional content. Barley is becoming increasingly popular as a substitute for, say, rice in a risotto (a farrotto!) – it's a full and very wholesome grain.

Buckwheat (gluten free) – Not actually a grain but a seed, buckwheat has a strong earthy flavour and is best paired with other big hearty ingredients. Buckwheat flour adds something a little different when added to baked goods, and makes a mean pancake.

Bulgur wheat – This is like a rougher, more nutritious cousin of couscous. It has been parboiled, meaning it takes only a short time to cook. Bulgur is used extensively in the southern Med and Middle East. For me, it's best served as a warm salad, with luxury adornments like almonds, dried apricots, herbs and spices.

Couscous – Made by rubbing wheat and flour together and parboiling. In some places in North Africa this is still done by hand. Couscous is a labour of love, a grain that is now a staple in the UK and rightly so. Very easy to cook, with a lovely light texture. You should always fluff up couscous with a fork, and I also like to add a glug of olive oil just before serving. It doesn't need much more!

Millet (gluten free) – This is another very nutritious grain and has been eaten in the UK for millennia – it's cheap to buy and makes a hearty accompaniment. Like buckwheat, millet is best roasted slightly before cooking, to lessen the stickiness. Its stickiness makes it ideal for forming vegan burgers and sausages.

Corn (gluten free) – Boasts plenty of nutrition and again, contains no gluten. Ground corn makes polenta and, like all grains, whole grain is best as it retains all the nutrition. Corn also has an awesome colour that brightens up the plate or bowl.

Quinoa (gluten free) – A high-altitude, super-nutritious grain (well, it's actually a sprout) that the Incas couldn't get enough of. Quinoa is a delicious and highly nutritious option, but the price and distance it travels means that I only use it on occasion.

Oats – Very rich in nutrients and good fats, oats actually lower cholesterol when eaten. We all know them as porridge, but they can be used as a coating before frying, in soups and stews, and make a great ingredient for baking (they add substance to all they touch). Gluten-free oats are readily available and are almost identical to the full-gluten varieties.

Rice (gluten free) – The Daddy grain. Most of the world lives on the stuff and they all cook it in different ways. Many people struggle with rice cooking, but it doesn't need to be taxing. It is actually very simple, and there are a couple of techniques that are foolproof (even I have mastered them!). I always cook basic, steamed rice in the same way and it never fails. Rice should always be washed before cooking – rinsed with cold water until the water runs clear. Brown rice is more nutritious and flavourful than white, but will take a little longer to cook. I normally keep brown rice (without it vegans wilt), red, black (if I'm feeling flush), wild, Arborio, jasmine and basmati rices. What can I say – I eat a lot of rice!

Semolina – A wheat-based grain. It is milled in a variety of grades which produce fine, medium or coarse. Fine and medium are good for pasta and for desserts like halwa, while coarse is normally made into couscous.

Tips for cooking grains:

- *Do not stir grains when they are cooking, it makes them mushy and sticky.*
- *Never remove the lid when grains are cooking, the trapped steam is what cooks the grains evenly.*
- *Add flavourings to your grains, i.e. stock, herbs, chopped onions, tamari, seaweed, etc., to give them an interesting edge.*
- *Always cook grains on a very low heat after initially bringing them to the boil. The slower they cook, the lighter the results.*
- *Leftover grains make perfect frying material. Pop them into the fridge, once cooled, and the next day they can be mixed with vegetables in a frying pan and transformed, with a little sauce, into a super-quick meal.*

Dried Beans, Pulses, Peas or Legumes…

Beans are powerhouses for lean plant protein and nutrients. Wherever these legumes grow, they actually enrich the earth with nitrogen and are therefore a very beneficial crop. Beans do need soaking and cooking properly, as they contain proteins that are hard for the body to break down (leading to bouts of whistling windiness), especially red kidney beans. Lentils and split peas do not need soaking, but do need washing before cooking. Sometimes I will soak beans and lentils just until softened and then blitz them into a purée. This is great for a twist on a pancake batter or for thickening soups and stews.

There is such a variety of beans on offer that I normally keep a few staples, like chickpeas, mung beans, red kidney beans and yellow split peas, and vary the rest as and when I need them for a recipe. Of course, it doesn't always work out like this, and you can end up with a kaleidoscope of beans in your larder.

Most beans and pulses take different lengths of time to cook, depending on variety, size, age and how dry they are. Just test them: if they're remotely 'chalky' between the teeth, let them simmer on.

Dried or tinned?

Dried. For me, always dried. You need to be a little bit ahead of yourself, as most beans need at least 6 hours soaking, and overnight is best. Dried beans are always cheaper and have a fuller texture.

Tips for cooking beans and pulses:

- *Soak all dried beans overnight, roughly 8 hours, in fresh cold water. They will expand to at least their original size, so always cover the beans with three times their volume of water. Little pieces of grit, stones or weird-looking beans may float to the top – remove them.*
- *Always preserve the cooking liquid from beans, it contains vitamins and bags of flavour and is ideal for soups and stews. I normally try to incorporate it into the dish involving the beans.*
- *Cooking beans and pulses on a low simmer will preserve their shape and texture. Do not add salt to the cooking water for beans: this will make the skins tough. Chickpeas and kidney beans foam when being cooked – just remove the foam with a slotted spoon.*

Below are some guidelines to how long different beans, peas and lentils should take to cook:

- *45 minutes–1 hour – aduki, black-eyed peas, haricot, red kidney beans, soya, mung beans (or less), all lentils and peas (red split lentils, think more like ½ an hour).*
- *1¼–1½ hours – black beans, chickpeas, flageolet, pinto, butter beans.*

NB – Check the beans by pressing one against the side of the pan with a spoon. If it's soft all the way through, it's cooked. I always like to nibble one, just to double check.

NNB – Stir salt into the pot just before the cooking time ends.

NNNB – If you'd like to cook your beans more quickly, add ½ teaspoon of bicarbonate of soda to the water. This will cut the cooking time by roughly a third.

INDICACIÓN GEOGRÁFICA PROTEGIDA

DENOMINACION ESPECIFICA

LENTEJA DE LA ARMUÑA

LENTEJA DE LA ARMUÑA
CATEGORIA EXTRA
Peso Neto: 1 kg.

tierra de sabor

LEGUMBRE
MONTES

Tierra
Guareña
CATEGORIA EXTRA

ENVASADO POR:
SOCIEDAD COOPERATIVA "LOS ZAMORANOS"
CAMINO VALPARAISO, S/N
Teléfono/Fax: 980 601 136
e-mail: cooperativa@loszamoranos.com
www.loszamoranos.com
49400 FUENTESAUCO (ZAMORA)

These are what I normally keep handy:

Beans – aduki, butter beans, red kidney beans, black beans, pinto, rosecco, flageolet, haricot, mung (whole and split), black-eyed beans, soya

Peas – chickpeas, brown chickpeas, split green and yellow peas, dried whole green peas

Lentils – green, brown, Puy and red lentils (I'll normally have a variety of indian lentils kicking around, but they are only recommended for the hopeless daal addict)

Soya bean products

I believe in the wonders of soya. Yes, there is bad soya. Parts of the Amazon are being chopped down to grow them, and they are then fed to livestock reared in the meat industry but generally, if we buy organic and fermented non-GMO (see pages 46–9) whole bean soya products, from reputable companies, there should be no problem. Most supermarkets now stock soya bean products.

Miso – Traditionally a fermented soya bean and grain product, miso has been produced for thousands of years in Japan and has a thick consistency and pungent aroma, ideal for flavouring soups, stews and sauces. Miso is naturally very salty. It is very rich in nutrients and vitamins and is good for calming the digestive system. The flavours of miso can range from nutty to winey and fruity. There are even some great people in Wales making some of the finest miso I have tasted (see Suppliers, page 338).

Tamari – Just like soya sauce, but always produced in a traditional and healthy way. It has more flavour than most soya sauces and, when used properly, accentuates the subtle flavours in food. It is also gluten free.

Tofu – Probably the ultimate vegan food, tofu is versatile and often misunderstood. Tofu loves nothing more than soaking up flavours and marinades, and boasts a whole range of textures that can complement any dish, savoury or sweet. That is part of its beauty: tofu can sneak effortlessly into a cheesecake, offering its wonderful smooth and rich texture and perfectly mingling with the flavours on offer. It has one of the highest levels of protein found in plant foods and is virtually cholesterol free.

Tempeh – Similar to tofu, but fermented. Tempeh uses whole beans and generally comes in jars, but can also be found, mainly in Asian food shops, in the freezer section. In this frozen form, I'd advise defrosting and steaming the tempeh for 10–15 minutes, which softens it a little and makes it more receptive to flavours. Then use as normal.

Seitan – This is a very meaty fella. Called mock duck by some, it is used throughout South East Asia to fool vegan tourists into thinking they're eating chicken! You can make your own seitan at home using a flour called Vital Wheat Gluten. It's dead easy. Having some VWG in your cupboard means that you can add real texture to veggie burgers and sausages and some swear by a couple of tablespoons in their bread. Seitan is the ultimate vegan trick up the sleeve, to impress people new to veganism. It's not just a crazy name for a food, but a delicious (dare I say it) meat substitute. Carnivore approved. It's basically pure gluten.

Pasta

Yes, have some. You already know your favourite shades and shapes and you know what I'm going to say. I like wholewheat pasta, etc., etc. Organic, etc., etc. Buy good stuff. There are also some pretty acceptable gluten-free pastas out there now, sans wheat. A simple plate of pasta, prepared with love, can change everything!

Tins, jars and cartons

I generally try to avoid tins. I know they are so much easier and sometimes cheaper, but the lining of tins is coated with all kinds of nasty chemicals that can enter the food. I'd always opt for jars or fresh.

Coconut milk – Unless you have a decent supply of fresh cocos, coconut milk is an essential larder superstar, adding smooth, plant-based creaminess to dishes.

Milk – Plant-based, of course. I keep soya milk as a staple, but also love almond and oat milk. Even lentil milk is interesting. You can milk most things nutty or pulsy (see pages 46–9).

Capers – I always have them lurking somewhere. Briny little buds that add so much piquant fruitiness to the fare, I don't know what I'd do without them. Once opened, stick them in the fridge.

Mustard – Dijon, wholegrain and English. The holy trinity of mustards can resurrect a sorry dressing and make it well nice.

Jams, marmalades and chutneys – As you begin to approach middle age, friends and family no longer seem to buy you strange gifts, but offer jars of jams, marmalades and chutneys. The perfect gift in my eyes. Of course they are heaped with sugar, but Sunday morning toast sessions are a must in the BHK.

Marmite – Love it or hate it (love it), vegans can actually get a little vitamin B boost from Marmite. It adds brilliant depth to sauces and stocks, but is best enjoyed off the end of a teaspoon.

Gherkins – Some call these cornichons, pickles, etc. I like gherkins. In fact, I love 'em. I eat them whole, my preferred late-night snack.

Pickled chillies/peppers – Called by many different names around the world, pickled chillies are a ready-made, ideal accompaniment to so many southern Mediterranean and Mexican dishes.

Margarine – In baking, it does add butteriness, which vegans can miss out on. Find a good brand and avoid anything with strange-sounding fats in it (see Suppliers, page 338).

Chipotle paste (or whole dried chipotle chillies) – I always have some of these tucked away and they're getting quite popular – even my local shop is stocking them. Super smoky and sweet, chipotle is the taste of Mexican cooking, used extensively in their soups, stocks and stews.

Sweeteners

Ethical, inexpensive sweeteners can be thin on the ground and normally cost a packet. But there are options. Sugar is of course the cheapest, but sugar is sugar is sugar, no matter how we swing it. It just ain't doing us any good. I like to used dried fruits to sweeten things, and Jane regularly laments my lack of sugary tendencies (she has a super-sweet tooth). I tend to use unrefined brown sugar to bake with, but admit that it will not produce as light and fluffy a cake as regular white granulated sugar.

Here are some sweeteners I use:

Unrefined brown sugar – Always look for organic fairtrade sugar if you can. Normally called soft light brown sugar, this is my staple baking sugar.

Brown rice syrup – This is my staple liquid, gooey-style sweetener. It's relatively cheap and has a delicious caramel flavour, ideal for dressings and cakes. It's also low GI and even boasts a few minerals.

Maple syrup – Lordy, lordy! What a thing. Delicate, evocative, fragrant, scrumptious, maple syrup is the sap of a tree from North America, particularly Canada. Spend a bit more on maple syrup and you will be rewarded – just a dab here and there will light up cakes and desserts.

Pomegranate molasses – Sweet and sour, something like a southern Mediterranean tamarind/citrus substitute. Used almost exclusively for a special touch with dressings, and adds a surprise element to marinades and stews.

Date syrup – I love to use this rich, dark sweetener in dressings and dishes that have an exotic flavour. Makes a very mean muffin.

Molasses – Dark as tar, its potent stickiness is used mainly in marinades – especially good in barbecue-style sauces and some sticky Chinese-style marinades. I also like popping it into bread recipes.

Jaggery – An Indian version of unrefined sugar cane juice. Very sticky, like a fudge. I absolutely love it, and this is my exception to my sweetness scepticism. I use it in baking and chais. It has a very strong flavour which can be a little domineering in the wrong place.

Muscovado sugar – Darker and stickier than soft brown sugar, muscovado is normally raw and unrefined, keeping all of that deep, dark molasses flavour.

Barley malt extract – Cheap and cheerful, with a lovely malted flavour. Great in hot, milky drinks, and I love it in bread. Not quite as sweet as sugar, agave, etc., so add a little more.

Apple juice concentrate – Organic is always best here. Good apple juice concentrate is amazing for adding fruity sweetness to bakes and dressings, and I even use it to flavour burgers and sausages.

Agave nectar – Made from the agave cactus (of tequila fame). Some regard it as a wonder sweet elixir, and some folk with sugar intolerances can get away with it.

Baking

Flours – Wholewheat (staple), unbleached white flour (for a lighter touch), spelt (for bread and cookies, lower in gluten), buckwheat (no gluten, but can have mad results when backed with), gram (chickpea flour, very healthy and ideal gluten-free replacement, with a strong flavour), rice (I use it mainly in baking, especially handy when making gluten-free bread), polenta (or cornmeal, ideal for cornbread and of course, for polenta, soft or baked) and rye (for bread . . . gorgeous, dark bread).

Baking powder and bicarbonate of soda – The main difference between these two is that baking powder makes things rise when paired with acidic ingredients, like lemon juice or vinegar. Bicarb is generally a better all-rounder, releasing carbon dioxide when combined with moisture, i.e. in soda bread. I always have both. I also brush my teeth with bicarb of soda, mixed with tea tree oil.

Vanilla extract – Costly, but lasts ages.

Nut extract – Almond and hazelnut normally do the trick.

Booze – You may need a little bit of liqueur when baking; one for the cake, two for chef is the normal ratio in most kitchens! Whisky, brandy and coffee liqueur especially can be added to cakes for that sozzled dimension. I always have a good bottle of malt for when Dad visits.

Oils and vinegars

Oils

Good fats and oils don't make you fat! Fat doesn't necessarily make you fat. If you eat too much of anything, it's not going to do you any good, but nutritionally, fats are essential. Our bodies love them. They need them, especially unsaturated fats, which are present in all plant-based foods. Without sounding like a smug tree-hugger, we vegans are very lucky to not have to monitor our saturated fat intake. There are hardly any bad fats present in the multifarious world of plants. Of course, eating a kilo of Brazil nuts per day is still not cool for the body, but generally, we are free to munch away.

We all want a healthy heart and brain (they seem like good bits to look after). Fats can either assist or pollute these vital organs, depending on the types we choose to consume. Good fats, poly and mono unsaturated fats and some saturated fats (like lauric acid, found in coconuts), are filled with essential fatty acids and are the ones we want. They are easier for the body to utilize and less likely to be stored as fat. They also help our cells and nerves to function more efficiently, protecting them from nasty invaders; they keep our hearts healthy, actually lessening cholesterol in the blood; they make our skin bright with vitality, our hair shine. Good fats make us fuller for longer and help us to absorb the vitamin content in our foods and even protect us from things like strokes and high blood pressure.

You will notice quite a lot of oils being used in these recipes. I love the Med and their lifestyle and have taken on board that large glugs of oil lead to longevity. Good oils also give vegan food richness and shine. Please do not fear good oils, they are your friends. If we are eating a vegan diet regularly we need the fat anyway, it is essential in maintaining a healthy body and mind.

- *Top 5 sources of healthy plant fats:* Avocado, coconut, nuts and seeds (including nut and seed butters), olives.
- *Top 5 healthiest oils:* Hemp, grapeseed, flax, olive, rapeseed.

Here are the ones I use most often:

Coconut oil – Always buy good-quality, unrefined and organic if you can. Good coconut oil has outrageous health-giving properties, poor-quality coconut oil has the opposite. Used extensively in vegan and raw desserts and offers a subtle, shimmering coconut-ness to anything fried in a pan. You can now buy it unflavoured.

Olive oil (light) – You know the score. Good stuff, mechanically pressed, is the only way to go. I use olive oil a lot for frying, mainly because I love the flavour and it's really healthy. Olive oil should never be used at high heat, keep it medium or low. Ideal for sautés.

Extra virgin olive oil – Only used for dressings and dipping warm bread into. It also adds a last-minute shine to sauces, stews, etc. Never use for frying or roasting: it is a shameless waste of the amber nectar.

Vegetable oils – Basic all-rounders that get the job done nicely. Good at high heat.

Rapeseed oil – Increasingly popular and improving in quality. Rapeseed oil used to be the standard option, but now it can be made using the same techniques as the finest olive oils. Dark golden and strongly flavoured, it doesn't suit every dish, but when married with bold flavours it can make all the difference. Operates well at high heat and smoking point if refined.

Toasted sesame oil – You can opt for untoasted, if you are not into the full-power flavour of toasted. Used in moderation, it adds a quintessential Japanese/Chinese twist to dishes that cannot be replicated (unless you sprinkle toasted sesame seeds over). Best for marinades and dressings, not a fryer.

Vinegars

Balsamic, apple cider, sherry, red wine, white wine, rice, white, malt (for chips).

Herbs and condiments

Fresh is normally best, but sometimes, in baking especially, you're looking for that intensely POW kind of thyme, not the delicate fragrant thyme. Herb mixtures are quick and easy and can be very good quality. I am lucky enough to have a herb garden, but otherwise, I'd always keep at least two types of fresh herbs in the fridge to use as toppings or additions to salads.

Dried herbs

Thyme, mint, basil, dill, marjoram, rosemary, oregano, tarragon, sage.

Fresh herbs

Parsley, coriander, thyme, mint, basil (weekly staples).

Condiments

I use some of the following ingredients regularly, but none could be classed as essential. Fortunately, they do last for a while.

Nutritional yeast flakes – In your average cupboard, few things get more random than this vegan delicacy. 'Nutritional yeast flakes, you're having a laugh.' I'll have you know they impart a very savoury, almost cheesy flavour to dishes and are also full of vitamin B. They do look like fish food and cats are very interested in them, but apart from that, they are an irrefutable vegan classic. NYFs add a delicious, umami background to soups, salads, stews and even baking. Like a salt, with bells on.

Vegetable stock – It's better to make your own, but not always practical. There are some really decent stock cubes and bouillon out there. Several brands offer organic and low-salt options.

Others – Dried mushrooms, tamarind (paste or dried), rose water, orange blossom water, mirin, Chinese rice wine, pickled pink ginger (for sushi) . . . things you pick up along the way.

Spices

Where would we be without a little spice in our lives? Everything would taste like school dinners! Good spices are essential to a cook's repertoire, and our bodies love them as they're a great way to boost the immune system.

There is a huge difference between good spice and not-so-good spice. Buy it fresh, keep it fresh, use it . . . fresh. I keep mine in the fridge, tucked away in a sealed container, far away from air or sunlight. I am lucky enough to travel frequently and have little pouches of special powders from all kinds of spice markets, from Marrakech to Delhi. Whenever I open them, it takes me right back to my first waft of spice in an alleyway somewhere in the world.

I sometimes use a coffee grinder at home to make my own spice mixes. Keeping spices in their natural state is a good idea – they can last for years at room temperature, but when ground will lose their essential oils (aka flavour, aroma . . .) very quickly. Grind small quantities, often. A pestle and mortar is also an essential tool in the true spice aficionado's cupboard. Once you've roasted and ground your own cumin and coriander, you'll never go back to the shop-bought packets – it fills the house with such stunning aromas.

Due to the essential oils in spices, prolonged cooking is generally not cool. You'll lose some of their zing. Spice mixes like garam masala are usually added towards the end of cooking curries, and over cooking spices is anathema. Grind your spices just before cooking, just enough for that particular dish.

Spices don't just have to be used in cooking, they can make great infusions with wonderful health-giving properties. Try boiling anise seeds, caraway seeds, fennel seeds and coriander seeds together for a totally ancient take on Rennie's. This is bound to awaken your digestive fire and soothe any stomach-aches.

When using spices, it's a good rule to rub them between your finger and thumb or in your palms. This should get the oils going and a strong aroma should be wafting around your nose. If spices look and feel dry or crumbly, they are well past their best.

Here is a quick shakedown of the spices that I generally have stashed away:

Ajwain seeds – Used extensively in Indian cooking, but rarely found in home spice collections. Ajwain is something you only need to keep in small quantities. I use it in a few recipes, but I am a curry nut. I find that dried thyme can be used as a reasonable substitute, as both contain the same essential oil.

Health benefits – *anti-fungal, anti-bacterial, rich in fibre and anti-oxidants. Used a lot in traditional medicine to treat indigestion, coughs and asthma.*

Allspice – Caution! This one is a live wire. It is very popular in Latin American and Caribbean food and is sometimes called pimento or Jamaica berry if you're on the road. If you like anything 'jerked', allspice is the main flavour. Generally used in baking, but may also pop up in stews, curries and soups. Use sparingly, it packs a real punch.

Health benefits – *soothing, warming, increases digestive power, anti-inflammatory, anti-flatulent, high in vitamins and minerals (like vitamin C and iron).*

Anise seed/star anise – If you like ouzo or Pernod, you like anise. Used throughout the world, especially China, the exotic anise seeds are generally used in the UK when tucked away in star anise (the rust-red husk).

Anise has a fragrant, sweet and aromatic aroma and a strong liquorice-like flavour. It is stuffed full of anti-oxidants, which fight disease and promote good health. Mixed with hot water or served in a chai (see page 81), anise becomes a potent health elixir, great for treating colds, stomach-aches and coughs. In India, it is a tradition to serve anise seeds at the end of a meal, especially a large ceremonial meal. The seeds are chewed and aid good digestion.

Health benefits – *tonic, stimulant, antiseptic qualities, high in copper and iron, good levels of the B vitamins, decent vitamins C and A, used to treat bronchitis, indigestion and asthma.*

Asafoetida – Asafoetida is the traditional Persian name for the spice that in India is referred to as 'hing', and some people also call it 'devil's dung'. It has quite a savoury flavour, reminiscent of onions, and for this reason is used in a lot of cooking, such as Jain or yogic, to substitute for onions and garlic. Both of these are believed to be stimulants and to stir up the mind. Asafoetida must be kept in its own well-sealed container. It is a very strong spice and will corrupt the flavours and aromas of other spices it is stored near.

Health benefits – *anti-flatulent, lowers blood pressure, anti-bacterial, aids digestion, soothing.*

Bay leaf – The dark green leaves of the bay tree have been used since very early times as a subtly sweet and aromatic flavour addition to soups and stews. Buying bay leaves is generally unnecessary, as there will be a local bay tree that you can visit and borrow some leaves from. You can use them fresh, but they are best dried out of direct sunlight (a dehydrator is very handy here). Bay leaves are a brilliant sub when making curries, if you can't get hold of good curry leaves for example. I use far too much bay and find it hard to cook lentils or beans without dropping at least one leaf in. It adds a subtle background flavour that you can build on.

Health benefits – *contains compounds that are said to fight cancer, and also boasts antiseptic, anti-oxidant and digestive qualities. Fresh leaves are a brilliant source of vitamin C and A, also high in minerals and folic acid. Bay leaves sooth the stomach, making them helpful when treating ulcers. Very high in iron.*

Black pepper – We sometimes toss black pepper into our meals almost without thinking, it's so commonplace on European tables. Salt and pepper are our condiments of choice, but this has only caught on in our part of the world. I love to find freshly ground cumin on a North African restaurant table, or freshly ground Szechuan peppercorns on a Chinese table. Tastes change all over the world, but black pepper, as a spice, is a sensation, especially when freshly ground or cracked. I love using it as the driving force of a spice mix, or pairing it with big bold flavours.

Pepper originated in Kerala, Southern India, and its use spread all around the world like wildfire. Sometimes known as the 'king of spice', peppercorns are actually berries obtained from a tropical plant. They come in many colours, generally relating to the maturity of the peppercorn and how it has been treated. Black peppercorns are the most popular, picked red and dried until they shrivel. Green peppercorns are picked early and white peppercorns are soaked in a brine to remove the black colour. Whole peppercorns keep for years at room temperature, but when ground, use straight away.

Health benefits – *anti-inflammatory, calming, anti-flatulent, stimulates digestion, great source of the B vitamins, good for vitamins C and A.*

Capers – Piquant, fruity little suckers from the Med. Capers are the bud of a spindly plant, and are always picked early in the day. They are one of the essentials in every Mediterranean kitchen and I use them a lot as a sneaky treat in many of my recipes. The smaller or finer the caper, the better and more intense the flavour. Capers are generally bought in brine or vinegar, and this pickling process brings out their flavour. They can have high levels of salt added to them, which is well worth bearing in mind.

Health benefits – *powerful anti-oxidant qualities, promotes smooth circulation of blood, lowers bad cholesterol, decent levels of vitamins A and K. Capers have been used to treat rheumatic pain and stimulate appetite.*

Caraway seed – A traditional European spice, caraway is a member of the parsley family. The seeds look a lot like cumin, but when sniffed they have a unique, peppery aroma. I don't use caraway loads, but find it mostly crops up in Eastern European food and plays a major role in making borscht, one of the world's finest soups. I also sneak it into our homemade sauerkraut.

Health benefits – *speeds up digestion, high in dietary fibre, absorbs toxins, several powerful anti-oxidants present, good for iron and zinc, used in remedies for IBS.*

Cardamom – Well renowned for its health-giving properties, cardamom comes in two colours, green and black. It's the little black, highly aromatic seeds we're interested in here – they have a 'camphor-like' flavour that really comes to life when crushed (although the skins do contain beneficial essential oils). Cardamom is used almost equally in savoury and sweet dishes and brings a whole new dimension to our traditional rice pudding.

Health benefits – *digestive, antiseptic, anti-spasmodic, calming, diuretic, general tonic, high in potassium, ridiculously high in manganese (helps clean out free radicals).*

Chilli – I could write a whole book on these feisty nightshades. I use lots of chilli in my cooking, both dried and fresh. Chillies come in many varieties and some recipes are much better made with specific chillies.

Health benefits – *capsaicin (an alkaloid compound) is what gives chillies their distinct flavour and spiciness. It has been shown to reduce cholesterol and to fight cancer and diabetes. Chillies have high levels of vitamin C and decent levels of minerals.*

Cinnamon – Very much one of those spices that is as much medicine as food. Cinnamon has the highest strength of anti-oxidants found in nature – 100 times more than an apple. Generally bought as 'quills', cinnamon is the outer bark of the cinnamomum tree, which during the drying process rolls up into neat tubes. Cinnamon is so good for us, it makes sense that when winter comes it begins to appear in many traditional recipes. It has long been regarded as an excellent cold-beater.

Health benefits – *warming and soothing, antiseptic and with anaesthetic qualities. Helps against arterial diseases and strokes.*

Cloves – Little dried black flower buds, cloves have a strong, fragrant aroma and bring a good biryani to life. Cloves have well-known anaesthetic qualities and I remember sucking on them as a child to get rid of toothache. Not my preferred serving suggestion.

Health benefits – *warming and soothing, antiseptic, anaesthetic, kills stomach para-sites. Clove oil is great for arthritis and aching muscles.*

Coriander seeds – Used since ancient times to treat ailments and in cooking, coriander seeds are one of the common spices in most kitchens. They have a strong, earthy orange flavour and I find they are best gently roasted and ground just before cooking, releasing all those crazy aromatics. Coriander seeds are packed with healthy fatty acids and essential oils. When added to soups and stews, they can also act as a thickening agent. A bonus feature.

Health benefits – *calming, digestive stimulant, very high in iron, generally great levels of minerals and vitamins. Coriander seeds can even help to combat bad breath!*

Cumin – There is no mistaking the distinct, pungent aroma and flavour of cumin seeds. Cumin is strong and warm, always best roasted and crushed before cooking. I like to sprinkle cumin, neat, on to curries and soups in place of pepper.

Health benefits – *high in dietary fibre, anti-flatulent, aids digestion, very good source of iron, high in copper (good for the red blood cells) and calcium, high in carotenes and the B vitamins, helps colds and indigestion.*

Fennel seeds – Fennel has been revered in Britain since Anglo-Saxon times, when it symbolized longevity, courage and strength. These seeds are full of sweet and herby anise flavours and aromas. They are a little softer and greener than anise seeds, but they come from the same family, so are quite similar.

Health benefits – *great stores of vitamins A, E and C, and the B vitamins. Good levels of dietary fibre and a famed anti-flatulent!*

Fenugreek seeds – Not one for the spice tourist here, fenugreek is strongly aromatic and flavourful. Overdo the fenugreek at your peril! In their raw state they are very bitter, but mellow out when lightly roasted.

Health benefits – *helps get the bowels going, full of fibre, great for stabilizing blood sugar levels, laxative, given to mothers to aid milk production, helps coughs and bronchitis.*

Horseradish – You may know it as creamed horseradish, lathered over Sunday roasts, but there is more to horseradish than a mere condiment. Very pungent and hot, horseradish is a real eyebrow raiser. It comes from the same family as cabbage, radish and mustard, and that unmistakable fiery flavour is present, at one level or another, in all these ingredients. Horseradish grows well in the UK, and is best enjoyed for its one-off flavour contribution as opposed to its awesome nutrition. Horseradish should be firm and

young when bought – the older it gets, the less flavour it has and the more fibrous it is. Grate and serve fresh, combined with a little vinegar to keep the flames down!

Health benefits – *soothes the nerves, diuretic, anti-inflammatory, gastric stimulant, increasing appetite and stimulating digestion.*

Mustard seeds – I normally use the black or yellow mustard seeds, but they come in all sorts of colours: brown, white, etc. Mustard seeds are used throughout the world as a flavouring, be it in mustard (paste), mustard oil, or just the seeds on their own. Mustard seeds come to life when crushed and mixed with water or roasted. This kickstarts the essential oil and brings out the pungent nuttiness.

Health benefits – *high in niacin, riboflavin and thiamine, lowers cholesterol, plenty of good fats, helps with muscle pain and rheumatism, also has excellent levels of vitamin E (protecting our cells).*

Nutmeg/mace – Wars have been fought over nutmeg, which does seem a little OTT, but these aromatic seeds used to grow on only one small cluster of islands in Indonesia. Nutmeg and mace are basically the same thing, mace being the crimson outside skin of the nutmeg, with nutmeg being the seed of a little fruit. Each has a similar warm and sweet aroma and flavour. The only real difference is that mace will give a light, saffron-like tinge to food. Nutmeg has long been regarded as a potent aphrodisiac and is also, bizarrely, a relaxant. In Chinese and Indian medicine, nutmeg oil has been used to treat digestive and nervous ailments. You should not ingest large quantities of nutmeg in one sitting, as this sort of behaviour may lead to hallucinations and delirium followed by death (probably best give it a miss).

Health benefits – *anti-fungal, aids digestion, calming, anti-depressant, jam full of anti-oxidants.*

Paprika – This is made from grinding dried red capsicums into a powder. It is very popular in Spain and Hungary. Paprika comes in three main varieties, smoked, hot or sweet. I use smoked paprika quite a lot; it is so distinctive and unique. Sweet paprika is mainly a colouring spice; vibrantly red, it contains high levels of superbly body-friendly chemicals that give it its wild colour.

Health benefits – *high levels of vitamin A, good for the eyes, heart and skin, decent levels of vitamin E to protect the nerves and organs.*

Saffron – The dried stigma or *threads* of a lavender-coloured crocus flower, saffron is one of the most expensive ingredients in the world and rightly so. Saffron has an unmistakable, subtle flavour and adds a light amber colour to food, not to mention incredible health-giving properties.

Health benefits – *contains chemicals that help fight stress, cancer and infection, boosts the immune system, therapeutic, anti-depressant, helps the heart and digestion. Basically, it's a super hero!*

Tamarind – Tamarind fruit is encased in long pods, hanging from massive trees, and adds a lovely sweet/sour tang to dishes, especially condiments. Tamarind can be nibbled straight from the tree, but is generally sold in the UK as a paste or in dried, compressed blocks.

Health benefits – *powerful anti-oxidant, high levels of thiamine, vitamin C and A, iron and fibre. Can be used as a laxative or digestive.*

Vanilla – Vanilla pods are traditionally from Central America and are extracted from an orchid which is only pollinated by hummingbirds. Good-quality vanilla pods cannot be replicated, although there are some very good vanilla extracts out there. There are several different types of vanilla, and normally price is a good gauge to where you're heading quality-wise. Vanilla is a special occasion spice and I use it as such.

Health benefits – *the Mayans used it as an aphrodisiac, but this is unproven. Vanilla is really all about the flavour!*

Nuts about nuts!

As a vegan you cannot avoid going a little nutty over our flexible, good-fat friends. Rammed full of richness and capable of adding a satisfying, creamy quality to dishes that just cannot be replicated in the vegan repertoire, nuts are indispensable. They are the plant world's nutritional powerhouses and even just a small handful a day can keep us topped up for protein, minerals, vitamins and healthy fats.

Nuts are always best bought in the shell. They degrade when they are cracked open and most nuts, unfortunately, have been processed when bought without their hard jackets. Buying roasted nuts is fine if you plan on eating them soon, but roasting your own nuts at home can be a real giggle – check it out on page 163.

Let's give our nuts a closer inspection:

Almonds – Almonds come from a beautiful pinkish-white flower dangling off an equally lovely tree. Almonds are full of things called phytochemicals, which have incredible health-giving properties, and they also contain high levels of mono unsaturated fatty acids, which help to protect from coronary disease and strokes. Almonds also contain very high levels of minerals like manganese, calcium and iron (the list goes on) and are very rich in vitamin E, a potent anti-oxidant. Almonds make a great milk (see page 49) and are popular all over the world. I tend to soak almonds overnight and have half a handful in the morning for a turbo-charged boost. A handful of almonds a day keeps the grim reaper at bay!

Brazils – It's all in the name really. Brazil nuts are from the Amazon, the seeds of the giant castania tree, which can grow to 50 metres tall and live for 700 years! Brazils are very high in energy and fats, and the latter actually lower cholesterol levels in the blood.

Cashews – Without glorious cashews, I'd be an 8-stone weakling! Delicately sweet, rich, totally delicious. I love 'em, and you can even eat the cashew 'apple' that the nut hangs from. Cashews, like most nuts really, are high in good fats and dietary fibre. They are packed with minerals like zinc, which is great for tissue growth and development along with helping digestion, and are also outrageously brilliant sources of copper.

Chestnuts – Ye olde chestnut. Chestnut trees are local to us. Members of the beech family, their nuts are a wonderful delicacy and relatively low in fat, from a nut perspective. I like to use chestnuts in purées and as a thickener in sauces or even desserts – they have a creamy, starchy, almost potato-like quality when broken down. Chestnuts actually have a nutritional profile more similar to a sweet potato than a nut. They should be stored like a vegetable and kept in the fridge.

Chia seeds – Chia seeds have been called the 'ultimate superfood' for a while now. The Aztecs knew this and have always cultivated this low-growing herb, a member of the mint family. They are full of poly-unsaturated fats, and contain a potent blend of vitamins, minerals, protein, anti-oxidants, dietary fibre, omega fatty acids . . . just a tablespoon per day contains much of your RDA of many of these things. Scatter them on your fruit salad, morning cereal, smoothie or toast to add magnificence to your day.

Coconuts – This rough kernel of the coconut tree comes with an added extra, water! Called a 'complete food', one average-size coconut contains the energy, minerals and vitamins needed daily by your average-size person.

Hazelnuts – Sometimes called 'cobnuts', hazelnuts belong to the birch family of trees. Very sweet, fatty and super-nutritious, hazelnuts are awesome sources of folate, a vitamin that battles anaemia and very good for expectant mothers. Added to this, hazelnut butter is one of the finest things you can spread on toast.

Macadamias – An Aussie nut. Super-sweet and über-luxurious (not to mention expensive), macadamias are a treat nut worth investing in. The gold bullion of the nut world yields not only supreme richness and moreish crunch but is very friendly to our hearts and has potent levels of the B vitamins. I use macadamias in many desserts, and when blended into a cream they are a dream.

Peanuts – These are actually a legume, but boast all the health-giving properties of a nut. The nutrient benefits of peanuts have been known since ancient times; they are a brilliant source of cheap, neat plant protein and a supercharged snack (if the salted ones are kept to a minimum). Sometimes called groundnuts, like all legumes they actually enrich the soil and grow very quickly – in roughly 100 days you could have a mature plant, laden with nut/pea goodness.

Pecans – I've always wished for a pecan tree (a hickory) and a mango tree in my garden, but it'd mean a commute between North America and India. Coupled with incredible tastiness, pecans are a rich source of wellness. Full of anti-oxidants, high in vitamin E and manganese, with a huge ship of minerals to boot. Pecans are normally used in desserts, but I like to play with their bold flavours in salads and baking especially.

Pine nuts – Creamy, buttery, delicate and sweet, nothing beats a pine nut (except the price). Very high in mono-unsaturated fats and essential fatty acids. Manganese is there in spades and really helps us fight infections. When blended, pine nuts make one of the smoothest butters/purées around, especially good for lathering on the top of cakes or cookies.

Pistachios – Pistachios always seem so exotic in a British store cupboard and generally pop up in some of my favourite global treats. The finest pistachios, in my opinion, are Iranian; they are the size of large grapes, deep green and rich. In fact, that green colour is a serious attraction – it can really light up a plate of food. Like most of these nuts, one handful of pistachios a day will mean your protein, anti-oxidant, vitamin and mineral levels are all taken care of.

Walnuts – Walnuts contain the highest level of anti-oxidants in any nut. Quite a thing. These friendly chemicals scavenge our bodies for signs of disease and wipe them out. The oil of walnuts has excellent astringent properties, making the skin supple and shining; much, much better than overpriced beauty creams.

Soak your nuts:

Soak your nuts in water for 2–12 hours before use, as this will release enzyme inhibitors, making them more digestible and the nutrients better available to the body. Soaking also softens the nuts and makes them easier to blend, which is especially useful when making nut creams and butters.

Fruits

When you're trying to eat a decent quantity of raw food, juicing and smoothie-making becomes a good habit.

Buying local and seasonal fruits would be ideal, but in Britain, it can be limiting. It is easy to be idealistic, but a world without mangoes is a bleak and hollow existence. We do, however, have so many seasonal opportunities to forage for berries and fruits. Hit the woods and hedgerows and freeze or make preserves with your bumper harvest. This will carry you through the leaner months of the year.

Many fruits contain plenty of vitamin C, which is a wonderful anti-oxidant. Try to keep fruits raw, or cook to a minimum to preserve their vitamin and enzyme content. Enzymes are an integral part of a healthy diet and are killed by cooking.

Dried fruits

Great food for when you're on the go, the ideal pick-me-up pouch, with the addition of a few nuts for good fats. Dried fruits keep brilliantly and are best when sun-dried or dried by other natural means.

Dried cherries, cape berries, the treat list goes on, but here are the staples: dates, figs, apricots or peaches (unsulphured), raisins, cranberries, sultanas.

Vegetables

Us lot wouldn't get very far without them! Good vegetables are at the heart of every vegan diet, and the fresher the better. Treat them with respect and you'll get the best out of them: scrub them tenderly, cook them with care and attention, savour their unique qualities . . . this may be getting into the realm of a romance novel, but it's true, love thy veggies!

I buy organic vegetables whenever I can, not because of the flavour (which I believe is generally better), but because of the ethics involved in growing them and the obvious fact that there are no harmful chemicals present. Organic generally means more nobbles, more lumps and more comical shapes, which is always a tell-tale sign of real veg. If they're covered in mud or leaves, even better.

Always scrub your veg with a little bristly scrubbing brush (it's the easiest way) and only peel when really necessary. If you do, you'll lose all the vitamins and minerals trapped just below and in the skin. If you do end up peeling, think about making a stock or soup with the peelings.

A good way to wash non-organic fruits and veggies is in a large bowl with half a cup of apple cider or white wine vineger and 1 tablespoon of bicarbonate of soda. Leave them to soak for 15–30 minutes, rinse well in water (filtered) and allow to dry naturally. This technique is said to remove more pesticides than scrubbing alone.

Veggies should never be overcooked. The best way to eat most vegetables, from a nutritional point of view, is raw, so be considerate in your cooking process.

A word on food waste: On average, a UK household throws away over £500 worth of food each year. A 'use by' date is a decent guide to the lifespan of foods, but I'd always opt for using common sense over following what it says on the packet. A sniff, a feel and a little taste is normally a very good way of discerning the freshness of food. 'Display until' and 'best before' dates are normally misleading, as the food will usually last longer than these stated times.

Mould is generally best avoided, but just because there is mould, it doesn't mean we need to bin something. Miso, for example, will form a light white mould, but in Japan it's perfectly normal and safe to skim it off and enjoy what lies beneath. This goes for most fermented products. There are, of course, good moulds and bad moulds. Bread with a bit of mould on it is still fine to eat, if the mould is cut off and the bread is toasted. If vegetables or fruits have gone slimy and rancid, they should be escorted to the compost bin. If there is just a little surface mould on a hard veggie, you can peel it off. With a little common sense and knowledge, we can easily minimize our food waste, especially if we are rotating and caring for our precious ingredients.

We throw away over 7 million tonnes of household food per year, half of which could be eaten. If we stopped wasting food, the environmental equivalent would be like taking one car in four off the road! Good news – in the last five years we've cut our food waste by 21 per cent.

Tips for cooking veg:

- *When boiling or blanching veg, always add salt to the water. This slightly increases the water temperature.*

- *Vegetables that grow in the ground, i.e. roots, such as potatoes, must be cooked in lots of cold water brought to the boil. Leafy vegetables, i.e. greens, must be cooked in minimal hot water at a rolling boil for a short time. There should not be enough water in the pan for the greens to move around and bash into each other.*

- *When boiling your roots, make sure that the water is at a steady simmer, otherwise the outsides will begin to disintegrate before the insides are ready.*

The 'What's up' With Dairy

Cow's milk is the most popular milk in Britain, but what do cows go through to produce our daily pint? To produce milk, animals need to be lactating and therefore pregnant, stimulating their milk production. A few decades ago, your average cow used to produce 4,000 litres of milk per year. Due to modern production techniques this has risen sharply, to around 5,800 litres. Cows are milked three times daily; this intense regime leads to lameness and other diseases, and these are treated with high doses of antibiotics, which can be present in the milk of the animal.

The vast majority of calves that are born will not be allowed to suckle from their mothers, and financially useless male calves are normally killed within their first few weeks. Many cows are given fertility drugs to increase their pregnancy rate. Dairy cows' life expectancy is obviously dropping the more intensive the farming techniques become, and a quarter of all dairy cows are culled before they are thirty-nine months old. About half of these are sold to the beef trade.

Fortunately, in the EU we are protected against the use of cow growth hormones, but milk bought from outside the EU may contain the growth hormone rBST, which is very bad news and has been linked with a number of serious illnesses, such as breast and colon cancer.

Dairy farmers are also struggling in the current dairy industry set-up. Since 1997 the average wage of a dairy farmer has been £2.90 per hour, including subsidies. Over-production has long been a problem in the dairy industry – famously, surplus milk used to be poured down the drains. Now, due to intensified production, animal welfare standards have slipped and smaller dairy farms cannot keep pace with the production levels, leading to many going out of business. This leaves the larger, industrial-scale dairy farms to monopolize the industry, potentially using GM feed on their cattle.

Having said all this, I personally know some cow farmers who treat their cows like family members, knowing the entire herd by name. Buying organically, and especially locally, means you can make an informed choice for yourself. As a vegan, I can just visit these farms and enjoy the company of the happy heifers, knowing that any milk they produce will go in some part to raising a new generation of comfortable cows that will have a long and more natural life.

The transport of milk also clocks up the food miles. Strangely, in Britain we export almost as much milk as we import (normally from outside the UK)! Normally this milk is turned into 'milk-based products' like yoghurt and drinks. As with anything we eat, provenance is important, and generally, the further it's travelled the more difficult it is to be confident of your produce. The 'keep it local' mantra seems ever more relevant.

From a nutritional point of view, we don't need milk in our diet, especially in the quantities in which many people consume it. The dairy industry has been promoting cow's milk for many years, and it's now the default milk of choice, but you may as well drink goat's, donkey's, llama's or ewe's milk. Even camel's milk, I have heard, has amazing properties, being very high in protein and low in fat. Our buying habits are directly affected by such promotion and advertising, and I can see, in the not too distant future, a shift away from dairy milks and more emphasis being placed on sustainably produced and organic soya, grain and nut milks. These can be a creamy treat and are perfect on your morning cereal. Maybe we'll leave the milk for the calves and reserve a nice bottle of silver top to be opened on a special occasion. Surely milk is a commodity worthy of respect, something to be truly savoured and enjoyed.

Homemade milks

'So how do you milk an almond then?' says the cow-milk fan to the nut-milk nut. I've heard it all before . . . Milking beans and nuts is actually a breeze, and only takes a little know-how and hardware (a blender or food processor, a sieve, some muslin cloth and a pan). Soak, blend, strain and drink. It's almost as simple as that. These milks are all pure plant and therefore have no cholesterol or nasty saturated fats and boast an impressive array of health benefits. Did I mention that they also taste creamy and delicious? I like to call them milks, though many companies and folk call them 'dairy alternatives' or simply 'drinks' – really it's all the same game.

You can't beat the flavour of a homemade milk, and best of all you know exactly what has gone into your daily pint. Most shop-bought milks are filled with preservatives and coagulating and thickening agents. Making plant milks also works out cheaper than buying good soya and nut milks. You will find that after soaking the beans or nuts, a few handfuls go a long way.

There are so many variations of non-dairy milk alternatives that it can be overwhelming sometimes. The basic guidelines when buying anything soya-related are to go for whole-bean and organic milks. Many soya milks are made with over-processed and potentially GMO soya, which takes a wonderfully nutritious food and makes it potentially bad for us. Also, the flavour of whole-bean soya cannot be compared to the other stuff – it's much, much richer and creamier.

There are many sources of plant milks, and on page 49 I've even included a recipe for lentil milk (which, while one of the healthiest things that could touch your lips, is probably not for splashing over your muesli), but I tend to stick to the basics: soya, oat, almond, coconut and cashew.

All these milks (bar the soya milk) are raw. Meaning that all their essential enzymes and nutrients are not denatured by heating. Enzymes are as important as vitamins and minerals in our diet and are only present in raw foods. Enzymes are the catalyst that starts the essential chemical reactions that our body needs to thrive and develop. They are necessary for digesting food, stimulating the brain, providing cellular energy, and repairing all tissues, organs and cells. Drinking these raw milks means that we are getting a serious dose of nutrients and good fats, the perfect way to start the day and promote good health.

Almond and cashew milks are especially delicious, but are not everyday milks as they cost a little more. Changing to plant milks, especially on a daily basis, has a huge effect on our health in the long run. In fact, if you make one vegan change in your diet, opting for regularly using plant milk as opposed to dairy is a huge step in a good direction. I have been known to add a little dark rum, cinnamon and nutmeg to a warm pan of almond milk, transforming it into a winter cocktail to get most vegans bleary round the edges and smiling. You may also like to try the healthy hot chocolate (see page 82) using your freshly made milks. Big yums!

These milks are quite creamy, and they may need thinning out using a splash more water. If you're a 'silver top' type, maybe you'd like to add less for extra creaminess. Halve the water quantity and you will have something resembling a vegan single cream to be used on desserts and so on. Just up the sweetness a little. All the milk recipes below are a blank slate for wonderful flavours – here are a few I love to add: vanilla extract, cinnamon, cardamom, soaked and puréed dried apricots/dates/figs, maple syrup, apple juice concentrate, nut butters, barley malt extract, cacao, banana, a shot of espresso, green tea, orange blossom water, elderflower, rose water, tahini . . . the list is completely open to the extent of your tastebuds' imagination. I keep these milks in sealable containers or old (well washed and rinsed) cartons. They keep well for a few days in the fridge. They can also be frozen if you are making a big batch.

Soya Milk

The vegan's everyday milk of choice, great in a cuppa, and loves nothing more than being poured over cereals. The leftover soya paste can be added as a binding 'agent' to burgers and sausages.

THE BITS

100g soya beans (organic, non-GMO), soaked overnight

2 tablespoons brown rice syrup

a pinch of sea salt

½ teaspoon vanilla extract

DO IT

Drain and rinse the soaked beans. Place in a pan with 250ml of filtered water and bring to the boil, then turn the heat down and cook for 15–20 minutes on a low simmer, skimming off any white foam that rises. Leave to cool.

Pour the beans into a blender and blitz for 2 minutes. Add the brown rice syrup, salt and vanilla extract plus another 250ml of filtered water and blend for another minute. Taste and adjust the salt/sweetness accordingly.

Pass through a sieve lined with muslin placed over a large bowl or pan. This is a slow process and the bottom of the sieve will need scraping with a spoon regularly to ensure a steady stream. Gather the muslin around the edges, then, once most of the milk is through, twist and squeeze out any more liquid. Pour 500ml of water into the beans as you are scraping and stirring.

Cashew Milk

MAKES 500ML

Rich, creamy and surprisingly refreshing. Very much treat territory, and not an 'every-dayer' in the Beach House. Best served in champagne flutes on special occasions.

Once you've strained the cashew milk, you will find some glorious plant cream in your muslin.

THE BITS

80g cashews, soaked overnight

1–1½ tablespoons maple syrup

DO IT

Drain and rinse the cashews, then place them in a blender with 250ml filtered water and blend for 3 minutes. Add the maple syrup and another 250ml of water and continue to blend for another minute. Taste and adjust the salt/sweetness accordingly.

Place a sieve lined with muslin over a pan or bowl and gradually pour in the cashew milk, stirring and scraping the muslin to ensure a steady trickle is coming through. Gather the muslin around the edges, then, once most of the milk is through, twist and squeeze out any more liquid.

Almond Milk

My mum likes to leave her almonds soaking for a couple of hours before straining – it makes the milk even creamier!

Blanching the almonds here does not result in a huge loss of nutrients. The almonds are still technically raw. You can dry the leftover almond paste and use it as almond flour (simply spread out on a baking tray and place in the oven on low heat for 30 minutes). It is also ideal as a binding agent in vegan sausages and burgers, used instead of breadcrumbs – much tastier.

THE BITS

150g almonds (blanched ones are best), soaked overnight

1½ tablespoons maple syrup (or other sweetener of your choice)

a large pinch of sea salt

DO IT

If using unblanched almonds, boil a kettle. Drain and rinse the almonds, then put them into a bowl, cover with boiling water and leave to sit for 10 minutes. Drain again. Now peel the skins off the almonds – they should just slip off.

Place the skinless almonds in a blender with 250ml of filtered water and blend for 3 minutes. Add the maple syrup and salt along with another 500ml of water. Continue to blend for another minute. Taste and adjust the salt/sweetness accordingly.

Place a sieve lined with muslin over a pan or bowl and gradually pour in the almond milk, stirring and scraping the muslin to ensure a steady trickle is coming through. Gather the muslin around the edges, then, once most of the milk is through, twist and squeeze out any more liquid.

Add 250ml more water to the milk (depending on how creamy you'd like it).

Sprouting Green Lentil Milk

I first tried this in a raw ayurvedic restaurant in Pondicherry, where it made the perfect accompaniment to a small plate of spiced coleslaw and a few crispy raw vadas. It was at this stage that I realized a vegan will milk anything!

This is one for the lentil fan. No question. You will be left with essence of lentil here, a savoury flavour that can be challenging for the pulse/legume sceptic. By way of gentle warning, if you try this out on anyone but a full-blown lentil-lover you may put them off lentils for ever. You can use any pulse/bean sprouts to make a milk. We also like to milk sprouting mung beans. The leftover paste here is perfect for thickening stews, curries or soups.

THE BITS

200g sprouted green lentils

1 tablespoon brown rice syrup

a large pinch of sea salt

½ teaspoon garam masala and ½ teaspoon ground turmeric (spicy options)

1 teaspoon wheatgrass or spirulina (health-boosting options)

DO IT

Drain and rinse the sprouts, then place them in a blender with 250ml of filtered water and blend for 3 minutes. Add the sweetener and salt (plus the spice and funky green powder), along with another 500ml of water, and continue to blend for 2 minutes. Taste and adjust the salt/spiciness/sweetness accordingly.

Place a sieve lined with muslin over a pan/bowl and gradually pour in the green milk, stirring and scraping the muslin to ensure a steady trickle is coming through. This takes some time. Gather the muslin around the edges, then, once most of the milk is through, twist and squeeze out any more liquid.

Breakfast

This is food first thing that is sure to brighten up your day. Not only is it colourful and packed with cheeky flavour combos and texture, it also gives your body and belly a big gentle hug. Vegan food is light and densely nutritious, just what we need to get us off to a flying start. Our minds generally need clean foods in the morning, the kind of foods that give us clarity and don't over-stimulate the mind like sugars and caffeine, but let us wake ourselves up steadily. Mornings are enough of a shock without a double espresso and donut to add to the equation!

The best things to eat and drink in the morning are green. Our bodies have been basically starving for eight or so hours and are ready and waiting to fully absorb anything we put into them. We have our belly's full attention at this hour and it can't wait to get started. Probably the number one way to start the day, and this is as old as the hills, is a glass of hot lemon water. It gets straight down to business, cleansing and stimulating our digestive tract and helping to detox our kidneys and liver. It gives all our internal organs a nudge and a tickle and reminds them to look lively . . .

Combine any of these breakfasts with a juice or a smoothie and you will hover to work in a cloud of peaceful well-being, radiating good health and sparkly eyes to everyone on the bus.

Raw-sli with Grated Apple, Blueberries & Macadamia Cream

FOR 4-6

I love muesli, but most shop-bought brands are packed with things I don't want and a hefty helping of sugar to boot. I like making my own – I can put all my favourite bits into the mix and balance everything perfectly. I have kept this dish mostly raw, which means all the enzymes and nutrients are there, so it's really healthy. The dried fruits are not exactly classed as raw, but most raw food folk permit them. Remember to soak everything the night before. Even better, sprout the groats and seeds. To do this, soak them for 24 hours in cold water, then leave at room temperature for 2–3 days, until little shoots start to appear. Rinse with fresh water twice daily.

The macadamia cream is not essential, but it does give the bowl a brilliant creaminess. Soya yoghurt would be a good substitute. Use soaked buckwheat and quinoa in place of the oats and barley for a gluten-free twist.

THE BITS

100g oat groats (wheat groats are also fine), soaked overnight

60g barley or wheat groats, soaked overnight

40g almonds, soaked overnight

2 tablespoons pumpkin seeds, soaked for 2 hours

3 tablespoons sunflower seeds, soaked for 2 hours

½ a handful of walnuts

40g sprouted mung or aduki beans

2 tablespoons pecan nuts, roughly chopped

2 tablespoons raw peanuts

2 tablespoons flax seeds or chia seeds

2 tablespoons hemp seeds or sesame seeds

4 dates, finely chopped

½ a handful of raisins, chopped

a big handful of fresh blueberries, raspberries, loganberries, etc.

2 bananas, halved lengthways and cut into small cubes

½ teaspoon ground cinnamon

For the macadamia cream

200g macadamia nuts, soaked overnight

2 large dates, e.g. Medjool, soaked for 2–4 hours

1 teaspoon vanilla extract

a splash of almond or soya milk

For the topping

2 green apples, cored and grated

juice of ½ a lemon

a large pinch of cinnamon

maple syrup, for drizzling

DO IT

Soak the ingredients for the stated times, as necessary, then rinse and drain well. Roughly chop the almonds and walnuts. Put them on to a plate lined with kitchen paper with the rest of the soaked ingredients and dry as best you can. In a large bowl, toss all the ingredients together and spoon into deep bowls for serving.

For the macadamia cream, simply blend the ingredients together until smooth. Grate your green apples for the topping and mix immediately with the lemon juice. Top each bowlful of raw-sli with a decent dollop of macadamia cream, a tall stack of grated green apple and a light sprinkling of cinnamon. Finally, drizzle with maple syrup. You may also like to pour over a little almond or soya milk to make it more like a traditional cereal.

Scrambled Tofu with Buckwheat Pancakes & Avocado Butter

FOR 6–8

A hybrid pancake/pizza that is an early morning feast for the eyes – worth getting up for! You can make these pancakes lighter and less full on (buckwheat has quite an earthy flavour) by replacing the wholewheat flour with unbleached white flour. Scrambled tofu is a wonderful morning meal and almost as simple as cracking an egg. It's comforting and vibrant and hearty and you'll get a great amount of protein from the bean curd. Avocado is a brilliant substitute for dairy products and is great on toast. It's hard to get a good ripe avocado sometimes. If yours are like green bullets, place them beside the bananas in your fruit bowl and a day or two later you'll have a beautifully creamy, ripe avo on your hands.

THE BITS

500g firm tofu, drained and mashed well with a fork

2 cloves of garlic, peeled and minced

1 red chilli, finely diced (check for heat – this is breakfast, after all!)

a large pinch of dried oregano

2 teaspoon tamari or a large pinch of sea salt

½ teaspoon ground turmeric

3 large ripe avocados, de-stoned and chopped into random chunks

juice of ½ a lemon

a large pinch of sea salt

4 teaspoons rapeseed oil (as needed)

3 spring onions, finely chopped, green parts included

For the buckwheat pancakes (makes about 14)

100g buckwheat or unbleached flour

200g wholewheat flour

200ml unsweetened organic soya milk

up to 500ml water, as needed

½ teaspoon bicarbonate of soda

a large pinch of sea salt

For the garnish

2 big handfuls of cherry tomatoes, thinly sliced

a big handful of fresh coriander, chopped

DO IT

In a bowl, mash your drained tofu with a fork and add the garlic, chilli, oregano, tamari and turmeric; combine well. The tofu should transform into something resembling scrambled egg.

In another bowl, sort out your avocado. Mash the avocado, lemon and salt with a spoon or fork until smooth and ever so buttery.

Put the flour into a large bowl and with a metal whisk, stir in the rest of the pancake ingredients. As they combine, begin to whip them into a decent batter, adding water as needed. The consistency should resemble double cream. A few lumps are not a problem here, they will merge into the pancake.

Get two frying pans ready (one big, one smaller) and a plate with a clean tea-towel (to wrap your pancakes in). In the big frying pan, heat 2 teaspoons of rapeseed oil on medium/high heat and begin to fry the spring onions. Fry for 2 minutes, then add the tofu mixture (draining off excess liquid before adding to the pan). Stir continuously and cook for 5 minutes – the tofu should start to colour and the garlic will lose its raw flavour. Set aside and cover. You're almost ready to eat!

Heat the smaller frying pan on a medium-high heat and add 1 teaspoon of cooking oil. When hot, add 2 tablespoons of the buckwheat batter. Spread out quickly in even circular motions with the back of your spoon, forming a decent-looking pancake that roughly meets the edges of the pan. Don't be too precious about holes, it will sort itself out. Batter tends to find a way.

Cook for 2–3 minutes, until the base is crisp and golden. Loosen the edges of the pancake with a flat spatula (some call this a duck's foot, which I like), then either flip the pancake over using your spatula (in one swift, graceful motion) or toss it like on Pancake Day. This will be exciting, and even if it sticks to the roof, you have more batter to play with.

Now that you're slightly more awake, cook the other side of the pancake for a minute or so and place on your plate (form an envelope with your tea-towel, meaning your pancakes are snugly wrapped). Repeat the pancake procedure until your batter runs dry, eating any excess pancakes later for 'breakfast dessert' (a new course I've added to breakfast, essential on Sundays, I find).

Place a pancake on a plate, spread it thinly with 1 tablespoon of the avocado, scatter over some tomato slices, then top with tofu and a sprinkling of coriander. I think they look lovely like this, but if you are in a rush, you could 'wrap and go'.

Extras

- Add some punchy sauce for a real wake-up call! Something like salsa verde (see page 157).

- If you are lucky enough to have avocado oil in your cupboard, drizzle 2 teaspoons over the tofu at the end of cooking.

Chestnut, Millet & Sage Sausages with Homemade Raw Ketchup

FOR 15 SMALL SAUSAGES

Chestnuts seem to have been a little neglected of late, and you rarely see the lonely chestnut roaster on the festive street corner these days. But chestnuts are so plentiful on our island, and can be used in a variety of dishes, both savoury and sweet. They come to life when paired with the robust and earthy sage, and will live with most herbs in harmony. I like to use them in sausages and burgers because they are quite starchy and help with the binding process, which can be a major failing in many vegan sausage and burger recipes. Most vegan sausages/burgers are best cooked straight from the freezer – they hold their shape better that way. The key with vegan sausages/burgers is to be gentle with them in the pan, and don't mess with them unnecessarily. They just need a precise flip on occasion and they are perfectly happy. To make things easy, you may like to use pre-cooked chestnuts.

THE BITS

75g millet

250g cooked chestnuts

300g firm tofu, mashed with a fork

3 tablespoons nutritional yeast flakes (see page 30)

a handful of toasted sunflower seeds

1 onion, grated

3 cloves of garlic, peeled and minced

2 tablespoons very finely chopped fresh sage

2 tablespoons very finely chopped fresh rosemary

1 red chilli, deseeded and finely diced

a large pinch of ground allspice

2 tablespoons lemon juice

150g very fine wholewheat or gluten-free breadcrumbs

1 tablespoon tamari or ¼ teaspoon sea salt

vegetable oil

1 x homemade raw ketchup (see page 328)

DO IT

To cook the millet, put it into a small pan and cover with 2cm of cold water. Bring to the boil, then pop a lid on, lower the temperature and leave to cook for 20 minutes. Fluff up with a fork – the millet should be soft and tender but quite sticky. This is perfectly normal. Allow to cool.

In a food processor, blitz your chestnuts to fine crumbs. Add half the tofu and pulse a few times until quite smooth. In a large bowl, mix the chestnuts and tofu with the rest of the ingredients apart from the vegetable oil. The mixture should be firm enough to form into sausages, slightly tacky to the touch. Check the seasoning and add more tamari or salt if needed.

Using dampened hands, form your sausages, making them look like big chipolatas. Roughly 15 will do, but you may prefer just a few longer ones instead. Place them on a plate and cover lightly with clingfilm, then pop into the fridge and chill them for 30 minutes (you can also freeze them at this point). Put ½ tablespoon of oil into a large frying pan on a medium heat and fry your sausages for 5 minutes, turning them regularly to get a good colour all over.

Serve with a big blob of homemade raw ketchup and some warm toast. And normally I'll have a few green leaves for the plate. Sausage sandwich, anyone?

The 'Oh So Simple' Apple, Jaggery & Walnut Breakfast Muffin

MAKES 6 MONSTER MUFFINS

Simple, tasty, hearty and robust, this is my ultimate breakfast muffin. It's based on a muffin I lived on for six very tough months, when I was running a restaurant near Harrods. It pulled me through many a 4:30 a.m. start. Jaggery is an unrefined Indian sugar, made by simply boiling sugar cane. It's my favourite sweetener and I use it in a lot of my baking. Some people say it's like a fruity fudge. It's a chewy, rich, sweet thing with a flavour like light molasses. The perfect sweet baking partner.

THE BITS

85g dates, soaked, de-stoned and roughly chopped

1½ tablespoons jaggery (or unrefined brown sugar)

120g unbleached white flour

100g wholewheat flour

1½ teaspoons ground cinnamon

1½ teaspoons baking powder

45g walnuts, roughly chopped

2 tablespoons toasted sunflower seeds

1 tablespoon poppy seeds

1½ tablespoons flax seeds or chia seeds

40g sultanas

zest of ½ an orange

2 green apples (1 coarsely grated, 1 finely diced)

1 small carrot, scrubbed and finely grated

DO IT

Preheat the oven to 180°C/gas mark 4.

In a bowl, combine the dates and jaggery. Add 250ml of water and mash them up together, making sure the jaggery is dissolved.

Sift the flours, cinnamon and baking powder into a large mixing bowl. Fold in the remaining ingredients and stir in the date mixture, combining well but not overdoing the mixing. It should be nice and sticky. Spoon into a non-stick deep 6-hole muffin tray (like the one you do your Yorkshire puddings in), filling each dimple with at least 2 heaped dessertspoons of mix. Don't attempt to bake these in muffin cases, as it is likely they will stick.

Bake for 25–30 minutes, until the muffins are golden (check out that smell!). Stick a cocktail stick, or a thin wooden chopstick, into the middle of one of the muffins – if it's very sticky and wet, they need another 5 minutes. Because of the apple, these muffins are quite moist in the middle, so don't worry about a little wetness.

Turn out the muffins and cool on wire racks.

Serve warm (almost essential). Also good cold. Jane is old-fashioned and likes a buttered muffin. Cut in half and lather on some sunflower butter.

Muffins tend to dry out after a day or two. In this situation, I recommend toasting your muffin under the grill to revive it.

Banana & Almond Toast with Strawberry & Maple Syrup

MAKES 6 SLICES

This is my twist on French toast, with the added wonder of almonds and bananas (not to mention strawberries). I can't resist maple syrup at breakfast time, and in this recipe the strawberries go some way towards reining in its outrageous sweetness. Always remember, the lighter in colour the maple syrup, the better the quality. We're looking for radiant amber. Maple syrup contains decent amounts of zinc and manganese, and it also boasts fifteen times more calcium than honey. As a treat I sometimes use it to flavour tea or coffee.

THE BITS

2 large ripe bananas

1 teaspoon brown rice syrup (or other sweetener of your choice)

240ml oat or soya milk

½ teaspoon vanilla extract

6 tablespoons ground almonds

2 tablespoons linseeds (golden look best)

3 tablespoons rolled oats (gluten-free are fine)

a small pinch of sea salt

⅛ teaspoon ground cinnamon

1 tablespoon coconut oil or vegetable oil

6 slices of wholewheat, sourdough, spelt or rye bread (your favourite toast)

For the strawberry & maple syrup

3 handfuls of strawberries, trimmed and roughly chopped

120ml maple syrup

For the garnish

a handful of flaked almonds

DO IT

Blend the bananas and the rest of the ingredients (apart from the bread) in a food processor until smooth. Pop into the fridge for 20 minutes.

Put the ingredients for the strawberry and maple syrup into the food processor or a blender and blitz together, adding a splash of water if needed. This syrup can be served hot or cold. I don't have a rampant sweet tooth – maybe you'd like to add more maple syrup. Have a taste.

Heat a grill to medium and toast one side of the bread. Flip the slices over, give them a good layer of the lovely banana mix and toast until golden brown.

Serve the toast fresh from the pan and with a good drizzle of the syrup, topped with some flaked almonds.

Raw Chia Seed Breakfast Pudding with Seasonal Berries & Rocket

FOR 2

When the body wakes up it needs gentle, nutritious food. It craves a good start to the day, and chia seeds mixed with healthy berries are just the ticket. Use any berries you prefer – summer and early autumn are the finest times for making this breakfast pud. Chia, a member of the Mexican mint family, is a hero of the plant world that can seed within days of planting. They have more omega 3 fats than salmon, are a complete source of protein, boast more fibre than flax seeds and have a huge amount of anti-oxidants and minerals. You can mix them into a cake/bread mix, use them as a sprinkle for soups and salads, and pop them into smoothies.

I sometimes like to serve this kind of breakfast pudding with rocket. It's a real surprise to the tastebuds, as you can imagine, but it completes the amazing nutritional properties of this bowl and adds a dash of greenery.

THE BITS

80g chia seeds

2 tablespoons pumpkin seeds or hemp seeds (sprouted is best)

2 teaspoons brown rice syrup (adjust sweetness accordingly)

½ a handful of fresh mint leaves, finely chopped

4 tablespoons organic coconut milk or unsweetened soya yoghurt

½ teaspoon vanilla extract

1 peach/nectarine/small pear, or 2 plums, finely diced

½ a handful of raspberries or strawberries

a handful of blackberries or blueberries

a handful of rocket leaves (optional)

DO IT

Put the chia seeds into a bowl and cover with about 2.5cm of fresh water. Leave to sit for 15–20 minutes. Make sure all the chia seeds are soaking, and add a little more water if needed. The chia seeds should resemble a cold rice pudding crossed with frog spawn (YUM!).

Stir in the rest of the ingredients, sprinkling the berries and rocket over last.

Plantain Breakfast Burrito
with Pico de Gallo

FOR 4

Most of us need a quick breakfast that is easy to prepare, and burritos are ideal. In Mexico, home of the burrito, breakfast differs from lunch in only minor detail – restaurants serve dishes almost identical to any other time of day. Pico de gallo is a classic, and easy enough to assemble for breakfast – although having a bowl of pico de gallo in your fridge is never a bad idea at any time of day. It can be found all over Mexico and Central America and bizarrely translates as 'beak of rooster'. If you're not serving your burrito with pico de gallo, I recommend mixing some fresh coriander leaves and tomatoes into the filling. *Qué rico!*

THE BITS

2 large green plantains

2 tablespoons cooking oil

1 onion, finely diced

1 red pepper, deseeded and finely diced

240g firm tofu or tempeh, well drained and mashed with a fork

3 cloves of garlic, peeled and crushed

½ teaspoon ground cumin

½ teaspoon ground coriander

½ teaspoon ground turmeric

½ teaspoon sweet paprika

½ teaspoon oregano

1–2 green chillies, deseeded and finely sliced (jalapeños would be perfect)

a large pinch of sea salt

4 large wholewheat tortillas (must be fresh – stale tortillas will crack when rolled – and they dry out very easily, so keep them covered; gluten-free tortillas are available)

1 x pico de gallo (see page 146)

DO IT

Make the pico de gallo. Peel the plantains with a potato peeler, then halve them lengthways and chop them into 1cm chunks. In a large frying pan, heat half the oil on a high heat, then add your plantains and toss well. They will become nicely caramelized. Stir them regularly to prevent them sticking and remove when they have some nice crisp brown bits – roughly 5–7 minutes. Set aside, uncovered.

Add the rest of the oil to the pan. On a high heat, sauté your onions and peppers (that's posh frying) and stir well. After 5 minutes, when they are beginning to caramelize, add the tofu, garlic, cumin, coriander, turmeric, paprika, oregano, chillies and salt. Cook and stir for a further 5–7 minutes, adding 1 tablespoon of water to ensure the spices are not sticking to the base. Now stir in the cooked plantains and check the seasoning. Cover and set aside.

Wipe out the frying pan with kitchen roll and warm your tortillas for a minute on each side (or you can warm them beforehand on a medium grill). They should be just warmed through, fragrant and still soft and pliable. If they are too toasted, they break when wrapping.

Spoon 3 tablespoons of plantain filling into the centre of each tortilla and top with 2 tablespoons of pico de gallo. Fold in the two opposing edges, pressing gently down, then roll the whole thing over. A burrito is like a tucked-in wrap, a fat tortilla parcel if you like.

Salsa verde (see page 157) is also amazing lathered over burritos or served on the side. Serve these burritos warm, with more fresh chillies or chilli sauce. POW!

Tostada con Tomate
(aka Spain on Toast)

FOR 4

This dish is one of the best things about eating in Spain, and can be found in every sleepy café bar. Few dishes could represent Spain more. It's light and packed with nutrition; tomatoes are a great way to start the day, as they contain loads of anti-oxidants and nutrients. Everyone has their favourite way of preparing tostada con tomate – a sprinkling of herbs here, a scrub of garlic there. I regularly spread the toast with tofu ricotta (see page 128) before spooning on the tomato, to give it some bulk and creaminess. Black olive tapenade (see page 332) spread on the toast is lovely too, and I also like to add a few capers to the tomatoes, negating the need for salt. The permutations are as wide as the plains of La Mancha!

GF folk, you know the score: reach for your favourite, delicious, *sans* gluten loaf.

THE BITS

4 medium-sized, awesomely fragrant and ripe tomatoes

4 slices of spelt, sourdough or wholewheat bread (or treat yourself to a fresh baguette – whatever's your favourite bread, basically)

1 clove of garlic, peeled and halved lengthways

a small pinch of dried mixed herbs (optional)

glugs of fruity olive oil

a good sprinkling of sea salt

a scant pinch of cracked pepper

DO IT

Coarsely grate your tomatoes into a sieve over a bowl. Allow to drain, pressing the pulp lightly through the sieve with the back of a spoon (drink the juice chilled, it's delicious). Place the drained tomato pulp in a bowl.

Toast your bread and straight out of the toaster or grill rub it all over with the cut side of the garlic. Spoon over a good layer of grated tomatoes. Serve soon after, sprinkled with a few herbs, drizzled with olive oil and finally seasoned with a little sea salt and cracked black pepper.

Buen provecho!

Getting some fresh air on
Dinas Dinlle Beach.

Smoothies, Juices, Steamers & Hot Drinks

Smoothies and juices are the first port of call for the dedicated nutrition-seeker and offer an intense spot of detox in daily life. We don't need to go crazy to grab a superbly healthy start to the day – a green smoothie will more than do.

S and Js are the perfect way to get going early on. Most days I skip breakfast altogether and feel bursting with energy from just one glass of juice. The nutrients, vitamins and minerals are all there, easily accessible to the body and absorbed very quickly, so the benefits are felt after only a few minutes.

Go to town with your smoothies and juices and make them special. Dig out some cocktail glasses or dust off those champagne flutes. The glassware will make all the difference – everything tastes good out of a champagne flute!

Frozen bananas and berries are ideal for all things smoothie. Just chop bananas that may be past their best and freeze them in sealable plastic bags. Berries can be bought frozen or saved from a summer glut. In late summer and early autumn the price of berries and fruit in general drops – take advantage of this and stock up the freezer with gorgeous fruits. Come a dark chilly December morning you'll be delighted to find a bag of bright red strawberries waiting for you to make smoothie magic with.

Tropical fruit in this country is a bit hit and miss – you can caress a mango all you like, it may have fragrant skin and be soft to the touch, but often you cut it open and there's no flavour. One more reason to stay local and seasonal, but who can resist a little tropical sun sometimes? Life would be dull without pineapples.

I am not a huge fan of food supplements – I believe it's all there for us if we eat a balanced and varied diet. I do, however, appreciate the addition of what I call the 'green powders' to juices and smoothies, things like spirulina, wheatgrass and barley grass. They are concentrated hits of chlorophyll, calcium, protein and other wonderful nutrition. They can be a little expensive, but you don't need much. Try them out and I'm sure you'll feel and see the difference. I remember when I was in India once, eating a pretty meagre diet of lentils and rice, a friend bought me some spirulina and after a week I noticed that my nails were really strong. I also had more energy, and I have been a funky green powder convert ever since.

We use brown rice syrup a lot in smoothies – it's one of our favourite vegan sweeteners. Barley malt extract is also lovely, although neither are as sweet as honey or sugar. If you find any of these smoothies and juices too sweet, balance them out with a little celery or lettuce. Sounds strange, but it works a treat and adds minerals to the mix.

Your juicer may prefer it if you chop harder root vegetables into chunks. I have killed a juicer by trying to force a beetroot through it. Use the lower setting first for the softer, less dense bits, then ramp up the power for your tough roots. The pulp left over from juicing can be added to soups and works well in burgers and salads. I've even heard of a pulp sorbet!

I like a good thick smoothie, so add a little more water if you'd prefer it thinner. These recipes make large glasses, around 300ml, normally with leftovers. Some of these recipes do require a juicer, but who's to say that you can't make a perfectly amazing juice into a perfectly amazing smoothie. Try them out in your food processor/blender. The higher power the kit, the smoother things get.

There are so many awesome nut and other plant-based milks that can make hot drinks rich and superbly comforting. You will never, ever, miss your saturated-fat-laden cappuccino or sugar-laced mocha frappé something-or-other.

There is so much scope when preparing a vegan milk (see pages 46–9). I recently tried sprouting green lentil milk, which was surprisingly rich and delicious. Not one for making hot chocolate with, but ideal for adding to smoothies, curries or soups.

Vegans are generally an unassuming, health-conscious lot, and this mentality filters down into everything we eat and drink – treating ourselves to a satisfying hot drink does not necessarily mean lacing ourselves with bags of nasty fats and sugars. There is another way to treat yourself, and here it is . . . hugs in a mug just got a whole lot nuttier!

All these steaming beauties can be chilled in the fridge and reheated, or even enjoyed chilled over ice. And all are gluten free.

Peaches &
Cream Smoothie
FOR 4 GLASSES

This is like dessert in a glass. Not your everyday smoothie, and quite filling for the mornings, with all those nuts. A smoothie to savour in its sweet, fruity decadence and richness. Try this one out on a lazy Sunday morning. It's the perfect breakfast-in-bed smoothie. If you can't get hold of good peaches, nectarines or even apricots will suffice. I have used dried apricots too – soak them in water for a few hours and they're ready to blend. This smoothie can also be frozen into a wonderful ice cream – just follow the chilling techniques for the chocolate and maple ice cream on page 314.

THE BITS

150g macadamias, soaked for
2 hours or more

200g peaches, de-stoned and sliced

½ a vanilla pod, insides scraped out,
or 1 teaspoon vanilla extract

240ml filtered water

3 large dates (Medjool are best),
soaked for 20 minutes in warm water

DO IT

Pop it all into a blender and blitz until nice and smooth. Eat with a spoon (think 'Flake' advert).

Strawberry
Ice Cream Smoothie
FOR 2 GLASSES

Frozen bananas make anything taste like ice cream – it's an easy vegan cheat. Strawberries are outrageously healthy and a potent healing food. They are very rich in vitamin C, as well as vitamins B12 and D – add to that a whole host of beneficial minerals and you're looking at a wonder berry (aren't they all). Strawberries are calming for the liver and joints, and our bodies generally love 'em.

THE BITS

260g strawberries, chopped

1 large ripe pear, cored

3 bananas, chopped and preferably
frozen beforehand

a drizzle of soya milk (if needed)

DO IT

Place it all in a blender and blitz until it looks thick and ice-creamy, adding a drizzle of soya milk if needed.

For a slightly more refined smoothie, you may like to juice the strawberries and pear beforehand and then add to the smoothie.

Green Banana Detox Smoothie

FOR 4 GLASSES

After drinking this smoothie, you are officially ready for anything. Scale tall mountains, climb a tree, or just go to work with bags of energy. Full of green things and a helpful banana boost, this is shining health in purée form. If you drink one of these every morning, you'll probably live until you're a hundred!

THE BITS

2 bananas

2 celery stalks

3 handfuls of spinach or kale leaves

1 apple, cored and quartered

½ cucumber, seeds and skin removed

2.5cm fresh ginger, grated

juice of ½ a lemon

150–200ml filtered water (depending on whether you prefer a thicker or thinner smoothie)

a handful of ice

1 tablespoon funky green powder
(i.e. spirulina, wheatgrass, barley grass, etc.)
or a small handful of fresh parsley

DO IT

Pop it all into a blender and blitz until smooth.

Spiced Apple & Pear Juice

FOR 2 GLASSES

If you're going to juice, it's best to get green. The broccoli here adds a lovely savoury edge and the fruits are the perfect combo for autumn and winter, the time of year when we need to be reaching for our spicy green friends. Cinnamon is one of those medicinal spices that we regularly use and seldom realize the incredible healing potential of when they're alive and kicking in our muffins or our curry. Drinking smoothies like this in the winter months can ward off any nasty colds and other unwanted sniffles – proper medicine!

THE BITS

3 apples

2 pears

3 large florets of broccoli

2.5cm cube of fresh ginger, peeled

juice of 1 lime

2 pinches of ground cinnamon

DO IT

Juice all the fruit and veg. If your juicer is up to it, juice the lime with them. However, I normally use a manual squeezer to get at the lovely citrus juice, negating the potential bitterness of the seeds. If you are blending, core the apple and pear.

Pour into two nice glasses and top with a light dusting of cinnamon.

Mango, Coconut &
Lime Smoothie

Straight out of *Castaway*! All you need is a tropical island and a hammock.

Fragrant, ripe mangoes will make all the difference here. I know a guy, who knows a guy, who can get me something resembling what you munch on in Thailand or the Philippines. It's always that kind of deal, as the supermarkets just don't cut the mustard, mango-wise. Coconuts, however, seem to be ever easier to get in the UK and are a real treat. Ideally we'd use young coconuts here, but the old husky varieties are fine. The milk is actually more flavourful and better to use in smoothies, I find.

THE BITS

1 large mango, peeled and chopped

2 green apples, chopped

juice and zest of 1 lime

225ml coconut water (normally the
water from one big coconut is enough)
or coconut milk

2 large dates, de-stoned and soaked
in warm water for 20 minutes

To serve

2 tablespoons chia seeds
(for an even healthier smoothie)

1 tablespoon grated coconut

DO IT

Pop it all into a high-powered blender and blitz until smooth, stirring the chia seeds after-wards, sprinkling with grated coconut and hopping into your hammock!

Green Dream
(Watercress, Kale &
Sunflower Seeds)

The ultimate green juice. There is no better detox . . . it's an elixir for the real high life. All those green things with the added bonus of super-charged seeds. This juice is best topped with alfalfa sprouts for that final, supersonic touch. If you are a home sprouter, using sprouted sunflower seeds in this smoothie is quite wonderful too.

THE BITS

1 apple

3 carrots

3 celery stalks

5 large kale leaves (any type is good,
and dark green cabbage also works well)

a handful of fresh flat-leaf parsley

juice of ½ a lemon

2 handfuls of watercress (or spinach)

80g sunflower seeds, soaked in cold water
for 1 hour or sprouted beforehand

1 tablespoon chia seeds (optional)

For the garnish

a handful of alfalfa or mustard seed sprouts
(or any other sprouts)

DO IT

Juice the apple and all the veggies, then blend with the seeds in a blender. Sprinkle with some sprouts and you're well away!

Always juice your leaves first, followed by the harder stuff, as this will help to flush the juicer out. A drizzle of water also helps to extract all the juicy bits hiding in the pith and the leftover cellulose.

Raw Cucumber Mojito

One of the best things I consumed in Mexico, and there were many, was surprisingly a cucumber juice. Mixed with a little sugar, it was sensational. Cucumber is very soothing for the body and mind, an ideal way to start the day, especially if stress is on the horizon. Of course, this can be enjoyed at any time of the day and can be made rather boozy with the addition of white rum or tequila/mezcal. You're looking for a strong sweet and sour kick here, a decent balance of syrup and lime. Best served in something resembling a cocktail glass, with a thin slice of cucumber sitting on the rim.

THE BITS

1½ cucumbers, juiced
juice of 3 limes
a handful of mint leaves, finely sliced
2–3 teaspoons brown rice syrup, to taste
480ml sparkling water
crushed ice (optional)

For the garnish
2 sprigs of fresh mint

DO IT

This mocktail is best when all the ingredients are shaken in a cocktail style, but they can also be mixed in a jug and poured over crushed ice. Make sure the syrup is well mixed in, as it tends to dwell in the bottom of the glass. You may prefer to strain the cocktail (use a sieve) if you don't like the idea of mint leaves floating around in your drink.

Garnish with mint leaves.

Avocado 'Red Eye' Smoothie

FOR 2 GLASSES

We all sometimes wake with the dreaded 'red eye', for a variety of reasons (I hope they were fun!). This is the raw vegan bloody Mary. The raw, super-savoury smoothie that is going to drag you back into the land of the living (or get you out of bed and down to the kitchen at the very least). This smoothie has been rigorously trialled and tested, and I can confirm that this green delight could resurrect Tutankhamun himself!

THE BITS

140g soya yoghurt or silken tofu
1 avocado, de-stoned and peeled
½ a red pepper, deseeded
2 large handfuls of spinach
leaves or kale leaves
juice of ½ a lemon
½ a red chilli, finely diced, or a dash
of Tabasco, to taste
225ml soya milk
a small handful of coriander leaves

DO IT

Pop it all into a blender and blitz until smooth. Scrape down the side of the blender a few times, as the spinach leaves will try to climb out. Enjoy in moderation.

Almond Rooibos Chai

FOR 4-6 CUPS

Chai is the finest beverage for a chilly winter's night. Nothing comes close. It's basically a potion of warming spices wrapped up in a cloak of steaming creaminess. It's equally great when chilled and served ice cold, and can easily be made boozy with the addition of some rum or brandy. I use the richness of almond butter in the almond milk and decaffeinated rooibos tea to make this almost guilt-free treat spectacular, but if you prefer you can use Assam tea leaves, which give it a more traditional appearance. Loose-leaf rooibos infuses better and seems to pack more of a punch flavour-wise. If you are using bags, split them open and pour the leaves in.

THE BITS

4cm fresh ginger, scrubbed and grated

7 green cardamom pods, seeds removed and crushed in a pestle and mortar, or just cracked

4 black peppercorns

240ml water

4 rooibos tea bags, cut open, or 3 heaped teaspoons loose-leaf rooibos

1 cinnamon stick, broken into 3 pieces

4 cloves

2 star anise

740ml almond milk (why not make your own? – see page 49)

2 teaspoons almond butter

sweetener of your choice

DO IT

In a pestle and mortar, bash up your ginger, cardamom and black peppercorns.

In a small pan bring the water to a boil and add your tea and spices, then lower the heat, cover and simmer for 10 minutes. Leave to infuse, the longer the better.

Using 2–3 tablespoons of almond milk, thin out the almond butter into a loose paste. Add this along with the rest of the almond milk to the pan and bring back slowly to the boil (keep your eye on the pan, as this has a habit of bubbling up all over your lovely sparkling hob). Allow to simmer vigorously for 10–15 minutes.

Strain the chai using a sieve (a small one is perfect) when serving, which is easiest done with a ladle. Add a sweetener of your choice – I like to let people add their own sugar. Remember, chai is normally served sweet, sweet, sweet.

Chai is usually served in small cups – think slightly larger than espresso size. You can always come back for seconds! Though as you can see, our mugs are a bit bigger.

Healthy Hot Chocolate

FOR 6–8 CUPS

Raw cacao powder is seriously dark and flavoursome, nothing like cocoa powder, which can be laden with quite a few freaky ingredients and non-vegan nasties. Raw cacao powder is pure, with incredible health-giving properties – it has a wickedly potent chocolate flavour, to be used sparingly when compared to standard cocoa. It can be easily found in health food shops, and you'll probably find cacao butter on the same shelf. If cacao butter is hard to track down, try nut butters such as cashew, almond or Brazil. I love using almond milk, which adds great richness to a plant-based potion like this one and, as we all know, nuts and chocolate are always a brilliant pairing. This hot chocolate can also be chilled in the fridge and used as a chocolate sauce. If it's a little bitter, sweeten it up, but we love the contrast between a sweet dessert or ice cream and a bitter choc sauce.

THE BITS

750ml almond milk (or unsweetened vegan milk of your choice)

45g raw cacao powder (or vegan cocoa – check the packet!)

1½ tablespoons cacao butter (for optional gorgeous richness)

3 tablespoons unrefined brown sugar (or other sweetener of your choice)

DO IT

To make this supremely healthy, warm the almond milk in a pan until it is just steaming, then whisk in your cacao and cacao butter. If you are using raw cacao, take care not to heat the milk above 40°C as this can decrease the nutrient content. But if you like it hot, go for it! Whisk in your cacao and cacao butter, which will give the hot chocolate a nice frothy look. Now sweeten as you like and wrap yourself around a hearty mug.

Cacao is quite bitter, so you may need to add a little more sweetness than usual.

Lavender, Rosemary & Lemon Infusion

FOR 4 CUPS

A quick infusion that takes minutes to make. Great for an early morning detox/herbaceous pick-me-up, it's more like a health tonic than merely a tasty beverage. A zesty infusion to lift spirits, steeped in well-being. I don't use boiling water, as it would kill all the vitamins and the subtle aromas of the herbs. Leaving the boiled water for a couple of minutes before you use it means you don't scorch the herbs, but have just the right amount of heat to convince them to release their fragrant oils. I like to drink this out of a small bowl, or a large flat mug – this way you get to see the herbs in all their glory.

THE BITS

2 big handfuls of mint leaves
3 sprigs of fresh rosemary
8 thin slices of lemon (2 per mug)
2 sprigs of dried lavender
3 sprigs of fresh thyme
sweetener of your choice (as needed)

DO IT

Place an equal amount of the bits into each small bowl or wide, large mug.

Boil a kettle and leave to sit for a couple of minutes, then pour the hot (but not boiling) water over the herbs.

Allow to infuse with a saucer over the top for 5 minutes, then pour into cups. Enjoy the revitalization!

Warm Apple Mull

FOR 4 CUPS

British apples are something to really savour and be proud of. For me this is the quintessential taste of winter splendour, all steaming and golden in a mug. There is something intoxicating, and almost alchemical, about the combination of apple and cinnamon, and in this mull we have the perfect expression of their potential, potent nature. Try to source some nice apple juice for this magical mull, as it makes all the difference. Try the cloudy stuff out for size. Adding glugs of dark rum to the finished mull can only lead to a wonderful sense of merriment and rosy cheeks. As with most of these hot drinks, I make a double batch of this and have it the next day as well.

THE BITS

2 cinnamon sticks, broken
into small pieces
6 cloves
3 star anise
4cm fresh ginger, peeled
and finely grated)
1.25 litres apple juice
sweetener of your choice
(I like a nice dark unrefined sugar),
if the apples aren't sweet enough

DO IT

Place all the spices in a pestle and mortar, add the ginger and give it all a decent bashing.

Put all the ingredients into a small pan and slowly bring to just below boiling. Pop a lid on the pan and simmer on a very low heat for at least 1 hour. Leave to sit and infuse.

Sweeten, then strain into cups and serve steaming.

Soups

I could happily eat soup for every meal. Starter, main and dessert could easily be covered (I recently had an incredible papaya and mango soup). The potential for variation in texture and flavour is seemingly endless, and with the backbone of a decent stock, you can hardly fail.

Everywhere you travel around the globe, there is the great soup constant. We all seem to love a good slurp! From the depths of winter over here to the bubbling pho stands of Ho Chi Minh City, we're all face down over bowls of steaming broth. I have even eaten a form of chickpea soup in the middle of the Sahara, with smiling Bedouins, cups of mint tea and desert-baked bread (bread buried and baked in the desert). The cooling and restorative qualities were amazing. I make many of my soups at lunchtime in a little retreat centre that I work in at the foot of Mount Snowdon, overlooking a tranquil lake with its own verdant biodynamic vegetable garden. It's one of the most spectacular places to cook in the world.

Soup takes us up in its simmering arms and whisks us off to a place of healing and nourishment. Why is it after soup we feel lifted? A bowl of soup is like a prolonged hug that only ends when the last dunk of bread or noodle has disappeared. Soup changes things! It's either alchemy or the fact that soup can boast so many concentrated flavours, from humble and, let's be honest, past their best ingredients. The finest soups don't always come from the finest cuts of carrot or the most perky bunch of spinach.

Slurping is a very important part of eating soup; people who eat soup in a polite, genteel fashion are always worrying and probably hiding something. The name 'soup' derives from Old French; 'sup' referred to the natural noise of the soup admirer when huddled up to their bowl. Call me a savage, but the louder the slurps, the greater the enjoyment.

Here is a selection of mainly simple soups that covers a decent wedge of the supping-sphere.

Braised Pumpkin & Butter Bean Soup
with Orange Chilli Oil

FOR 6–8

This is a beautifully creamy soup, even if I say so myself. It's the kind of soup that pleases everyone – meat-eaters especially like the hearty richness that the pumpkin and beans combo brings to the bowl. Toasting and grinding your own coriander seeds is essential here.

THE BITS

200g dried butter beans, soaked overnight

3 teaspoons coriander seeds

1 tablespoon olive oil

700g pumpkin, peeled and cut into 2.5cm cubes

3 teaspoons toasted sesame oil

2 onions, roughly chopped

125g white cabbage, roughly chopped

4cm fresh ginger, finely diced

2 bay leaves

1.5 litres vegetable stock (or bean cooking liquid)

2 large pinches of freshly grated nutmeg

sea salt, to taste

1 big handful of fresh coriander (optional)

For the orange chilli oil

3 teaspoons coriander seeds

a pinch of sea salt

zest of 1 orange

2 red chillies, deseeded and finely chopped

5 tablespoons olive oil

DO IT

Drain the soaked beans and rinse with fresh water. In a small pan on a medium heat, toast all your coriander seeds (6 teaspoons) for a minute until fragrant and occasionally popping. Grind together in a pestle and mortar or food processor. Enjoy the aroma! Reserve half for the soup, half for the oil.

Put ½ tablespoon of olive oil into the same pan, on a high heat, and roast your pumpkin for 8 minutes, until slightly caramelized. Set aside. Put the sesame oil into a large, heavy-bottomed pan and warm on a medium heat. Add the onions and cook for 5–7 minutes, then add the cabbage, ginger, half the ground coriander seeds and bay leaves and cook for 2 minutes. Now add the stock or bean liquid, followed by the butter beans and pumpkin. Bring to the boil and pop a lid on the pan. Cook for 25 minutes at a steady simmer.

Meanwhile, to make the orange chilli oil, blend the other half of the ground coriander seeds, salt and orange zest in a pestle and mortar or food processor until you have a chunky paste. Add the chillies, then gradually add the olive oil while crushing or blending the ingredients together. Check the seasoning – there should be a nice orange kick to the oil. I like to do this the day before and keep the oil sealed in a cool place. You may have some left over, in which case don't worry, it keeps brilliantly for a couple of days and can be used on salads and mixed into stews. Try it stirred into some mashed potato!

The soup should now be ready, so stir in the nutmeg and pick out the bay leaves. Season with sea salt. Using a stick blender, whiz the soup in the pan until smooth and definitely thick and creamy. It should not resemble baby food, so dilute with warm water or more stock if needed. Serve topped with a good drizzle of your orange chilli oil or a scattering of coriander leaves.

Fennel, Dill & Saffron Soup

FOR 4

This soup combines some pretty wonderful flavours – fennel, dill and saffron – in one pan. Fennel is something I cannot get enough of – we buy ours from a local farm and it looks like aniseed-y rugby balls (this is Wales, after all). Saffron is something I tend to stockpile when I'm in Spain and then hoard for no apparent reason. It seems such a precious commodity and is so labour-intensive to harvest. It really cannot be replicated and adds an element of luxury to everything it graces. The more flowers in food the better, I say. The cauliflower adds a lovely smoothness without the weightiness of potatoes – it's a little trick I like to use. And tofu adds a lovely creamy richness to any soup. You won't believe this is all plant!

THE BITS

1 tablespoon olive oil

1 onion, chopped

3 medium bulbs of fennel, cut into chunks

1 small cauliflower, roughly chopped (including the stem)

1 teaspoon curry powder

¾–1 teaspoon saffron threads, soaked in 1 tablespoon warm water

100ml white wine (veggie)

800ml–1 litre vegetable stock

140g silken tofu

½ a handful of fresh dill or fennel fronds, chopped

DO IT

Heat the olive oil in a large pan and add the onions. Cook them for 10 minutes, until soft. Add the fennel, cauliflower and curry powder, stir and cook for 5 minutes, then add the saffron (with its soaking water) and white wine. Bring to the boil and pour in the stock, then cook at a low simmer with a lid on for 25–30 minutes, until the fennel is tender.

Now add the tofu and most of the dill, and allow to warm through. Then, using a stick blender, blitz the soup until smooth, loosening the consistency with more stock if needed.

Serve topped with a light scattering of dill or fennel fronds.

Smoked Cuban Black Bean Soup with Avocado & Lime Salsa

FOR 4

This is made in a similar way to the Portuguese/Brazilian feijoada, a stew/soup which is normally served with lots of pig parts, smoky and fatty. To add richness here I've used diced smoked tofu and the wonderful chipotle pepper. The recipe came about after Jane returned from a recent visit to Havana with an array of dried beans and one giant avocado. I like to cook this in the oven, like a good old feijoada – it seems to taste better that way. You can of course make it on the hob. If you can't track down smoked tofu, just use firm tofu instead or leave it out. The protein in the beans will keep you rocking for a long time.

THE BITS

250g dried black beans, soaked overnight

2 tablespoons coconut oil

1 large onion, peeled and finely diced

5 cloves of garlic, peeled and minced

2 celery stalks, finely diced

1 red pepper, deseeded and diced

2 bay leaves

2 carrots, scrubbed and finely diced

3 large smoked chipotle peppers, roughly chopped, or 2 teaspoons chipotle paste, or 2 teaspoons smoked paprika

3 teaspoons balsamic vinegar

1 teaspoon dried thyme

700ml vegetable stock or water

250g smoked tofu, cut into 1cm cubes

For the avocado & lime salsa

2 avocados, peeled and diced

2 spring onions, finely sliced

3 tablespoons fresh coriander

juice of 1 lime

a pinch of salt

DO IT

Drain the soaked beans and rinse them in fresh water. Warm a large cast-iron oven dish (or something like that) on the hob, and when warm add the coconut oil, followed by the onion, garlic, celery, red pepper, bay leaves, carrots and chipotle or chipotle paste (if using paprika, see below). Cook through, stirring, for 10 minutes, until soft.

Preheat the oven to 180°C/gas mark 4.

Add the balsamic vinegar to the veggies and allow a moment for it to evaporate. Then pop in the drained beans, paprika (if using) and thyme, stir, and add the stock or water. Cover and place in the oven for 1¼ hours. The slower the cook, the more flavour to be expected! The beans are tough and can take longer in the oven. Check the beans by tasting one, and pop back in for another 15 minutes if necessary. Meanwhile, make the avocado salsa by putting all the ingredients into a bowl and mixing well.

When the soup is ready, pick out the bay leaves, then ladle out roughly a third of the soup and blend it in a food processor (or pop a stick blender into the soup and give it a few whizzes). Return the blended soup to the pan and stir in the smoked tofu. Season well with sea salt and black pepper. Serve topped with a couple of spoonfuls of avocado salsa and for some added richness try the Creamy Cashew Cheese Sauce (see page 327).

Aduki Bean & Oat Soup

FOR 6

This soup reminds me of the rustic origins of vegan food, on the periphery since the 60s, when vegan restaurants were tucked away in alleyways and disused churches. It's got bags of soul and there's hardly any preparation required. Aduki beans are one of the most health-boosting beans going, and combined with oats they produce a potently healthy concoction of robust flavours and nutrition. I enjoy popping a handful of oats into soups, as they add substance and a little creaminess.

Gluten-free option: use GF oats.

THE BITS

1.75 litres water (use the bean cooking water)

175g dried aduki beans, soaked overnight

2 bay leaves

1 large onion, finely diced

2 celery stalks, finely diced

1 large carrot, scrubbed and finely diced

1½ handfuls of oats (big flakes, rolled are fine but the traditional style, not quick-cooking)

2 tablespoons brown miso

1 tablespoon light tahini

1 teaspoon ground coriander

⅔ teaspoon dried thyme

1 teaspoon sea salt, if needed

DO IT

Put the water, drained aduki beans and bay leaves into a large pan and bring to the boil, then cover the pan and simmer for 30 minutes.

Add the onion, celery, carrot and oat flakes, followed by the miso, tahini, coriander and thyme. Reduce the heat to low and cook, still covered, for a further 30 minutes. Check that the carrots are tender, then fork out the bay leaves and add the salt. Thin down the soup with more hot water as needed, check the seasoning, and add more miso (or salt) as needed.

I like this soup chunky, but you can blend it into a nice smooth soup with a stick blender if you like. If you choose chunky, make sure you cut your vegetables neatly – there is nothing worse than an uneven celery chunk!

Zen Noodle Broth

FOR 4

Food plays a large role in the daily life of a Zen monastery. It is not merely about nutrients, but about energy to replenish and nurture the spirit. I try to think about this whenever I cook, putting as much positive energy into my cooking as possible. (Fortunately this is easy, as I love bashing pots and pans.) The idea for this Zen-style broth came about first because a friend lived on it while practising to be a Zen Buddhist monk (near Manchester!), and also because this soup is really simple to prepare and yet almost infinitely complex. A pleasant paradox.

Soba noodles are made primarily with buckwheat and are generally much better for the body and digestion than other noodles. They have a wonderfully full texture. In Britain, the best miso you can buy is, surprisingly, made in Wales. Sometimes I will add a splash of sake or mirin to the frying vegetables, which adds even more flavour to the stock.

Still the mind, feel the love, stir the soup. Enjoy the whole process (including washing up).

Gluten-free option: use 100% buckwheat noodles.

THE BITS

1.6 litres water

3 carrots, halved lengthways and finely sliced into half-moons

2 onions, very finely chopped

3 large green cabbage leaves, finely shredded (kale/cavolo nero works well)

1 red chilli, finely diced

½ tablespoon cooking oil

3 strips of dried wakame (seaweed)

12 dried shiitake mushrooms

3–4 tablespoons brown miso

150g soba noodles

For the garnish

3 spring onions, finely sliced at an angle

DO IT

Bring the water to the boil in a large pan, then reduce the heat and let it gently simmer while you fry the vegetables.

In a wok on a high heat, flash-fry the carrots, onions, cabbage and chilli in the oil for 3–4 minutes. Then add the vegetables to the simmering water. Add the wakame, shiitake mushrooms and miso (diluted in 4 tablespoons warm water) and simmer uncovered on a low heat for 15 minutes.

Place your noodles in a separate pan of boiling water and cook for 4 minutes (or see packet instructions). Drain, then refresh with cold water.

Taste the soup and add extra miso if more saltiness is needed. Add the cold noodles to the soup and warm through for a minute.

Serve straight away, topped with slices of spring onion.

Courgette, Cumin & Mint Soup

FOR 4

This was a traditional Turkish-style soup until I got my hands on it. A real taste of the Med here, via Wales. Welsh courgettes grow like wildfire, and each summer we are inundated with wheelbarrows full of them. The kitchen at work suddenly becomes like an industrialized processing plant – barrels of courgettes enter at one end and come out the other puréed, roasted, pickled and poached. This soup is best served in the sunshine, but is also perfect for lunch on a bright, crisp November day. It is traditionally made with lots of yoghurt, but the silken tofu steps in and adds wonderful creaminess to the proceedings. No need to be too precious with the prep here, as it's all going to be blended!

THE BITS

2 tablespoons olive oil

1 onion, sliced

1½ teaspoons cumin seeds

1 teaspoon salt

4 cloves of garlic, diced

4 courgettes, chopped

2 celery stalks, sliced

1 large potato, peeled and cubed

¼ of a white cabbage, chopped

1 teaspoon dried mint

⅓ teaspoon black pepper

950ml good veg stock or water

150g silken tofu/unsweetened soya yoghurt

a handful of fresh mint, finely chopped

For the garnish

½ a handful of fresh mint leaves

½ teaspoon freshly ground cumin seeds

a glug of fruity olive oil

DO IT

In a large thick-bottomed pan, warm the olive oil on a medium heat. Add the onions, cumin seeds and salt and sauté for 10 minutes, until beautifully golden. Now add the garlic, courgettes, celery, potatoes and cabbage, and continue to sauté and stir for 5 minutes. Add the dried mint and black pepper and stir well.

Pour in the stock and bring to the boil, then cover and simmer for 25–30 minutes, until the potatoes are nice and tender.

In a bowl, whisk up your silken tofu with a fork and stir it into the soup. Blend it all together with a stick blender – I like to leave it slightly chunky. Sprinkle in the chopped mint and stir.

Garnish with fresh mint leaves, a sprinkle of freshly ground cumin and a good drizzle of olive oil.

Apple & Beetroot Borscht with Horseradish Sour Cream

FOR 6-8

This is one of the simplest soups I know – no messing, just all into the pan and boil. And I really think that borscht is the finest thing to come out of the Russian kitchen. It's the colour that gets you with this one: deep purple. Horseradish works in perfect harmony with borscht – I wouldn't serve it with anything else. The soup can be served cold or hot and has untold health benefits.

THE BITS

4 beetroots, peeled or scrubbed, and cubed

3 cloves of garlic, peeled and minced

2 onions, thinly sliced

2 tablespoons tomato paste

1.25 litres vegetable stock or water

¼ of a red cabbage, thinly sliced, hard stems in the compost bin

2 carrots, thinly sliced

1 potato, peeled and diced

2 green apples, peeled, cored and diced

3 tablespoons apple cider vinegar

2 tablespoons molasses (not blackstrap) or brown rice syrup

3 tablespoons cream sherry

2 tablespoons tamari

1 tablespoon caraway seeds

½ a handful of fresh dill

For the horseradish sour cream

400g tofu, drained well

2 tablespoons grated horseradish

1 tablespoon lemon juice

1 teaspoon rice vinegar

½ teaspoon salt

1 small clove of garlic, peeled and well crushed

For the garnish

½ a handful of fresh dill, chopped

DO IT

Place all the soup bits, except the dill, in a pan and bring to the boil, then reduce the heat and simmer for 2 hours.

Meanwhile, make the horseradish sour cream by placing the ingredients in a food processor and blending until smooth and creamy.

With a stick blender, smooth most of the soup. Some lumps are good. Now add the dill, check the seasoning and add sea salt if needed.

Serve topped with more chopped dill and a large spoonful of the horseradish sour cream.

Raw Avocado & Lime Gazpacho

FOR 4-6

This is a simple summer cooler with the richness of avocado and all the wonderful flavours of a bright and breezy summer's day. Raw soups can be spectacular and all you really need to do is gather and blend. Without a food processor, preparing raw soups and stews is pretty tough, however. I don't like the term 'processing', it's a little industrial for my liking, but a food processor is an essential kitchen tool for the modern cook with hungry mouths to feed and a head full of ideas.

You may like to serve this chilled soup in nice glasses with spoons, or glass bowls.

THE BITS

3 large ripe tomatoes, diced

1 cucumber, peeled, seeded and diced

3 spring onions, sliced

1 small green pepper, diced

2 avocados, peeled, de-stoned and diced

250ml tomato passata

100ml water

1 teaspoon unprocessed brown sugar

juice of 1 lime

zest of ½ a lime

1 teaspoon sea salt

a large pinch of cayenne pepper

2 handfuls of fresh coriander leaves

For the garnish

½ a handful coriander leaves

DO IT

Put all the ingredients into a large bowl or pan and combine well together.

Place two-thirds of the mixture in a blender and blitz until smooth. Stir the rough with the smooth, then taste and season accordingly.

Serve slightly chilled (out of the fridge 15 minutes before serving), topped with a few fresh coriander leaves.

Salads

Now as this is a vegan cookbook you'd expect there to be a half-decent salad section; after all, that's what the majority of people think we live on! For those who think salads are 'rabbit food', get a load of this!

For me, salads are simply a way of arranging beautiful, complementary, eye-catching ingredients on a plate. Normally they're raw. I don't mind if they're vegetable or fruit, nut or leaf, pulse or preserve; all are welcome in my salad realm.

What is a salad anyway? We thought we knew: something to do with icebergs, tins of sweetcorn and salad cream. Jeez, we've come a long way, brothers and sisters. My parents remember a time when olive oil could only be procured from the chemist!

These are vibrant, evolving times. Our diets are shifting and keeping pace with this rapidly changing world. Technology and science are steaming ahead and this is leading to huge advances in all things nutrition. We know now that you can actually live on leaves (although admittedly it wouldn't be that interesting). We can certainly live on plants: fresh plants, bursting with life force. Nowhere else is this freshness and crunch better shown off than in a colourful platter of vegetation.

The very best salads are easy to arrange. They can get a bit Jackson Pollock, scattering chopped mint here, flicking some sweet paprika over there, as your imagination runs wild. Your seasonal produce and spice rack form a palette of sorts, a handful of nuts adds richness, a squeeze of lemon lightens the tone. This is art on a plate. Don't over-arrange – go wild!

The ultimate rule with salads is fresh, fresh, fresh. If it's limp, it fails the audition and should be utilized in something cooked or shown the compost bin. No food goes to waste in the Beach House Kitchen – either we eat it or the worms do.

Couscous Salad with Tempeh, Preserved Lemon, Yellow Courgette & Almonds

FOR 6

Tempeh is like chunky, funky tofu, with a slightly fermented taste. It has a little bit more about it than tofu, more substance. It stands up to the full flavours of the preserved lemons in this dish admirably. If you can get your hands on yellow courgettes, they look great in any dish. There is no difference in flavour from their green buddies, they just make a refreshing change sometimes and have some good nutrients in their skins. Preserved lemons are becoming more commonplace in supermarkets and are of course found in the corners of Middle Eastern shops around the land.

Gluten-free option: use quinoa or millet instead of couscous.

THE BITS

300g couscous

525ml boiling water or vegetable stock

½ tablespoon olive oil

200g tempeh (well drained, then cut into thin 5cm slices)

1 teaspoon cumin seeds

2 red chillies, deseeded and finely diced

3 cloves of garlic, peeled and crushed

3 tablespoons finely chopped preserved lemon

a handful of flaked almonds, toasted

60g dried apricots, roughly chopped

a handful of green olives, stoned and chopped

sea salt and freshly ground black pepper

3 small courgettes, sliced lengthways into thin strips

½ a handful of fresh mint, finely chopped

a handful of fresh parsley, finely chopped

For the dressing

100ml extra virgin olive oil

2 teaspoons light tahini

juice of ½ a lemon

1 clove of garlic, peeled and well crushed

½ tablespoon white wine vinegar

DO IT

Pour your couscous into a large bowl (preferably a heavy one) and cover with the boiling water or stock. Pop a lid on immediately and leave for 15 minutes. Fluff up with a fork a couple of times when ready to use, otherwise leave covered. You have to love that simplicity!

Grab a large frying pan and warm ½ tablespoon of oil on a medium-high heat. Add the tempeh and sauté for 5–7 minutes, to get a little colour on the chunks. Now add the cumin seeds, followed by the chillies and garlic, and cook for 5 minutes, stirring well. Pop in the preserved lemons, most of the almonds, the apricots and olives and season with salt and pepper, warming everything through. Take off the heat and cover.

Warm a small griddle pan, then brush the courgette strips with a little oil and griddle in batches. Thin strips should take only 1–2 minutes per side. The strips should still have a little spring to them. Whisk the dressing ingredients together in small bowl.

Now fluff up the couscous and gently mix in the tempeh, dressing and most of the fresh herbs, followed by the courgettes (try not to break them up too much). Sprinkle the rest of the almonds and herbs over the top. Serve in a large shallow bowl or on a large plate.

Fennel, Walnut & Celeriac Salad
with Caesar-ish Dressing

FOR 4

Here is an untraditional Caesar salad, without the unmistakable anchovy, but with the positively pokey caper and a decent dab of mustard. All invoking something along the lines of the classic dish. Good enough for me! It's nice to use the salad leaves to help in the scooping and eating of this salad – Caesar salad was traditionally eaten this way. The dressing should cling to the leaves. You want crisp leaves here, so maybe reserve the outer ones for another salad, wrap, etc.

THE BITS

1 large handful of toasted walnuts

1 fennel bulb, finely sliced lengthways, fronds and all

3 celery stalks, halved lengthways and cut into 2cm dice

½ a red onion, finely diced

⅓ of a medium celeriac, peeled and grated

2 green apples, cored and cut into 2cm dice

6 radishes, finely diced

½ a handful of raisins

3 tablespoons fine capers, well rinsed and drained

2 tablespoons toasted pumpkin seeds

2 small romaine lettuces, outer leaves placed in the fridge to crisp up, hearts thinly sliced

For the Caesar-ish dressing

4 tablespoons cashew nuts, soaked for 4 hours, then drained

2 cloves of garlic, peeled and crushed

100ml olive oil

2 teaspoons capers, rinsed and well mashed

juice of 1 lemon

sea salt and freshly ground black pepper, to taste

For the garnish

a handful of fresh dill, chopped

For a decadent touch

pine nut Parmesan
(see page 336)

DO IT

To make the Caesar-ish dressing, place all the ingredients in a food processor, drizzling in the olive oil as the blades are running, to give you a shimmering, thick dressing. Check the seasoning – I like it with a good peppery poke and a decent garlic kick.

Roughly chop the walnuts and set aside half for sprinkling over at the end. Put the rest of the walnuts and all the other salad bits, including the shredded romaine hearts, into a big bowl. Add the dressing and combine well. Arrange the crisped-up lettuce leaves around the edge of a large serving plate in a big circle. Mound the dressed salad in the centre, then sprinkle with dill and the reserved walnuts, or, if you're feeling frisky, some pine nut Parmesan.

Hazelnut, Buckwheat &
Greens Salad with Watercress Oil

FOR 4-6

When did we lose buckwheat? What a travesty. I am so chuffed to see its reappearance – like Led Zep at the O2, it is one worthwhile comeback. Buckwheat, we salute you and your impressive range of nutritional benefits. You are a gluten-free grain, you are a tasty sucker and you also take as much effort and thought to cook as couscous (which is actually easier than toast).

THE BITS

400g raw buckwheat

1–2 tablespoons balsamic vinegar, to taste

1 teaspoon sea salt

½ teaspoon cracked black pepper

½ a small head of broccoli

150g runner beans, sliced diagonally in half

a handful of fresh dill, finely chopped

½ a handful of fresh parsley, finely chopped

½ a handful of fresh chives, finely chopped

½ a red onion, finely diced

100g baby spinach leaves (if larger leaves, roughly chop)

a handful of raisins, soaked and roughly chopped

a handful of roasted pumpkin seeds

a large handful of roasted hazelnuts, roughly chopped (reserve some for topping)

For the watercress oil

4 tablespoons olive oil

1 clove of garlic, crushed

80g watercress

a large pinch of sea salt

DO IT

On a medium high heat, dry roast the buckwheat in a pan for 7 minutes, until darkening. Cover with 3cm of cold water and bring to the boil, then cover the pan, turn down to a very low heat and cook for 20 minutes.

Pour the balsamic vinegar over the warm buckwheat and season with salt and pepper, fluff with a fork, then leave to cool.

Bring a large pan of salted boiling water to a steady simmer on the hob. Blanch your broccoli for 2 minutes, then remove and place in a large bowl of very cold water. Leave for a few minutes, then drain. Set aside in a large bowl, covered with cold water.

In the same pan, blanch your runner beans for 2 minutes, then repeat the process for the broccoli and set aside. Make sure both broccoli and beans are cold – if not, dunk them in cold water again. They should be nice and firm, crisp, with a good crunch. Vibrant greens! Put your watercress oil ingredients into a blender and blitz until nicely smooth.

Combine the dill, parsley, chives, onion, spinach, raisins, pumpkin seeds, hazelnuts, broccoli and beans in a large bowl (saving some hazelnuts and herbs for topping). Sprinkle over the buckwheat with your hands (making sure it's well broken up). Toss nicely and turn out on to a lovely serving platter.

Drizzle with the watercress oil and sprinkle with the rest of the hazelnuts and fresh herbs.

Seaweed, Fennel & Avocado
with Udon Noodles

FOR 4–6

This salad is best served chilled. It's hearty, yet light, full of zing and vitality. A perfect salad for a contemplative, lazy summer lunch. If you do not live by the coast with a readily available supply of seaweed, head to the supermarket or health food store and look for some Japanese sea greens – here I have used one of my favourites, wakame, which is packed full of life-giving properties.

Gluten-free option: use brown rice noodles.

THE BITS

270g udon noodles

2 handfuls of ice cubes

60g wakame seaweed, sliced into thin strips

2 teaspoons toasted sesame oil

2 tablespoons rice vinegar

1 teaspoon light brown sugar

2 teaspoons tamari

3 teaspoons lime juice

4 teaspoons sake (mirin or even dry sherry will do)

1 avocado, peeled and cut into small cubes

½ a medium bulb of fennel, fronds trimmed, very finely chopped lengthways

1 small cucumber, peeled, deseeded, halved lengthways and chopped

1 small carrot, peeled and cut into thin batons

For the garnish

1 tablespoon lime zest

3 tablespoons pink pickled ginger

DO IT

Bring a pan of water to a rolling boil and cook your noodles for 4–5 minutes (see the pack for the best cooking time noodle-wise, as they can vary). Drain and run under cold water until cool.

Put the ice cubes into a large bowl, fill with water, then plunge your noodles and wakame seaweed into the seriously chilled water. Leave for a few minutes, to ensure the noodles are nice and cold (you can pop them into the fridge for a while too). Drain the noodles and wakame well and toss them in a bowl with the sesame oil.

Whisk the vinegar, sugar, tamari, lime juice and sake together. Taste and add more tamari if necessary. Lightly toss the avocado, fennel, cucumber and carrot with the dressing.

On a large plate, make a shallow bed of the noodles and scatter over your green salad. Top with a sprinkle of lime zest and pink pickled ginger.

Red Med Tofu Tostada with Murcian Salad & Fey's Dressing

FOR 4-6

We spend a lot of time in Spain, down in the wild red deserts and craggy mountains of Murcia. Jane and I don our backpacks and raid the local Sunday farmers' market, with its year-round abundance of fresh, seasonal and cheap produce. Fey, who came up with the dressing, is a superstar, living in a beautiful valley not far from our little *casita*. This is a 'rustic' salad, so don't bother chopping the vegetables too finely – the key is arranging them in a symmetrical way on the plate. I use three big slices of wholewheat bread, cut into triangles; though traditionally tostada uses the whitest of white bread.

Gluten-free option: use your favourite GF bread.

THE BITS

12 small pieces of bread

1 head of soft-leaf lettuce (such as oak leaf), roughly chopped

2 little gem lettuces, quartered lengthways

½ a small red onion, finely chopped

½ a cucumber, quartered lengthways and diced

1 carrot, quartered lengthways and diced

3 tomatoes, quartered and roughly diced

½ a courgette, quartered and roughly diced

2 handfuls of good black olives, pitted and halved widthways

5 piquillo peppers or 1 red pepper, finely sliced

3 tablespoons fine capers, well drained

a handful of fresh parsley, finely chopped

1 teaspoon sea salt

½ teaspoon cracked pepper

For the Red Med tofu

400g firm tofu, drained

1 large clove of garlic, minced

1 small celery stalk, finely diced

2 teaspoons sweet paprika

½ teaspoon smoked paprika

½ teaspoon dried thyme

½ teaspoon dried oregano

¼ teaspoon dried dill

a pinch of dried rosemary

8 sun-dried tomatoes (soaked, then finely chopped)

4 tablespoons green olives, chopped

2 tablespoons fresh parsley, finely chopped

½ tablespoon tomato purée

2 tablespoons olive oil

1 tablespoon nutritional yeast flakes (optional, see page 30)

sea salt (if needed)

1 x Fey's parsley and lemon dressing (see page 327)

DO IT

Toast your bread under a grill on a medium heat or in a toaster – the crisper the better. Let it cool on a wire rack. To make the Red Med tofu, place all the ingredients in a food processor and blend until nice and smooth. It should be a thick, rich and creamy paste. Check the seasoning – you should only need a little salt. Now make Fey's dressing.

Arrange your salad in a large flat bowl or on a serving platter. Start with your soft leaves, then arrange your quarters of little gem around the edge of the bowl. Scatter over the rest of your vegetables, leaving the piquillo pepper and capers until last, then top with the fresh parsley.

Spoon a big, neat blob of the Red Med tofu on to each of your cooled tostadas. Place the tostadas all over the salad, tucking them in a little bit. Season and serve in a sunny spot, with smiles.

Braised Cauliflower & Puy Lentil Tabouleh

FOR 4-6

Tabouleh is a proper southern Med classic. Combined with great olive oil and sweet roasted cauliflower it makes a substantial salad. I love the spice mix baharat – if you can find it, substitute it for the ground spices. I like to use pomegranate molasses in the dressing – it gives a funky reddish tinge and has a sticky tang all of its own. For a special occasion, go the whole hog and sprinkle over herbs, baharat, pomegranate and chopped toasted almonds.

Gluten-free option: replace the bulgar wheat with millet.

THE BITS

100g Puy lentils

1 bay leaf

220g bulgur wheat, rinsed in cold water

about 450ml boiling water or veg stock

1 small cauliflower, cut into small florets, roughly 2cm in size, stalks finely diced (waste nothing!)

a large pinch of ground cumin

a large pinch of ground coriander

a large pinch of sweet paprika

a large pinch of ground turmeric

a small pinch of ground cinnamon

½ teaspoon sea salt

4 spring onions, finely chopped

½ a cucumber, deseeded and finely diced

2 ripe tomatoes, deseeded and finely diced

1 tablespoon great olive oil

½ a handful of dried apricots, soaked for 2 hours, then drained and finely chopped

a handful of fresh flat-leaf parsley, finely chopped

½ a handful of fresh mint leaves, finely chopped

seeds from 1 small pomegranate

1 tablespoon toasted sesame seeds

1 x pomegranate dressing (see page 328)

For the garnish

4 tablespoons pomegranate seeds

a handful of chopped fresh parsley and mint

DO IT

Put the lentils into a pan and cover with water. Leave for 5 minutes, then pick out any floating lentils. Drain, cover with fresh water, and add the bay leaf. Bring to the boil, then reduce the heat and simmer for 30 minutes, stirring and checking the water level (add more if needed). The lentils should be springy, but cooked. Drain if necessary, though there should be very little liquid left.

Put the bulgur wheat into a large bowl and pour over the boiling water or stock, enough to cover it by about 2cm. Tightly cover and leave for 30 minutes. Once cooked, fluff with a fork and cool.

In a frying pan, heat the oil on a high heat, then add the cauliflower and begin to fry. Stir regularly and cook for 10–12 minutes. Once the cauliflower has softened and the edges are slightly charred, sprinkle over the ground spices and salt and cook for a further 2 minutes, stirring well. Cover and leave to cool. The cauliflower should be nicely coated with the spices.

Make the pomegrante dressing. Add three-quarters of the lentils to the bulgur wheat, along with the cauliflower, herbs and the rest of the ingredients, then pour over the dressing and mix gently together with your hands until well combined.

Place in a wide, shallow serving bowl and spread out evenly. Sprinkle over the remaining lentils and garnish with pomegranate seeds and herbs.

Charred Fig & Rocket Salad
with Lemon Tofu Feta

FOR 4

I struggle to eat vegan in France. However, when we were visiting Sancerre, and sipping our way around the surrounding countryside, we stopped in a tiny little place where the kindly chef offered to roast me some figs in balsamic vinegar with rocket salad. The natural sweetness of the figs and the sharp rocket lit up my mouth.. Here I've added a little fragrance with the basil and a good dollop of tofu feta, which makes it more of a light lunch salad.

THE BITS

3 handfuls of rocket leaves

a handful of fresh basil leaves

6 ripe figs, quartered

2 tablespoons balsamic vinegar

3 tablespoons toasted pine nuts

For the lemon tofu feta

1 tablespoon nutritional yeast flakes (see page 30)

juice of ½ a lemon

½ teaspoon lemon zest

1 tablespoon olive oil

400g firm tofu, well drained, crumbled

1 clove of garlic, peeled and crushed

a large pinch of sea salt

a pinch of cracked black pepper

For the dressing

1 tablespoon lemon juice

1 teaspoon brown rice syrup

½ tablespoon balsamic vinegar

a pinch of sea salt

1 tablespoon extra virgin olive oil

DO IT

To make the tofu feta, put the nutritional yeast flakes into a bowl with the lemon juice and zest and leave to dissolve.

Heat the oil in a small frying pan on a medium heat and add the tofu and garlic. Pan-fry until slightly golden, then add the lemon mix, salt and pepper, bring to the boil and cook until the lemon juice has evaporated. Spoon into a bowl and allow to cool. Check that it's just a little too salty, like feta.

To make the dressing, whisk together the lemon juice, syrup, vinegar, salt and extra virgin olive oil in a small bowl.

Mix the rocket and basil leaves together in a bowl. Drizzle 1 tablespoon of the dressing over the leaves and toss together. Keep the rest of the dressing for further dipping and drizzling.

Warm a griddle pan on a high heat and brush with a little oil. Just as the oil begins to smoke, place your figs widthways in the pan. Allow to cook for 2 minutes, basting them with balsamic vinegar as you go. Turn them when well caramelized, then remove the now sticky figs from the heat.

Scatter the leaves beautifully on plates, and top with the warm figs, a couple of spoons of the tofu feta and a sprinkling of toasted pine nuts.

Fragrant Wild Rice, Curly Kale & Pistachio Salad

FOR 4-6

I was raised on rice – I grew up in the Philippines, and rice is a 24/7 constant for the Pinoys. I went back there recently and clambered up some very impressive rice paddies in the mountains of Luzon – I was pleased to see that many of these ancient step-like structures are still being used, stretching and winding across many miles of green verdant valleys, hugging the most gravity-defying crevices and nooks. This is a simple salad that combines some wonderful ingredients. There are a lot of flavours going on here: the occasional sweetness from the raisins, the hunk of saltiness from the sun-dried tomatoes – it's a feast of a salad. It's also very tasty served warm – just leave the rice to cool for 20 minutes, rather than cooling completely. You can transform it into a wonderful big plate by adding pan-fried tempeh, cut into chunks.

THE BITS

250g wild rice

1 carrot, grated (if you have any carrot tops, finely chop them and add)

5 leaves of curly kale, cut from the stems and very finely sliced

3 tablespoons raisins, soaked for 2 hours and roughly chopped

½ a handful of roasted pistachios, roughly chopped

6 radishes, trimmed and finely diced

6 sun-blush or sun-dried tomatoes, including any oil, finely chopped

4 spring onions, finely sliced

½ a handful of fresh dill, chopped

½ a handful of chives, finely sliced

a handful of sprouted mung beans or green lentils

For the dressing

2 cloves of garlic, peeled and crushed

3 tablespoons olive oil

juice of 1½ limes

zest of ½ a lime

½ teaspoon sea salt

½ teaspoon freshly ground black pepper

For the garnish

a handful of roasted pistachios

3 tablespoons chopped fresh dill

DO IT

Rinse the wild rice in cold water a number of times until the water runs clean. Place in a pan, pour in water to cover by 3cm, then bring to the boil and put a lid on the pan. Reduce the heat to its lowest possible and cook for 45–50 minutes, until the rice is soft and all the water has evaporated. Fluff up gently with a fork and allow to cool fully. Spreading the rice out on a plate will help here.

To make the dressing, whisk the ingredients together in a small bowl.

Combine the rest of the ingredients in a large bowl and toss well to mix evenly (using your hands here is amusing). Add the dressing, spoon in the rice and combine well.

Serve in shallow bowls, garnished with the extra nuts and herbs.

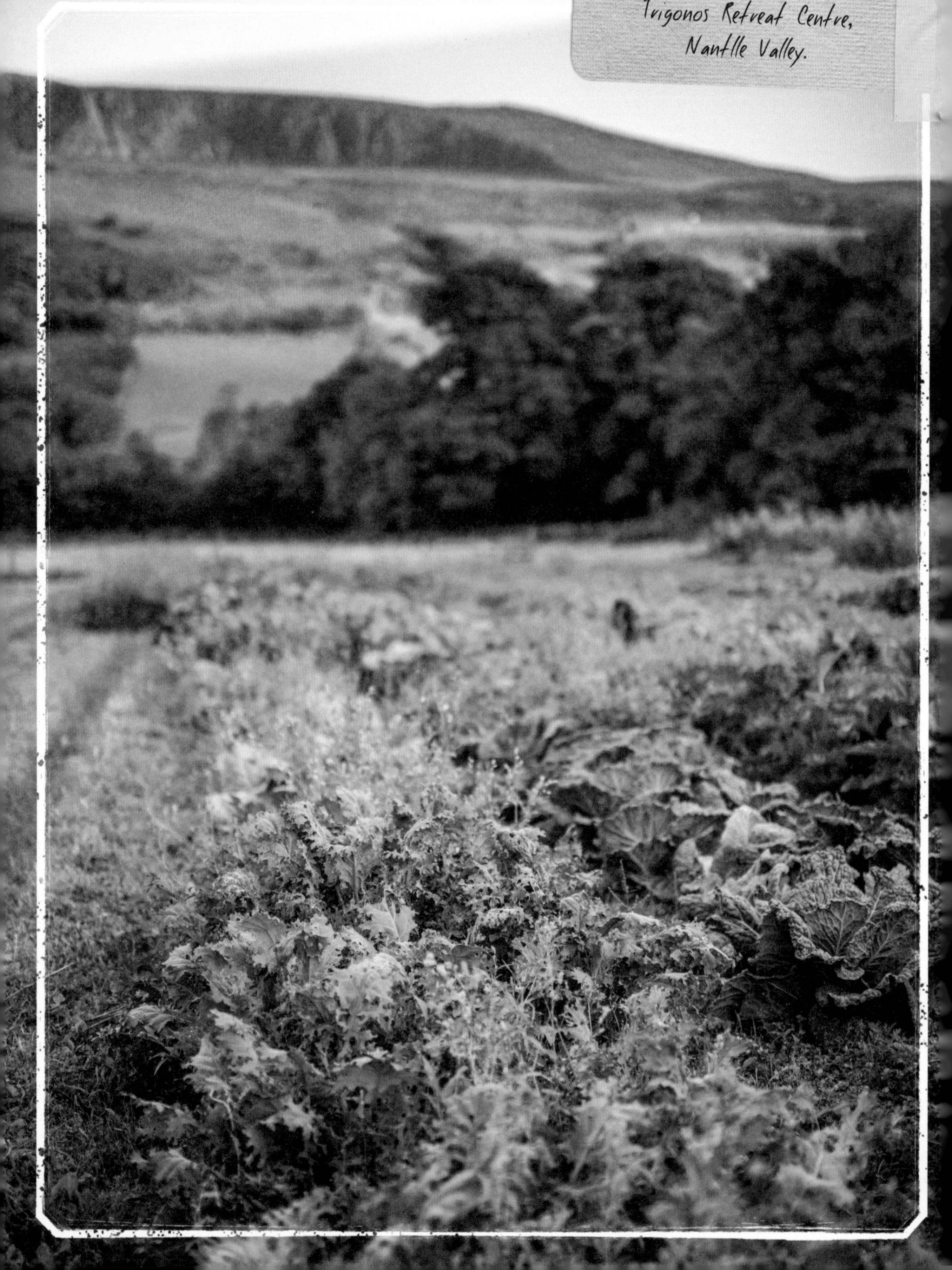

Trigonos Retreat Centre, Nantlle Valley.

Charred Pumpkin with Salsa Verde, Butter Beans & Piquillo Peppers

FOR 4

This is one of my favourite salads to make when I'm in Spain. The salsa verde cuts through the sweet pumpkin and rich beans nicely and you're left with happy mouth tingles. The main bits can be prepared in advance, so it's really just an assembly job. Adding cubes of tofu or tempeh to the salsa verde and leaving it to infuse overnight is a nice idea, and turns it into main course material. Chargrill your pumpkin on a griddle pan to get best results. Piquillo peppers are roasted Spanish sweet peppers and can be found all over the place, normally in little jars. If you like, you can grill red peppers with the pumpkin for a similar flavour and effect.

THE BITS

1 small sweet pumpkin, scrubbed, deseeded and quartered, then cut into 1cm thick half-moon wedges

12 cloves of garlic, unpeeled

2 tablespoons olive oil

sea salt

5 handfuls of baby spinach (slice larger leaves into thick green ribbons)

120g dried butter beans, soaked overnight, cooked and drained

2 ripe tomatoes, diced

1 x salsa verde dressing (see page 157)

For the garnish

150g piquillo peppers, cut into thick slices

3 tablespoons toasted pumpkin seeds

a handful of fresh coriander

½ teaspoon sweet paprika

2 teaspoons fruity olive oil

DO IT

Preheat the oven to 200°C/gas mark 6, and put a griddle pan on a high heat.

Put the pumpkin and whole cloves of garlic into a large bowl and add the oil and 1 teaspoon of sea salt. Rub the oil into the pumpkin, then place the chunks on the hot (probably slightly smoking) griddle pan. Leave them for at least a minute without moving them, then turn them over and do the same on the other side. You're looking for pronounced black lines. This is probably best done in batches.

Now place the pumpkin chunks on one half of a large baking tray and the garlic on the other. Pour over any leftover oil. Place in the oven and roast for 20 minutes, until the garlic is soft and gooey. Using a spatula, remove the garlic and place on a plate to cool. If the pumpkin is not quite soft yet, return it to the oven for a further 7–10 minutes.

Make the salsa verde. Sprinkle the spinach leaves over a large serving platter. Scatter over the beans, roasted garlic (skins on), pumpkin chunks and diced tomato, then drizzle over some of the salsa verde. Be creative here, go wild! Splatter sauce and toss beans around – the freer you are the better it looks.

Top with the sliced piquillo peppers and a sprinkling of pumpkin seeds and fresh herbs. Drizzle with a little more salsa verde, sprinkle with sea salt and sweet paprika and add a good glug of fruity olive oil.

Super Hero Raw Sprouting Salad with Cashew Hummus

FOR 4–6

Sprouting is a wonderful way to feed yourself cheaply with sparkling wonder foods. It's not fancy or expensive, but it is one of the finest examples of converting pennies into super-charged fuel for the body and mind.

This salad can be used to great effect with most sprouts, but mung beans, aduki beans and green lentils are the easiest to source and sprout. Alfalfa is a little more tricky, but can be found in many shops, especially your local health food shop. Very rarely does a plate of food scale such heady heights of vitality and potent nutritional hit. This salad is a head-turner, a gob-smacker, a lip-tickler and a full-on riot of plant power.

THE BITS

2 handfuls sprouted mung beans

2 handfuls sprouted green lentils

2 handfuls sprouted aduki beans

1 large carrot, scrubbed and grated

1 beetroot, peeled and grated

1 apple, cored and finely diced

6 Brussels sprouts or ¼ of a small cabbage (dodgy leaves picked off), very finely sliced

1 celery stalk, finely diced

½ a red onion, finely diced

1 yellow pepper, finely diced

2 handfuls of broccoli, chopped

3 tablespoons black olives, pitted and finely sliced, or fine capers

a handful of toasted sunflower seeds or pumpkin seeds (these can also be sprouted in the same way you sprout beans)

1 tablespoon chia seeds or sesame seeds

1 big handful of fresh parsley, finely chopped

Cos lettuce leaves, or any big lettuce leaves, for making a 'nest' (chicory leaves work well for smaller portions)

1 x super hero dressing (see page 327)

1 x raw cashew hummus dressing (see page 160)

For the garnish
a handful of sprouted alfalfa

sprinkles of wheatgrass, spirulina, etc. (optional 'super hero' topping)

DO IT

First make your super hero dressing and cashew hummus. Put all the salad ingredients, except the lettuce leaves, into a large bowl and add the dressing. Toss together, making sure everything is lightly coated.

Form a nest with the lettuce leaves in a large salad bowl, then scoop in the salad and sprinkle over the alfalfa and funky green powder (spirulina, etc.) if you have any. Alternatively you can use the individual salad leaves as 'boats' for your sprouts, spooning neat piles on to individual leaves. If the leaves you are using are soft and pliable, why not make some raw wraps?

This salad is magic with the cashew hummus. Avoid bread this time – the ridiculous amount of nutrients in this salad will keep you full for a long, long time. Give it around 20 minutes to digest and do its thing and you'll be well sated.

Beetroot, Apple & Raspberry Salad with Herb Millet

FOR 4–6

Millet is a magnificent whole grain and makes a delicious, gluten-free, low-carb alternative to potato, rice, wheat and all those other things we eat loads of. It grows very well in the UK and arrived here well before potatoes and wheat. I've had millet as porridge for breakfast in villages in the Himalayas, where the ground grains are also made into roti (flatbread). It is still used in many tribal communities around the world, especially Africa – in the places where wheat, especially, has not yet infiltrated.

Raspberries and beetroot are two powerful allies that add serious nutrition, colour and flavour to this salad. I sometimes like to throw in some tofu – it bulks it out and gives a nice rounded, protein-packed feel to the plate.

THE BITS

3 beetroots, with leaves on

1 carrot, scrubbed and grated

1 sour green apple, cored and roughly grated

½ a small red onion, peeled and roughly grated

200g firm tofu, diced into small cubes

a handful of raspberries

a handful of toasted walnuts or hazelnuts

For the millet

175g millet

300ml water

1 tablespoon olive oil

2 teaspoons fresh thyme leaves

½ teaspoon salt

3 tablespoons finely chopped fresh parsley

1 x raspberry dressing (see page 328)

DO IT

Cut the leaves off the beetroot, keeping them whole. Cut the stems into 2cm pieces, and scrub and roughly grate the roots.

In a small pan, toast the millet for 7 minutes, until it starts to become golden, shaking and swirling the pan to keep the millet moving. Add the water, lower the heat to minimum and cover the pan. Cook for 30 minutes. Fluff up the millet gently with a fork, and heat a little longer if it is still damp. Turn out on to a plate and leave to cool.

When the millet is just warm, stir in the olive oil, thyme, salt and most of the parsley. The millet may be sticky, which is fine. Break it up with your hands – the olive oil and parsley will help with this.

Make the raspberry dressing. Place all your grated bits in a large bowl and stir in most of the dressing, along with the chopped beetroot stems.

Arrange the sliced beetroot leaves around the edge of a serving plate and spoon the millet in the centre. Scatter the grated bits and tofu chunks over the top, followed by the raspberries and walnuts, then drizzle over a little more dressing and sprinkle with the rest of the parsley.

Sides

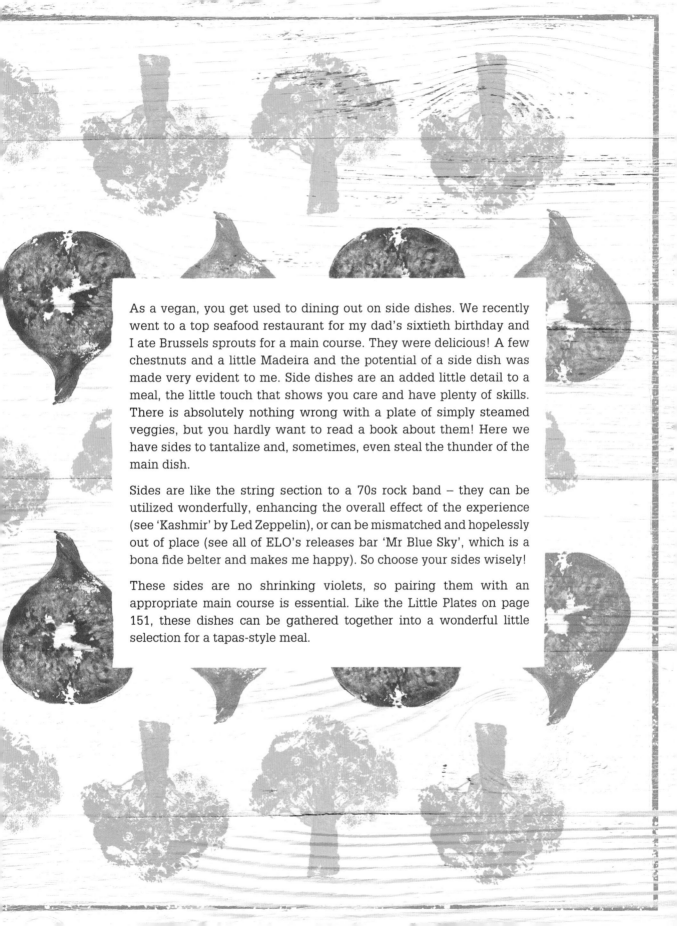

As a vegan, you get used to dining out on side dishes. We recently went to a top seafood restaurant for my dad's sixtieth birthday and I ate Brussels sprouts for a main course. They were delicious! A few chestnuts and a little Madeira and the potential of a side dish was made very evident to me. Side dishes are an added little detail to a meal, the little touch that shows you care and have plenty of skills. There is absolutely nothing wrong with a plate of simply steamed veggies, but you hardly want to read a book about them! Here we have sides to tantalize and, sometimes, even steal the thunder of the main dish.

Sides are like the string section to a 70s rock band – they can be utilized wonderfully, enhancing the overall effect of the experience (see 'Kashmir' by Led Zeppelin), or can be mismatched and hopelessly out of place (see all of ELO's releases bar 'Mr Blue Sky', which is a bona fide belter and makes me happy). So choose your sides wisely!

These sides are no shrinking violets, so pairing them with an appropriate main course is essential. Like the Little Plates on page 151, these dishes can be gathered together into a wonderful little selection for a tapas-style meal.

Turkish-style Oven-baked Spinach with Creamy Tofu Ricotta

FOR 6 AS A SIDE DISH OR 4 AS A BIG PLATE

Turkish food is stunning – I love the eclectic mix of influences and the incredible fertility of the land there. One of my favourite restaurants in the world is in Dalston, in east London, and to step through its doors is like a one-way ticket to the Bosphorus. This Turkish delight seems heavy on the spinach, but you know what it's like, it just disappears into a pile of gorgeous green. You can use any suitable greens here – kale works a treat, beetroot leaves are brilliant, and even the greener shades of thinly sliced cabbage will do. This dish can easily be made into a bigger plate by adding sliced cooked potatoes and cherry tomatoes to the spinach.

THE BITS

1 tablespoon olive oil

4 cloves of garlic, peeled and crushed

½ teaspoon ground allspice

1kg spinach

2 large pinches of freshly grated nutmeg

a big handful of fresh dill

a good pinch of salt

For the tofu ricotta

700g firm tofu

½ teaspoon sea salt

2 cloves of garlic, peeled and crushed

1 tablespoon lemon juice

1 tablespoon nutritional yeast flakes (see page 30)

1 teaspoon dried basil or oregano

a good pinch of sweet paprika

olive oil, for drizzling

DO IT

Put the oil and garlic into the largest pan you have, on a medium heat, and fry for a minute. Then add the allspice and fry for a moment, stirring. Add the spinach in big fistfuls and stir to help it to wilt. You will need to do this in batches; covering the pan helps lots. Once all of the spinach has wilted down, stir in the nutmeg and dill with a pinch of salt and cook uncovered until most of the liquid has disappeared. Take off the heat and cover the pan.

Place the tofu, salt, garlic, lemon juice, yeast flakes and dried herbs in a blender and blitz until smooth. You will have even better results if you do this the day before and keep it in the fridge.

Preheat the oven to 200°C/gas mark 6.

Spread out the spinach in a medium baking dish and press it into the corners to make a solid layer. Top with the tofu ricotta, spreading it in a thick layer until it meets the edges. Sprinkle with the paprika and finely drizzle over some olive oil and place in the oven for 25–30 minutes, until the tofu is nicely browned.

Serve warm with flatbreads, roasted veggies, or maybe a nice glass of 'lion's milk' (raki – don't worry it's vegan!).

Sweet & Sour Aubergines

FOR 4

Over a billion Hindus and thousands of years' worth of tradition have resulted in a beautiful array of vegetarian fare in India; from north to south, east to west, the food varies so much in this fascinating country. I ate something like this dish on my first night in Delhi, many years ago, wondering why they didn't serve this kind of Indian food in my local curry house.

To make this dish more authentic, try to get some of the smaller aubergines. Baby aubergines would work perfectly. Leaving the top of the aubergine intact adds to the look. If you'd like a thicker sauce, add a couple of chopped tomatoes when you add the water. The tomato and basil pilaf on page 143 would be lovely with this dish.

THE BITS

1 teaspoon salt

8 baby aubergines, quartered lengthways, keeping the stem intact

3 tablespoons gram (chickpea) flour

2 teaspoons cumin seeds

2 teaspoons coriander seeds

1 tablespoon finely grated fresh ginger

2 cloves of garlic, peeled and crushed

½ teaspoon cayenne pepper

1 teaspoon sweet paprika

a handful of fresh coriander leaves, finely chopped

3 tablespoons coconut oil (or vegetable oil)

juice of ½ a lemon

3 teaspoons brown sugar (unrefined)

For the garnish
a handful of fresh coriander leaves, chopped

DO IT

Rub ½ teaspoon of salt into the aubergines and leave them to drain in a colander for 30 minutes.

Put the chickpea flour, cumin seeds and coriander seeds into a heavy frying pan and toast on a medium heat until the seeds pop and the flour becomes darker. Scoop out into a pestle and mortar and roughly crush the seeds. Add the ginger, garlic, cayenne, paprika, fresh coriander, ½ teaspoon of salt and the toasted flour and spices to the mortar and bash into a thick, sticky paste.

Pat the aubergines dry with kitchen paper, then rub the paste into them, giving them a good, tasty coating.

Put the oil into a large frying pan (or an Indian karhai if you have one handy) and heat on medium-high. When it is hot (test with a little of the mix), add the aubergines and begin to fry, browning them on all sides for around 3–4 minutes. Add 3 tablespoons of water. Pop a lid on the pan and leave to simmer gently for 15 minutes, depending on size, until the aubergines are beautifully tender.

Take the lid off, then whisk the lemon and sugar together and pour over the aubergines. Continue to cook for a few minutes, turning them once, until there is a thick sauce and the aubergines are almost falling apart.

Serve warm, topped with chopped coriander.

Nantlle Lake.

Tamarind Mashed Sweet Potatoes with Coconut & Cumin

FOR 4

Sweet potato and tamarind are such good bedfellows. They love each other dearly and the addition of coconut milk takes mashed potatoes intergalactic! This dish is so bursting with flavour, you'll probably want to serve something simple with it. It is perfect alongside roasted vegetables (with a little spice added) and some wilted greens for a wonderfully balanced meal. You can buy tamarind paste, without stones. If you use this, halve the quantity. We've all added butter and milk to mash, now try this for a change. It's mash, but not as we know it.

THE BITS

450g baking potatoes, peeled and cut into chunks

450g sweet potatoes, peeled and cut into chunks

1½ teaspoons salt

2 tablespoons tamarind pulp, soaked in 3 tablespoons warm water for 2 hours

1 tablespoon coconut oil

a big handful of cashew nuts

1 teaspoon cumin seeds

1 teaspoon methi (fenugreek) leaves

1 teaspoon mustard seeds

1 lemongrass stalk, halved, or 2 teaspoons lemon zest

1–2 teaspoons dried chilli flakes (to taste)

200ml coconut milk

For the topping

a handful of fresh coriander, finely chopped

2 tablespoons cashew nuts (optional)

DO IT

Place all the potatoes in a pan, cover with fresh water, add 1 teaspoon of salt and bring to the boil. Simmer until tender – around 25 minutes. Drain, saving the liquid for a soup or stew (it's delicious). Leave for 5 minutes to steam dry, then pop back into the pan and put the lid on.

Pass the tamarind through a sieve, pressing down with a spoon. Make sure most of the pulp passes through and none of the stones.

While the potatoes are cooking, heat the coconut oil in a frying pan and add the cashew nuts, cumin seeds, methi and mustard seeds. Allow to cook and pop for a minute, but be careful not to let them burn. Add the lemongrass and chilli flakes and cook for less than a minute, then stir in the tamarind pulp. Pour in the coconut milk, bring to a slow boil, then simmer gently for 15 minutes. Cover and leave to sit for a while, letting the flavours have a party.

Pour two-thirds of the coconut sauce into the potatoes (picking out the lemongrass stalk) and get your funky mash on, mashing well until smooth and adding more sauce as needed. Zero lumps are tolerated. Check the seasoning and add the rest of the salt if necessary.

Sprinkle with fresh coriander and a few more cashews, if you are that way inclined.

Kasha with Rosemary, Apricots & Walnuts

FOR 6

Kasha is just another name for roasted buckwheat, but it sounds so much more exotic! Buckwheat is superbly nutritious and is actually completely gluten-free. This method of roasting buckwheat before steaming it really brings out its earthy flavour and is the way to go for me. The grains hold their shape and it becomes less of a mush. You don't have to soak the apricots – it just plumps them up and makes them a little softer, which I like.

THE BITS

2 tablespoons olive oil

360g raw buckwheat

1 large red onion, finely diced

500ml vegetable stock or water

2 large sprigs of fresh rosemary

125g dried apricots, soaked in 2 tablespoons water for 1 hour), then roughly chopped

a large pinch of black pepper

1–2 tablespoons tamari, to taste

70g toasted walnuts, roughly chopped

a handful of fresh parsley, finely chopped

½ a handful of pumpkin seeds

For the garnish
a handful of toasted walnuts, roughly chopped

DO IT

Heat 1 tablespoon of oil on a low heat in a large heavy pan and roast the buckwheat gently for 5 minutes, stirring regularly. When its colour changes to a darker brown, it is ready.

Add your onions and continue to cook, stirring, for 6–8 minutes, then add the warm stock and the rosemary sprigs. Cover, lower the heat to minimum, and simmer for about 15 minutes.

Remove the rosemary sprigs, fluff up the buckwheat with a fork, then stir in the rest of the ingredients and add 1 tablespoon of olive oil. Check the seasoning, pop the lid back on, and leave to mingle for 5 minutes. Serve warm, sprinkled with toasted walnuts.

Kimchi

MAKES ONE LARGE CONTAINER

Kimchi is currently taking the world by storm. It's made by fermenting cabbage with flavourings, a process called lacto-fermentation, in which a salty brine kills all bad bacteria. We omit the fish sauce and shrimp paste that is traditionally used and substitute kelp and some shiitake-flavoured stock, adding a decent dose of umami taste to proceedings. The most important step is to taste the kimchi each day – it should be fiery and salty. Remember, a little goes a long way. It keeps well in the fridge. I serve it with simple wok-fried vegetables, flavoured with tamari and ginger and rice or noodles, but if you're a real kimchi fiend, grab yourself a spoon and eat it straight out of the jar! *Shazam!*

THE BITS

1kg Chinese cabbage

140g sea salt

1.9 litres spring water

2–4 tablespoons chilli flakes (depending on desired heat)

1 apple, cored and peeled

2.5cm fresh ginger, peeled and finely sliced

1 white onion, peeled and roughly chopped

4 tablespoons tamari

5 cloves of garlic, peeled

1 small cooked potato (roughly 2 tablespoons of potato – leftover white rice can also be used)

6 spring onions, cut into 5cm pieces

1 large hot red chilli, sliced into thin rings, seeds left in

1 tablespoon sesame seeds

For the stock

2 large pieces of kelp

6 dried shiitake mushrooms (or 1 mushroom stock cube)

500ml water

DO IT

Cut the Chinese cabbage in half and remove the thick stems lengthways. Cut widthways into 5cm strips. Put the salt and cabbage into a large bowl and massage the salt into the cabbage – once it begins to release some liquid, cover with the spring water and press down with a plate, making sure all the leaves are submerged. Leave for 2 hours.

Put the stock ingredients into a pan and bring to the boil. Allow to cook down until roughly 175ml of liquid remains. This should be a very flavoursome broth. Strain and allow to cool. Rinse the Chinese cabbage and leave to drain in a colander for 15 minutes. Put the chilli flakes, apple, ginger, onion, tamari, garlic and potato into a food processor, add the stock, and blend to a smooth paste.

Gently squeeze out excess moisture from the cabbage. Put it back into the large bowl with the spring onions, fresh chilli and sesame seeds. Pour over the vivid red paste and massage it into the leaves, making sure they're all well covered (you may like to use gloves here; the chillies can be rough on the hands and whatever you choose to scratch next).

Place in a sealable container (Tupperware will do) or a large clean jar or two. Leave about 2.5cm space between the kimchi and the top of the container. Place the container on a plate; it may bubble over when left to ferment. Leave at room temperature in a safe place for 1–5 days (3 days being the average). Taste daily and press the leaves back down into the brine. Store in the fridge once you're happy with the tang and kick.

Winter Roots Braised in Porter

FOR 4–6

This is a full-power way of roasting your precious winter roots with one of my favourite winter things: jet black and intoxicating porter. Liquorice meets deep espresso while flirting with a smidgen of cacao in a heady brew. This dish is nice made with baby carrots and little parsnips, roasted whole, but if you can't find the little versions of these veggies, just use their big brothers chopped into similar shaped chunks. The mini versions do retain their flavour and nutrients better when roasted. This makes a delicious main course served with kasha (see page 135).

THE BITS

100g parsnips

150g carrots

150g swede

4 celery stalks

200g small onions (such as pickling onions), peeled

2 tablespoons rapeseed oil

3 cloves of garlic, peeled and crushed

175ml porter

1 sprig of fresh rosemary

1 tablespoon tomato purée

250ml vegetable stock

1 tablespoon unrefined brown sugar

½ teaspoon sea salt and cracked pepper (to taste)

DO IT

Peel or scrub the parsnips, carrots, swede and celery as necessary and cut into small similar-size batons.

Bring a small pan of salted water to the boil, drop in your onions and cook for 10–15 minutes, until they are tender when stabbed with a sharp knife. Drain well and pat with kitchen paper.

Heat the rapeseed oil in a pan, add the onions and celery and cook on a medium heat until lightly golden – roughly 10 minutes. Add the garlic and cook for 2 minutes, then add the carrots, swede and parsnips. Stir, then pour in the porter. Add the rosemary, tomato purée, vegetable stock and sugar and bring to the boil. Cover the pan and cook until the vegetables are tender, checking after 10 minutes.

The cooking stock should now be nice and thick. If not, remove the vegetables with a slotted spoon and keep warm, then continue to cook the stock until it has thickened. Put back the vegetables, pick out the rosemary sprig, and serve alongside a hearty dish like parsnip rumbledethumps (see page 204) or nut roast (see page 197), like a proper Sunday dinner.

Catalan Spinach

FOR 4–6

This side dish is so tasty it makes a great starter, or can even be served as a main course with a hunk of bread or some couscous. I love tapas and ate this a lot in Cataluña – it can be tough being a vegan in Spain, and this traditional spinach dish is an utter saviour.

THE BITS

50g sultanas

1 tablespoon olive oil

1 onion, finely chopped

2 cloves of garlic, peeled and finely chopped

800g spinach, roughly chopped

4 tablespoons toasted pine nuts

sea salt and cracked pepper, to taste

DO IT

Soak the sultanas in a bowl of warm water for 30 minutes, then drain and set aside (drink the water – it's lovely and sweet).

Heat the oil in a large heavy pan on a medium heat. Add the onion, stirring and cooking for 6–8 minutes, then add the garlic and cook for 2 minutes more. Throw in your spinach leaves, stir, then cover the pan and continue to cook for another 4–5 minutes, until the spinach has wilted down. You may need to do this in batches.

Now add the pine nuts and sultanas to the pan and season with salt and pepper.

Warm through and serve with a few more pine nuts on top.

Sesame & Sweetcorn Pancakes

MAKES 10 SMALL PANCAKES

Lovely little pancakes to soak up your favourite stew or curry. The gram flour adds unmistakable earthiness and plenty of nutrition and the regular flour helps to bind things together nicely. A great pancake partnership. If you'd like to go for full-on nutrition and be gluten free, add buckwheat flour instead of the normal flour and you will have a very funky pancake indeed. If you leave it to cool, it may even turn pink for you (a strange habit of buckwheat).

THE BITS

100g unbleached white flour

100g gram (chickpea) flour

2 teaspoons bicarbonate of soda

2 tablespoons sesame oil (cold-pressed and not toasted)

2 teaspoons tamari

360ml soya milk (unsweetened)

30g sesame seeds, toasted

2 handfuls of fresh sweetcorn kernels (or 1 small tin)

2 spring onions, finely sliced

a little vegetable oil, for frying

DO IT

Sift the flours and bicarbonate of soda into a large mixing bowl. In a separate bowl whisk together the sesame oil, tamari and soya milk until well combined. Now fold the dry ingredients into the wet ingredients until a batter is formed. Stir in the sesame seeds, sweetcorn and spring onions. Cover the mix and place in the fridge for 20 minutes.

Lightly oil a small frying pan and put on a medium high heat. When it's hot, add roughly 3 tablespoons of the mixture at a time and fry until one side is brown, 2 minutes max. Flip over and fry the other side for slightly less time. This should leave you with a nicely cooked pancake to enjoy. You may need to add a little more oil to the pan as you go along. Wrap the pancakes in a clean tea towel when cooked, to keep warm.

Enjoy with anything in the curry section (pages 216–38) or make a flame-grilled vegetable and chermoula wrap (see page 158)!

Mujaddara with Crispy Onions

FOR 4

This dish is Arabic in origin, but I think many countries would consider this pulse and grain combo their own, and rightly so, as it's a sure-fire winner. My version sees lentils and wheat teaming up to make a flavoursome side and a base for many wonderful additions. Just add a dressing, chopped herbs and vegetables and you're looking at a very special pilaf. I've left it plain here for you to have a play with. If you feel up to it (bearing in mind this is a side dish), the crispy onions finish this dish perfectly. Ideal teamed up with seeded lentil falafels (see page 175) and blobs of shimmering hummus (see page 160).

For a gluten-free option, replace the bulgur with millet or brown rice (more traditional).

THE BITS

115g green or brown lentils
480ml vegetable stock
110g fine bulgur wheat
1 tablespoon olive oil
2 teaspoons cumin seeds
1 onion, finely chopped
sea salt and black pepper, to taste
a large pinch of chilli powder
a large pinch of ground cinnamon

For the topping (optional)
vegetable oil
2 onions, very finely sliced
a handful of fresh parsley, finely chopped

DO IT

Cover the lentils with cold water and soak for 5 minutes, picking out anything dodgy that floats to the top. Drain, then place the lentils in a heavy pan with the stock, bring to the boil and simmer for 35–45 minutes, until tender. Stir in the bulgur and add enough water to cover by about 2cm. Cook on a very low heat for 5 minutes, then remove from the heat, cover and let stand for 10 minutes.

Heat the oil in a frying pan and sauté the cumin seeds for a minute. When they are popping, add your onions and sauté for 6–8 minutes, until soft. Stir the onions into the pilaf with a fork and season with salt if needed, pepper and the chilli and cinnamon. Fluff up the mujaddara with a fork and cover, keeping it warm.

To make the topping, heat a decent amount of vegetable oil in a heavy-bottomed frying pan – we are shallow-frying these onions until very golden and crispy. Turn the heat to medium and make sure the oil is hot. When it's shimmering (and a piece of onion frazzles when dropped in), add your onions and fry for 15 minutes, until deeply gold and sweet. Drain well, using a slotted spoon, and place on a plate covered with kitchen paper. Pat the onions with more kitchen paper to remove any excess oil.

Serve the mujadarra topped with the crispy onions and chopped parsley. Best served hot, but also great cold.

Tomato & Basil Pilaf

FOR 4-6

This is a decidedly European twist to pilaf. A delicious rice dish that can be easily served as a big plate. In late summer, basil grows wild on our window ledges and works its fragrant way into most of my dishes. It's so pungent and intoxicating you can barely believe it's legal! I like to use brown basmati, for taste and health reasons, but white basmati will also do. Just take 10 minutes off the overall cooking time. Stir in cooked beans or chickpeas and more veggies to make a more substantial main course dish.

THE BITS

400g brown basmati rice
(white basmati is also fine)

4 tomatoes, coarsely chopped

2 big handfuls of fresh basil leaves

225ml vegetable stock

2 tablespoons olive oil

10 peppercorns

1 cinnamon stick (about 8cm)

6 cloves

2 bay leaves

1 medium onion, finely chopped

1 teaspoon sea salt

½ teaspoon chilli powder (if you like things spicy)

DO IT

Wash your rice, cover it with water and swirl with your hand. Continue until the water is clear when drained. Leave to soak in fresh water for 45 minutes or longer. Drain well.

Blend the tomatoes and basil in a food processor and mix with the stock in a large jug. There should be roughly 600ml of liquid, so make up the amount with water if you need to.

Now pour the oil into a heavy-based saucepan and heat on medium-high. When the oil is hot, add the peppercorns, cinnamon, cloves and bay leaves, stir a few times, then add the onion. Keep stirring for 5 minutes, then add your rice. Stir gently, scraping the bottom and coating the rice with the oil.

Now stir in the tomato mix and salt, and the chilli powder if using, and bring to the boil. Cover the pan and cook on a very low heat for 35–40 minutes. Never lift the lid on your rice – it needs the steam.

Fluff up the rice well with a fork and serve with a gorgeous curry of your choice (see pages 216–38 for more inspiration).

Cauliflower Rice

FOR 4–6

This is a brilliant alternative to rice – gluten-free, very simple and something really quite different. It's just like rice but with bags more nutrition, less carbohydrate and, dare I say it, more flavour. This rice is ideal for serving with curries and I like to add the turmeric for a little colour, but it can easily be omitted to give pure white rice instead.

THE BITS

1 large cauliflower, chopped
very finely

1 tablespoon olive oil or vegetable oil

1 teaspoon ground turmeric

1 tablespoon water

1 teaspoon sea salt

DO IT

Make sure that your cauliflower is very well chopped – the easiest way is to put it into a food processor and pulse about five times, until it resembles rice. Any big bits can be picked out and kept for a later pulsing.

Heat the oil in a frying pan on a medium-high heat and begin to fry your cauliflower. Stir it regularly, and after 5–7 minutes, when the cauliflower is getting a little colour, add the turmeric and water. Continue cooking for another 5 minutes, until the cauliflower has become tender but still has a bit of bite to it.

Season with salt and serve.

Pico de Gallo

MAKES A DECENT BOWLFUL

I love this salsa – it's greater than the sum of its parts. Pico de gallo adds freshness and zing to every plate and can be served with all sorts, from burgers to burritos. It also makes a wonderful topping for soups and stews. I spent some time working on a banana farm in Nicaragua and we ate pico de gallo with every banana-based meal. Getting good tomatoes can become a serious quest on our temperate little island. The finest tomatoes will shine in this dish – the sweeter, the better. You can add a little sugar to tart things up a bit.

THE BITS

3 ripe room-temperature tomatoes,
finely chopped

½ a red onion, finely diced

1 big handful of coriander leaves,
finely chopped

juice of 1 lime

1 chilli, deseeded and finely chopped

½ teaspoon salt

½ teaspoon unrefined light brown sugar
(if the tomatoes are not sweet enough)

DO IT

Combine all the ingredients in a bowl and allow to settle for half an hour.

Sweet Sake Sugar Snaps

FOR 4

You could use any other green peas, like mangetout or French beans, for this lovely combination of crisp beans and sweet and salty sauce. Sake is well worth having around – it's a light, wine-like alcohol made with rice. It is delicious served warm and is also very handy to use as a substitute for mirin in Japanese-style cooking.

THE BITS

450g sugar snap peas

½ teaspoon sunflower oil

2.5cm fresh ginger, peeled
and finely grated

2 tablespoons sake

2 teaspoons brown rice syrup

2–3 teaspoons tamari, to taste

2 teaspoons toasted sesame seeds,
for topping

DO IT

Bring a pan of water to a rolling boil, then drop in the peas and cook for a minute. Drain, cool thoroughly under cold water, and drain again. Put them on a plate covered with kitchen paper and make sure they are nicely dry, ready to be fried. Heat the oil in a heavy frying pan on a high heat. When it's very hot, add the peas and ginger, sauté for 2 minutes, then add the sake and brown rice syrup. Let the liquid reduce for a minute, then remove from the heat. Season with tamari to taste, sprinkle with the sesame seeds and serve immediately.

Braised Fennel, Pear & Radish
with Toasted Almonds

FOR 4

This is a robust autumn/winter side that can light up a dark night. The fennel and pears work brilliantly and the radish adds its unique pink sphere of charm. Use firm sweet pears here, or they'll end up in a mush.

THE BITS

2 tablespoons olive oil

a pinch of sea salt

1 tablespoon red wine vinegar

1–2 tablespoons wholegrain mustard

1 teaspoon unrefined light brown sugar

2 large fennel bulbs, sliced lengthways into 1cm thick slices

6 cloves of garlic, peeled and left whole

2 handfuls of radishes, washed and trimmed

3 sprigs of fresh thyme or 1 teaspoon dried thyme

50ml dry white vermouth (i.e. Noilly Prat or dry Martini), or 75ml white wine

2 ripe pears, cut lengthways into thick slices

For the garnish

a handful of toasted almonds, roughly chopped

DO IT

Whisk together ½ tablespoon of olive oil, a pinch of sea salt, the red wine vinegar, mustard and sugar to make a dressing. Set aside.

On a high heat, warm the rest of the oil in a wide, heavy frying pan. Add the fennel and fry for 3 minutes, then add the garlic and radishes and toss in the oil for a further 4 minutes. Now add the thyme and vermouth and lower the heat, covering straight away to trap the steam. Leave to braise for 10 minutes, shaking the pan regularly, until all has become nicely brown and sticky.

Add the dressing and cook uncovered for 5 minutes longer, stirring and allowing the flavours to intensify. Add the pears and toss together gently, warming everything through, and remove from the heat.

Serve on a warm platter, topped with toasted almonds.

Nibbles, Dips & Little Plates

Small but perfectly formed. Modest explosions of flavour set to tantalize the palate, sparking the imagination. A prelude to a perfect main course or maybe part of a table full of these tasty little critters, variety being the spice of life and all.

These plates baulk at 'size matters' and concentrate on intensity instead. My favourite food cultures in the world do not eat off massive platters with piles of things mounded on them. I like little plates, in the middle of the table, and plenty of open-hearted sharing. Bits and pieces, bites and morsels, plenty of chatting and sipping, everyone trying everyone else's food and then their own!

These dishes can be served as starters or gathered together into a smorgas-bord of joyous goodness. Now we're really vegan dreaming!

Let's face it, it's party time! We rarely make special nibbles without having something to celebrate. Making nibbles needn't be much tougher than opening a bag of Kettle Chips. Minimal fuss can produce something wonderfully homemade and creative. Nibbles are a celebration for the fingers.

Britain seems to have turned into a nation of professional grazers – hummus is now the national dip of choice, and the range of dips and nibbles in supermarkets is truly mind-boggling (I find that about the selection of most things in supermarkets. How many shades of hummus is too much?). Making your own nibbles is fun and, importantly, a lot cheaper. A few vegetables, a gentle fry and you have a large bowl of vegetable crisps! Little things like this make me happy.

Making your own always means more – your guests will really appreciate it and you'll get a lot more Christmas cards (most probably mentioning your spicy maple pecans). Here we have some roasted bites and perfect purées that are anything but shop-bought, and the best part about them is they are comparatively very healthy! Plus they have gone nowhere near a factory, which I think is hugely important.

These recipes are not too vexing to get together and are the perfect excuse to get a party started. You'll love sharing the results with your friends and loved ones. People won't even realize that you're feeding them vegan fare.

Homemade Vegetable Crisps

MAKES ONE LARGE BOWLFUL (ENOUGH FOR 8–10 NIBBLERS)

So simple you'll stop buying the overpriced shop-bought varieties. The great thing about these crispy beauts is that you can moderate the amount of salt and eat them warm. A warm crisp is a thing of deep and meaningful beauty. You can use most vegetables here, but the starchier the better. I like adding an apple to the mix as it's something a bit different.

Using a mandolin is very dangerous, so take it easy and always use the protective guard provided. You can use a thin blade on your food processor, although this has varying results. Most will be fine, but you'll be left with some dodgy chunks. Just cut these as thin as you can.

THE BITS

1 beetroot
1 parsnip
1 potato
1 carrot
1 small sweet potato
1 apple
cooking oil, for deep-frying
sea salt

DO IT

Preheat the oven to 150°C/gas mark 2.

Scrub all the vegetables and the apple, peeling any that are marked or bruised, and slice them very thinly, using a mandolin if you have one (be careful!) or the fine blade on a food processor. Fill a large, flat pan one-third full with oil and heat to 180°C or until a slice dropped in sizzles immediately – this takes about 4 minutes.

Dry off your veggies in batches on a plate lined with kitchen paper, press them quite firmly between more sheets of kitchen paper to remove as much moisture as possible, then fry them. They all take different times to cook, so keep them separate – don't mix potato with apple, for example. Give them a little stir, making sure they don't stick together. Fry the beetroot and carrot first, as they can become soft after frying and need longer in the oven to crisp up.

When the crisps are golden, they are ready. Drain each batch on kitchen paper to remove excess oil, then place on a baking tray and put them into the oven. Bake them for 10–15 minutes, until they are all crispy.

Serve warm, sprinkled with sea salt.

Broad Bean & Avocado Dip with Lemon & Thyme

MAKES 1 LARGE BOWLFUL

Superbly green and full of rich, smooth, fresh flavours, this dip makes the ideal sunshine accompaniment or spread. The broad bean harvest is one of my favourite times of year. I love podding them – it's very therapeutic, although many of the beans end up in my mouth. I have found that many people prefer broad beans cooked a little, so we are going to blanch them here. If the beans are not freshly picked or it's getting late in the season, I'd recommend you peel the sometimes leathery coats off them. Otherwise, just blend them up to a vibrant bowl of vivid green and enjoy with some sliced veggies.

THE BITS

300g broad beans, shelled and blanched

2 ripe avocados, peeled and stoned

2 cloves of garlic, peeled and minced

1 big handful of fresh mint, chopped

3 sprigs of fresh thyme, leaves only

juice of 1 lemon

zest of ½ a lemon

½ teaspoon sea salt

a large pinch of cracked black pepper

2 tablespoons olive oil

DO IT

Cook the shelled broad beans in salted boiling water for 5 minutes. Drain well and cool.

Put all the ingredients except the olive oil into a food processor, and trickle in the oil while blitzing. Use enough oil to give a shimmering appearance – 2 tablespoons should do nicely, but add a bit more if necessary.

Serve with long dippers of your choice – the ubiquitous carrot works well, but you could also try beetroot batons or kohlrabi shards, green apple chunks or even chicory boats.

Artichoke & Almond Purée

MAKES ONE BIG BOWLFUL

A purée that really highlights the potential of plant-based creaminess. The richness of the almonds balances the sharpness of the artichokes and lemon, a match made somewhere in the Med. I make this type of thing a lot in Spain, and it's a tried and tested 'carnivore friendly' dip. In fact, some people have said that this dip is the highlight of the meal, and I guess if the dip overshadows the rest, you know you're doing something right. I normally buy fresh artichokes if I have time to treat them with the care they deserve. But I also use jarred ones – they're much better than tinned.

THE BITS

400g artichoke hearts (jarred is fine)

2 big handfuls of almonds, soaked overnight, skins peeled off (blanched almonds are fine)

2 cloves of garlic, peeled and minced

1 teaspoon dried mint

juice of ½ a lemon

½ teaspoon sea salt

3 tablespoons olive oil

For the garnish

any leafy green fresh herb
(parsley, mint or even chives are cool)

a large pinch of sweet paprika

DO IT

Place all the ingredients in a food processor and blend until creamy.

Garnish with a sprinkle of fresh herbs and paprika. Note: Normally I'd serve this with some seeded breadsticks or, if the occasion is slightly fancy, in hollowed-out cherry/small plum tomatoes (striking to look at, but admittedly a little fiddly). Easier to thinly slice a carrot, cucumber, courgette, green apple, etc., spoon a small amount of purée on to each slice, and top with herbs and paprika. Stunning!

Watercress & Butter Bean Purée

MAKES ONE BIG BOWLFUL

Watercress grows all over the place in the UK, in clean streams and rivers, like a weed. If you are short of time, use tinned beans, though I much prefer to soak and cook my own. Anything tinned just doesn't have the same flavour or texture, and you also don't get the heavily flavoured cooking stock, which can be used in all sorts of ways. If needed, add it to this purée to thin it out. Think of nutritional yeast flakes as very nutritious vegan Parmesan – they are ideal when a little cheesy savouriness is required.

THE BITS

6 large handfuls of watercress

250g dried butter beans, soaked and cooked, or 2 x 400g tins, drained

2 large cloves of garlic, peeled and crushed

3–5 tablespoons olive oil

juice of ½ a lemon

1 teaspoon sea salt

For the garnish

a handful of dandelion leaves
(fresh and young leaves only)

2 tablespoons nutritional yeast flakes
(see page 30) (optional)

DO IT

Wash the watercress and trim off the very ends of the stalks if necessary. In a small pan of salted boiling water, blanch the watercress for 1 minute and drain well in a colander.

Place all the ingredients in a food processor and blend until thick and creamy. Add a little water (or bean cooking stock) to thin it out.

Serve on seeded crackers with some chopped dandelion leaves. Spoon on the dip and sprinkle over the nutritional yeast flakes.

Pinto Bean Pâté
with Walnuts & Raisins

MAKES ONE BIG BOWLFUL

This is a hearty vegan pâté, nice and chunky, with a smoky paprika twang. I generally serve it during the colder months, as it's quite filling. It's perfect to serve with drinks, as it's almost a meal in itself and happy hour will stretch long into the night. Smoked paprika can vary and will age badly. If you're using the good stuff, one teaspoon will suffice in this recipe.

THE BITS

285g pinto beans, soaked and cooked,
or 2 x 400g tins, drained

½ a small red onion, finely diced

3 cloves of garlic, peeled and crushed

2 tablespoons fresh thyme leaves

a handful of fresh parsley,
finely chopped

3 tablespoons olive oil

75g roasted pumpkin seeds

70g walnuts, roughly chopped

3 tablespoons raisins, roughly chopped

1 teaspoon smoked paprika

1 teaspoon sea salt

120ml water

For the optional garnish

a drizzle of olive oil

a pinch of smoked paprika

DO IT

Place all the ingredients except the water in a blender and drizzle in the water while blending, until a thick, chunky consistency is achieved. Don't overdo the blitzing. This is not a smooth pâté. You may like to drizzle over a little more oil and a sprinkle of paprika to round things off.

This dip is awesome served on soldiers of pumpernickel toast or any German-style heavy bread. If you can get Schwartzbrot (black bread), the daddy of all German baked goods (and that is quite an achievement!), please use it liberally. The full flavour of this dense loaf works perfectly with the pinto pâté.

Salsa Verde

FOR 6

The party has not started until salsa verde lands on the canapé table – the ultimate expression of zest, herbs and fiery chilli, all mingling in some form of green gorgeousness. This kind of green sauce (salsa verde!) is made all over the world, from Italy to Mexico. Most people have their favourite balance of flavours, and this is a really simple recipe. A few warm tortillas and you're away . . . If you can't find green tomatoes, just use red ones instead. Slightly unripe is probably best for this salsa. Tomatillos, if you can find them (you can sometimes buy them online), have a lovely tart and citrus twang, taking things in a proper Mexican direction.

THE BITS

4 large green tomatoes or tomatillos

2 big handfuls of fresh coriander

1 big handful of fresh parsley

1–2 fresh red chillies, finely diced

2 cloves of garlic, peeled and crushed

juice of 1 large lemon or 2 small limes

zest of ½ a large lemon or 1 small lime

½–1 teaspoon sea salt

DO IT

Place all the ingredients in a food processor and blitz until well combined, adding water as needed. Sometimes you want a thin salsa, sometimes you want something thicker. It depends on the occasion. For dips, go thick! This can be served warm or cold.

Flame-grilled Vegetables with Chermoula & Raw Cashew Hummus

FOR 4

Vegan barbecues can sometimes be a damp squib, but these veggies are perfect for the barbie and the punchy chermoula and creamy hummus make up for the lack of cremated sausage. I love the zest and vibrancy that chermoula brings to the party. It's one of those relishes that is the real star of the plate and the raw cashew hummus is even richer and more decadent than its chickpea cousin.

THE BITS

1 red pepper, deseeded and cut into chunky strips

1 yellow pepper, deseeded and cut into chunky strips

1 medium aubergine, cut into 2cm chunks

2 medium courgettes, cut into 2cm chunks

3 small red onions, quartered

2 bulbs of fennel, fronds trimmed, cut into 1cm slices lengthways

4 tablespoons good olive oil

2 teaspoons cumin seeds

2 teaspoons caraway seeds

sea salt and black pepper

2 handfuls of cherry tomatoes

1x raw cashew hummus (see page 160)

For the chermoula

1 teaspoon coriander seeds, or ½ teaspoon ground coriander

1 teaspoon cumin seeds, or ½ teaspoon ground cumin

100g fresh coriander

50g fresh parsley

2 cloves of garlic, peeled and crushed

2 tablespoons lemon juice

2 teaspoons lemon zest

8 tablespoons olive oil

DO IT

Warm a griddle pan or barbecue. Toss all the vegetables (except the tomatoes) in a large bowl with the oil, then griddle for around 10 minutes on a high heat, turning every so often, to char all over. You may need to do this in batches. Keep the cooked veggies covered and warm.

Preheat the oven to 200°C/gas mark 6.

Place all the vegetables on a baking tray with the cumin and caraway seeds, then drizzle over any leftover oil from the bowl. Season with salt and pepper.

Bake the vegetables for 25–30 minutes, turning them twice and basting them with the juices. Add the tomatoes 5 minutes before the end. Meanwhile make the cashew hummus.

To make the chermoula, dry roast the coriander and cumin seeds in a small frying pan on a medium-high heat for about 1 minute (they will pop). Keep them moving and make sure they don't burn or they will become very bitter. Tip the seeds into a pestle and mortar and grind them down into a powder. Now add all the ingredients (except the oil) to the mortar and continue pounding and stirring, then drizzle in the oil. The chermoula should resemble a thin sauce, so add more oil if needed. Put into a bowl and set aside.

Serve the vegetables on large warmed plates, drizzled generously with chermoula and with the cashew hummus alongside. Piles of light fluffy couscous finish this dish perfectly. Alternatively you can take things in a different direction by serving as a wrap with sesame and sweetcorn pancakes (see page 141).

Raw Cashew Hummus

MAKES ONE BIG BOWLFUL

Cashews are like the double cream in the vegan repertoire. Most vegans have a long and committed love affair with the cashew – it has such a gorgeous silky smooth feel and subtle, creamy flavour. Soaking nuts unlocks the enzymes within and allows the nutrition of the nut to be better utilized by the body. Soaking also makes them nice and soft, which is ideal when blending these precious little gifts. I like a decent amount of tahini in my hummus. It boosts this recipe into the stratosphere of outrageously healthy and delicious. This hummus is quite rich, and you only need a small spoonful. Enjoy it responsibly! Sometimes I mix two handfuls of fresh basil leaves in here.

THE BITS

300g raw cashews, soaked overnight

1–2 big cloves of garlic, peeled and crushed

juice of ½ a lemon

½ teaspoon sea salt

3 tablespoons light tahini

½ teaspoon freshly ground cumin seeds

100ml olive oil, plus extra for drizzling

75ml water

DO IT

Place the cashews, garlic, lemon juice, salt, tahini and cumin seeds in a food processor and blitz, turning off the machine and scraping down the sides regularly to incorporate the mix.

Once combined, blitz continuously and drizzle the olive oil in. When you are getting towards the right consistency, add the water (this lightens the hummus a little). Keep blitzing and drizzling in oil until the desired shimmering hummus texture is achieved. Cashews don't thicken up in the fridge like chickpeas, so don't make it too thin.

Serve drizzled with olive oil, with long celery stick dippers and a smile.

Oven-baked 'Gigglebeans'

SERVES 6

Superbly simple party food and homemade nibble goodness. They're very nutritious and even cheaper than buying loads of cheap crisps. Gigglebeans are what our German brothers and sisters call their *Kichererbsen*, or chickpeas. Healthy nibbles are far too rare, and most chickpea snacks are deep-fried. The vast amounts of oil tend to negate the shining health properties of your gigglebeans. Granted there is a hefty glug of oil in these chickers, but you can always add less and they still turn out wonderfully well. You can do all sorts with these chickpeas when roasted – I normally like to add some warm and smoky spices.

THE BITS

350g dried chickpeas, soaked overnight

250ml sunflower or groundnut oil

1½ teaspoons sea salt

½ teaspoon smoked paprika

¼ teaspoon cayenne pepper

¼ teaspoon ground cinnamon

DO IT

Preheat the oven to 180°C/gas mark 4.

Drain your chickpeas really well and pat them dry with kitchen paper. Combine the chickpeas and oil on a baking tray, allowing enough space for the chickpeas to spread out. You don't want them stacked up. Bake for 20 minutes, give them a good stir, then bake for 10–15 minutes more. They should be golden and very crispy at this stage.

Pour them on to a large plate covered with lots of kitchen paper to absorb any extra oil, then put them into a serving dish. Mix the salt and spices in a small bowl and sprinkle over the hot chickpeas.

Reserve a few of the gigglebeans for yourself, because these suckers don't last long in the wild. Serve immediately.

Spicy Maple Pecans

FOR 4

This is a great way to spice up your nuts – I love the combination of sweet and spicy. Pecans and maple go together like a mountie and moose. Canada's answer to chapatti and chai, tequila and nachos, black coffee and a slab of dark chocolate. This is a special occasion snack – pecans are precious, and it's a full-on celebration nibble. You can use any nut you like with this recipe and the results will be similarly spectacular. Real maple syrup is costly, but I would always recommend keeping some stashed in your cupboards. Less is more with maple syrup, and you cannot replicate that flavour.

THE BITS

200g pecan nuts

2 tablespoons unprocessed brown sugar

1–1½ teaspoons sea salt

⅓ teaspoon cayenne pepper

a large pinch of ground cinnamon

1 teaspoon sweet paprika

a large pinch of ground ginger

3 tablespoons maple syrup

1 tablespoon water

2 teaspoons cooking oil

1 teaspoon fresh orange zest

DO IT

Put a large, heavy-based frying pan on a medium heat, then throw in your nuts and gently toast, stirring almost constantly and making sure they don't burn. After 7–8 minutes you should be getting gorgeous aromas of toasted nut-ness – add the rest of the ingredients to the pan, then heat through and stir for 2–3 minutes on a low heat.

Spread the nuts out on a baking tray or a large plate – the coating should be clinging to them. Leave to cool slightly, and serve warm.

Mixed Nut Cheewra

FOR 6

Now this is a real nut-fest! Spicy at that. Indians know how to nibble and have the most outrageously complex methods for producing savoury snacks, or namkeen. Most of these salty snacks are deep-fried and they come in piles of glorious colours and varieties. It seems that all grains and pulses, all shapes and sizes, are given the namkeen treatment. The perfect snack to eat while ogling the Indian countryside from a train window. Magnificent served with grated onion, tomato and fresh coriander (don't forget the healthy pinch of spices). In winter, you may like to add chestnuts to the cheewra, which cuts down the amount of fat in the dish.

THE BITS

3 tablespoons vegetable oil

1 teaspoon cumin seeds

2 teaspoons black mustard seeds

3 tablespoons unprocessed brown sugar (or sugar of your choice – jaggery works well)

2 teaspoons garam masala

½ teaspoon ground turmeric

a large pinch of cayenne pepper

a large pinch of black pepper

1–1½ teaspoons sea salt

a handful each of raw almonds, walnuts, peanuts, cashews and raisins

2 handfuls of plain puffed cereal (rice is traditional, but anything puffed up will do)

DO IT

Preheat the oven to 180°C/gas mark 4.

Put the oil into a large frying pan on a medium heat, heat for a minute, then add the cumin and mustard seeds and allow them to splutter and pop for 30 seconds. Add the brown sugar and wait for it to melt a little, then pop in the spices and salt. Stir constantly and let it bubble for a minute, making sure the sugar doesn't burn. You don't want a full caramel here, just slightly melted sugar.

Add the nuts to the pan and give them a good coating of sticky spice mix. Spread the nutty goodness out on a foil-lined baking tray and bake for 15–20 minutes, until golden brown (texture like sun). Stir a few times during the baking, and keep your eye on them.

Set aside and let them cool slightly on the tray, then place in a bowl and mix in the raisins and puffed grains.

Serve warm, to a few 'oohs' and 'aahs' from your guests.

Young Leeks, Watercress & Asparagus with Tofu Gribiche

FOR 4–6

Some of my most magical memories are of camping in the Côte d'Or in France during *le vendange* (the grape-picking season). We were tipsy by 9 a.m. (purely medicinal for the back pain!) and by 10 a.m. had already munched our first whole baguette, the grape-pickers' version of an express lunch, containing lashings of butter, marinated artichokes, local cheese and slabs of chocolate (this was in pre-vegan times of rampant indigestion). I returned to Britain like an overweight lump of salted *beurre*, with Beaujolais-tinted cheeks and a smile painted on my face. Many things have changed since then, but my love of old-fashioned romance, good French wine and gribiche are undiminished. I have tampered in a vegan fashion with the traditional recipe, but have always loved the tangy herbiness of this little condiment.

THE BITS

500g young leeks, trimmed and cleaned

400g young asparagus, trimmed

300g watercress, well washed and dried

1 tablespoon olive oil

3 tablespoons toasted pine nuts

For the tofu gribiche

240g firm tofu, well drained

3 teaspoons capers, drained and roughly chopped

2 tablespoons chopped fresh tarragon leaves

1 tablespoon chopped fresh chervil or parsley

sea salt and freshly ground black pepper, to taste

3 tablespoons olive oil

½ teaspoon unrefined light brown sugar

1 tablespoon lemon juice

1 teaspoon Dijon mustard

DO IT

Make the gribiche, preferably beforehand. Put the tofu into a bowl and break it down, using a fork – it should resemble hard-boiled eggs. Now mix in the capers and herbs and season well. Mix together the oil, sugar, lemon juice and mustard in a small bowl and stir it into the tofu. Cover and pop into the fridge for at least 30 minutes (2 hours is ideal).

Fill a medium saucepan two-thirds full with water, add a little salt, and bring to a rolling boil. Dunk in your leeks and cook for a couple of minutes, then remove with a slotted spoon and set aside to cool. Allow the water to come back to the boil, plunge in your asparagus and cook for a couple of minutes, then remove and set aside. Bring the water back to the boil again, blanch the watercress for 30 seconds and set aside also. (Keep this water: it is awesome stock.)

When cooled, dry the asparagus and leeks on kitchen paper (the leeks may need a gentle squeeze). Put a griddle pan on a high heat and brush with a little olive oil. When very hot, chargrill the leeks and asparagus for 1 minute each side. This will bring out even more of their flavours and also looks very cool indeed.

Once the vegetables are cool, place them on a shallow serving plate with the watercress. Spoon over the gribiche and top with a scattering of pine nuts. It's a green feast!

Toasted Sourdough with Roast Courgette, Tomatoes, Marjoram & Almond Cream

FOR 4

This is the kind of thing I imagine millions of Italians tucking into on their leisurely lunch break. I don't eat loads of bread, but when I do, sourdough is my preference. As for the tomatoes, I rarely skin mine as I'm lazy! Here's a shining summer starter, or lunch, that takes advantage of glorious fresh seasonal produce and bread that is slightly past its best.

Gluten-free option: use your favourite GF bread.

THE BITS

350g ripe tomatoes, quickly blanched and skinned

2 small green courgettes, trimmed and cut into 1cm strips lengthways

plenty of extra virgin olive oil

3 cloves of garlic, peeled and crushed with 1 teaspoon sea salt

a handful of fresh marjoram leaves

a large pinch of cracked black pepper

3 thick slices of sourdough bread (slightly stale is cool)

a handful of fresh basil leaves

1 teaspoon lemon juice

For the almond cream

1 big handful of almonds (soaked, skins slipped off, or blanched)

50ml sugar-free almond milk (soya will do)

1 teaspoon nutritional yeast flakes (see page 30)

a pinch of sea salt

½ tablespoon extra virgin olive oil

DO IT

Preheat the oven to 200°C/gas mark 6. Bring a small pan of water to the boil, then cut an 'X' in the base of your tomatoes and drop them into the water. Blanch for a minute, then take them out and place them in a large bowl of cold water. Once cool, peel them – the skins should leap off!

Rub the courgette slices with extra virgin olive oil and place them on a baking tray. In a small bowl, mix together the garlic, marjoram leaves and 2 tablespoons of extra virgin olive oil and season with salt and pepper. Drizzle this mix over your courgettes and roast for 15–20 minutes.

Meanwhile, tear your sourdough into roughly 5cm cubes, place them on another baking tray and drizzle with a good glug of extra virgin olive oil. Toss the bread with your hands to coat with the oil. Pop in the oven for 5–7 minutes, then toss again and put back into the oven for 3–4 minutes. The bread should be crisped on the outside, but still chewy in the middle.

To make the almond cream, put the soaked almonds into a food processor and blend until creamy – you should have something resembling a loose peanut butter (but almond!). You will need to scrape the sides of the processor a few times. Add the rest of the ingredients and blend until a smooth sauce is formed.

On a large serving platter, lay out your warm sourdough pieces. Cut all the tomatoes in half horizontally and squeeze the juice and seeds from half of them over your bread. Roughly chop the tomato flesh and sprinkle on top. Lay over your courgette slices in a lattice fashion and scatter on the rest of your halved tomatoes. Tear your basil leaves gently and shower them over the dish then sprinkle with the lemon juice. Now spoon over your almond cream and serve immediately.

Beetroot & Cumin Fritters with Horseradish & Dill Yoghurt

MAKES 8–10 FRITTERS

These little fritters are bursting at the seams with flavours, and the herbaceous horseradish yoghurt tops things off very nicely. A punchy, zesty sauce is perfect with any fried food, lighting the palate up. The sweet earthiness of the beetroot and the fragrance of cumin were, very simply, made for each other. I like to use any green peas or beans for this, but the edamame probably have the edge due to their nice crunchy texture, which adds an almost nutty bite to the fritters. Use any flour you like, but I prefer to keep them gluten free. Gram (chickpea) flour would work well.

THE BITS

1 large potato, scrubbed and cut into cubes

125g firm tofu, drained and well mashed

40g buckwheat or wholewheat flour

a handful of fresh mint leaves, finely chopped

zest of 1 lemon

1 teaspoon sea salt

¼ teaspoon freshly ground black pepper

300g beetroots, scrubbed and coarsely grated

a handful of edamame/green peas/broad beans

1½ teaspoons cumin seeds, toasted and roughly ground

vegetable oil, for frying

1 x horseradish and dill yoghurt (see page 330)

For the garnish

1 big handful of watercress or spinach leaves

2 spring onions, thinly sliced

DO IT

Put the potato into a small pan, cover with water, add a pinch of salt and bring to the boil. Cook for 25 minutes, until soft. Drain in a colander, mash well and leave to cool.

Make the horseradish and dill yoghurt. This can be done well in advance.

Once the potato has cooled to handling temperature, mix with the tofu, flour, mint leaves, lemon, salt and pepper. Now gently mix in the grated beetroot and peas, until all is well combined – using your hands is best. We'd like these fritters to be chunky and packed full of texture.

In a large, heavy frying pan, dry-toast your cumin seeds on a medium-low heat for a minute. They should pop and give off a lovely aroma. Put them into a pestle and mortar and bash them up a little, then stir them into the fritter mix.

In the same pan, warm ½ tablespoon of oil on a medium heat, ensuring that the base of the pan is evenly covered with a film of oil. Spoon in 2 heaped tablespoons of fritter mix per go, pressing it down a little with the back of the spoon until roughly 1cm thick. Cook for 3–4 minutes on one side and slightly less on the other. Repeat until you have a few fritters cooking at the same time, and continue to cook in batches. Drain on kitchen paper and keep them warm in a low oven.

Serve warm and crispy on a bed of vibrant green watercress or spinach leaves, garnished with the spring onions and with the horseradish and dill yoghurt on the side.

Muhammara (Syrian Roasted Pepper & Walnut Dip) with Warm Black Olives

FOR 1 SMALL BOWLFUL

This dish goes above and beyond the call of a dip. The combinations of flavours are quintessentially of the southern Med, some kind of Eden for the vegan-leaning foodie. Many cultures call muhammara their own, and I'm not weighing in to that debate. I just know that all is good in the world when warm pitta encounters muhammara and the salty twang of good olives. Red peppers are one of nature's best sources of vitamin C – they are so sweet and fruity and work brilliantly in Med-style food.

Gluten-free option: swap the bread for your favourite GF variety.

THE BITS

2 large red peppers

2 tablespoons fruity olive oil

1 teaspoon chilli flakes

2 slices of wholemeal bread, crusts taken off (stale bread works best)

2 big handfuls of walnuts

1½ tablespoons pomegranate molasses (add the juice of ½ a lemon if you can't get this)

1 teaspoon unrefined brown sugar

½ teaspoon smoked paprika

125g firm tofu

½ teaspoon sea salt

For the garnish

a glug of olive oil

½ a handful of fresh parsley, finely chopped

a large pinch of smoked paprika

For the warm olives

2 tablespoons olive oil

½ teaspoon cumin seeds

½ teaspoon fennel seeds

½ teaspoon chilli flakes

1 clove of garlic, crushed

200g nice black olives

zest of ½ a lemon

2 tablespoons fresh parsley

DO IT

Preheat the oven to 220°C/gas mark 7.

Using your hands, rub the peppers with a little of the olive oil and place on a baking tray, then roast them in the oven for 15–20 minutes, turning them over once, until the skins are slightly blackened and the peppers are very tender. Place in a bowl, covered with a plate or clingfilm, to cool. Once cooled, cut the peppers in half and scoop the seeds out with a spoon. Peel the bitter skin off – it should slip off nice and easily.

Place the peppers and all the other muhamarra ingredients in a food processor and blitz until creamy.

For the warm olives, place the oil, cumin seeds, fennel seeds, chilli flakes and garlic in a small pan and fry for 30 seconds, then add the olives and lemon zest and bring to a gentle simmer. Remove from the heat and stir in the parsley. Cover and set aside until you're ready to serve.

Serve the muhammara in the centre of a large serving platter, drizzled with olive oil, sprinkled with parsley and smoked paprika, with toasted pitta breads around the edge and a warm bowl filled with the olives.

Shiitake Tempura with Wasabi Mayo

FOR 4-6

The Japanese know all about the art of frying. I mean frying that results in the lightest of batters, crispy and retaining very little oil. This form of deep-frying is actually healthier than most shallow-frying. It's all about the temperature – if that's right, the food doesn't absorb so much oil. It just happily fizzes and bubbles away towards golden perfection. Tempura is only good when the oil is very hot and the batter is chilled. If you have any batter left over, just fry it on its own – it makes a great little snack. If you can't get your hands on shiitake mushrooms, any mushroom will do and can be cooked in the same way.

THE BITS

500ml cooking oil (or enough for deep-frying)

4 tablespoons unbleached white flour, for dusting

300g fresh shiitake mushrooms (oyster mushrooms are also rather nice)

For the batter
240g unbleached white flour

475ml cold (iced) water

½ teaspoon sea salt

For the wasabi mayo
250g silken tofu

juice of ½ a lemon

3–4 tablespoons wasabi

2 tablespoons olive oil

sea salt, to taste

For the garnish
3 handfuls of watercress or spinach leaves

DO IT

To make the mayo, blend the tofu, lemon juice and wasabi together in a food processor. Drizzle in the olive oil, making it shimmer. Check the seasoning and spoon into a small bowl for dipping purposes. (I love wasabi and normally add another tablespoon.)

Lightly whisk together your batter ingredients in a flat bowl. Don't worry about lumps (this makes the tempura even lighter). Pop it into the fridge for 20 minutes, to chill.

Warm the oven on its lowest setting. Then heat the oil to between 160°C and 180°C in a heavy-based pan – a wide saucepan is perfect. The oil is ready when it's slightly smoking and a drop of batter sizzles vigorously.

Sprinkle the flour on a separate plate and gently dust the shiitake mushrooms. This will help the batter to cling to the 'shrooms.

Dip the 'shrooms into the batter, covering them all over, and put them straight into the hot oil. Don't be too precious here, quickly works best. The closer your batter bowl is to the pan, the less batter you'll dribble everywhere. Fry for 1–2 minutes, then remove using a slotted spoon and drain very well on kitchen paper.

Continue frying in reasonable batches (don't overcrowd the pan) until you've used all the shiitakes. The warm oven is handy for keeping the tempura crispy, so have ready a baking tray with a wire rack (to allow the excess oil to drain) when frying. This takes the pressure off a little to get everything done in double-quick time. Tempura MUST be crispy.

(cont.) ➡

Serve warm, with watercress or spinach leaves and small bowls of the wasabi mayo on the side. If you have any leftover batter, consider frying any other fruit and vegetables that are in the vicinity. Tempura is a batter bonanza for all fruits and vegetables!

Extras

- Tempura is so versatile. Mix the batter with chopped onions and some corn, spoon into hot oil, fry for a minute or so and you have yourself a fritter.

- Tempura parsnips are incredible and can be made in the same way as the shiitakes – just add one more minute to the cooking time.

Enochi Mushroom & Chestnut Gyoza with Teriyaki Dipping Sauce

MAKES 20 DUMPLINGS

Enochi mushrooms are Japanese in origin, but are widely available here nowadays. Egg-free dumpling wrappers are available from Asian food shops – they normally come in quite big packs and I freeze them in small batches to use later. If your dumpling wrapper looks yellow, it's probably got egg in it. Egg-free wrappers are normally quite pale, but still very tasty. The dumplings are a little fiddly to make, but once you get your groove on, they become easier and pack a heavyweight flavour punch. I pan-steam mine, but they can be fried if you like – the results are, as you'd imagine, crispy, golden and painfully moreish. Pan-steaming these dumplings means you get a nice soft top and a crispy base, like proper Japanese gyoza (jiaozi in China – these types of dumplings are sometimes called 'pot-stickers').

Gluten-free option: you can find dumpling wrappers made with rice.

THE BITS

10 roast chestnuts, peeled and finely chopped

2 cloves of garlic, peeled and finely grated

4cm fresh ginger, peeled and finely grated

½ a yellow pepper, finely diced

2 spring onions, finely sliced

½ an aubergine, finely diced

2 teaspoons toasted sesame oil

2 tablespoons vegetable oil

80g enochi mushrooms, roughly chopped, woody stems discarded

1½ tablespoons tamari

½ a pack of egg-free wonton wrappers

100–150ml water

chilli oil

1 x homemade teriyaki sauce (see page 329)

(cont.) ➡

DO IT

First make your teriyaki sauce.

If your chestnuts are not already roasted, make a small incision in the domed end and place on a baking tray. Preheat the oven to 180°C/gas mark 4 and roast for 20 minutes, turning them over once. They should be lovely and sweet and tender inside by then (and not exploding!). I'd normally do a load and save the rest to use in another recipe.

Put the garlic, ginger, yellow pepper, spring onions, aubergine and sesame oil into a food processor and pulse a few times, until well broken up and coarse.

On a medium heat, warm 1 tablespoon of vegetable oil in a frying pan. Add the aubergine mixture and cook for 5–7 minutes, then add the enochi mushrooms, chestnuts and tamari. Cook gently for a further 5 minutes until any liquid has evaporated.

Lay out your wonton wrappers. Lightly moisten the upper half of the wrapper with a light brushing of water. Spoon 1½ teaspoons of the aubergine mixture into the centre of the wrapper and fold the bottom half up to meet the top half. Press the centre down and gently press the edges down to seal.

Don't overfill the dumplings, they'll blow! You may exhibit your origami skills here – I like to fold them like mini empanadas – or you can just press the edges down lightly between index finger and thumb, making a classic-looking dumpling that stands up.

Brush a large frying pan with 1 tablespoon of vegetable oil and place on a medium-high heat. When it is getting hot and slightly smoking, add the dumplings and sizzle for a minute to get them lightly golden. Add the water, cover tightly with a lid and leave to steam away. The dumplings are done when all the water has evaporated and one side is nicely golden brown – 1–2 minutes will suffice. Add more water to the pan if it evaporates very quickly, and keep an eye on it. Take the lid off and cook in the remaining oil for another minute, until the bases are dark brown and crisp and the tops are steamed. The dumplings may stick to the base a little, which is fine – remove them gently with a thin spatula.

Serve straight from the pan, with chilli oil or the teriyaki sauce, or combine 3 tablespoons of tamari, 3 tablespoons rice wine vinegar and 2 teaspoons brown rice syrup to make a simple Japanese dipping sauce. Dig in!

These gyoza love to be frozen. I usually make a double batch and keep half to be cooked at a later date.

Seeded Lentil & Quinoa Falafel with Tahini Lemon Sauce

MAKES 20-24

I love falafel, and the greatest falafel wrap in the world can be found in Acton, in west London. Bread baked in a brick oven, hummus that melts in the mouth, crisp salad . . . you get the drift! All wrapped by a charming moustachioed man from Beirut.

This is a brilliant vegan barbecue idea. The tahini sauce adds wonderful richness and a heightened sense of a Lebanese street corner. Once you get the mix together you can manipulate it into whatever shape you like: quarter-pounders normally go down very well on the barbecue, or you can go for the usual rotund falafel shape. I have sometimes made these falafels gluten free by using gram (chickpea) flour instead of the breadcrumbs.

THE BITS

175g brown or green lentils

175g quinoa

1 small onion

3 cloves of garlic

2.5cm cube of ginger

1 teaspoon cumin seeds

2 teaspoons coriander seeds

1 tablespoon olive oil

½ teaspoon ground turmeric

¼ teaspoon ground allspice

¼ teaspoon chilli flakes or ¼ teaspoon chilli powder

1 teaspoon sea salt

100g silken tofu

80g breadcrumbs or 50g gram (chickpea) flour

½ teaspoon bicarbonate of soda

3 tablespoons toasted sunflower seeds

½ tablespoon sesame seeds

a handful of fresh parsley, finely chopped

2 tablespoons raisins, finely chopped

zest of ½ a lemon

For dusting

25g gram (chickpea) flour

½ tablespoons sesame seeds

For the tahini lemon sauce

100g tahini paste

zest and juice of ½ a lemon

50g silken tofu

1 large clove of garlic, peeled and crushed

¼ teaspoon ground cumin

a large pinch of sea salt

75ml water

To serve

4–6 wholewheat wraps

2 tomatoes, finely chopped

3 spring onions, finely sliced

¼ tablespoon toasted sesame seeds

½ a handful of fresh parsley, chopped

crisp salad leaves

1 teaspoon sumac (optional)

DO IT

The lentils and quinoa are best cooked in advance, cooled and mixed together. You can keep them in the fridge until needed.

(cont.) ➡

To cook the lentils, put them into a pan and cover with water. Pick out any funny-looking things that come to the top. Drain, then cover well with fresh water. Bring to the boil, then lower the heat to a slow simmer and cook for 30–35 minutes, until tender. Drain well and leave to cool.

Put the quinoa into the same pan and cover with 2cm of water. Bring to a light boil, then cover and leave to simmer for 15–20 minutes (according to packet instructions). Fluff up with a fork, then leave to cool. Mix with the lentils and set aside.

Put the onion, garlic and ginger into a food processor and blend to a thick paste.

Toast the cumin and coriander seeds in a large heavy-bottomed frying pan for a minute, until fragrant, then bash up in a pestle and mortar. Put 1 tablespoon of olive oil into the same frying pan and warm on a medium heat. Drop in the onion paste and fry for 5 minutes, stirring regularly until it turns slightly golden. Add the spices and salt and warm through for about 2 minutes, until fragrant. Now stir in the silken tofu and leave to cool.

Place the breadcrumbs/gram flour and bicarbonate of soda in a food processor with the onion mixture and two-thirds of the lentils and quinoa, and blend until smooth. Transfer to a large bowl and add the seeds, parsley, raisins, lemon zest and the rest of the lentils and quinoa. Combine well with a wooden spoon and place in the fridge for 30 minutes.

Preheat the oven to 180°C/gas mark 4.

Shape the portions, using your mitts (wet them a little, it's a lot easier), into falafel shapes (think golfball but slightly larger). Scatter the gram flour and sesame seeds for dusting on a plate and toss the falafels in this mixture, giving them a good coating. Place them on a large, well-oiled baking tray, turning them over to coat them in oil. Bake in the oven for 25–30 minutes, turning them once.

To make the tahini lemon sauce, place all the ingredients except the water in a food processor and blitz together, adding the water gradually. You should have a thin and rich sauce, easily pourable – think of single cream.

Serve the falafels on warm wholewheat wraps, with crisp salad leaves and chopped tomato and spring onion, drizzled with the tahini and lemon sauce (with more in a small bowl for dipping purposes) and with a sprinkle of sesame seeds and chopped parsley. If you have some sumac handy, sprinkle it over as well. This is proper!

These seeded falafels are also wonderful with the green tomato, ginger & orange chutney (on page 331).

Raw Lumpia with Dipping Sauce

MAKES 12 SPRING ROLLS

Lumpia are basically spring rolls from Manila (with love). They are usually served with a dipping sauce, but I also like Pinakurat, a fermented coconut vinegar (if you can get it), and malt vinegar is fine too. Lumpia are normally very simple – carrots, beansprouts and cabbage – but I have gone a little wild and added some of my favourite ingredients. I've also made them raw, because although the fried version is delicious, it has a habit of being quite greasy. These spring rolls are light and very easy to prepare. They should be nice fat spring rolls, two per person.

THE BITS

12 rice spring roll wrappers

1 x dipping sauce (see page 330)

For the filling

½ a small sweet potato, peeled and coarsely grated

2 big handfuls of beansprouts

½ a yellow pepper, sliced into fine matchsticks

6 leaves of Chinese cabbage or bok choi, finely shredded

200g firm tofu, well drained and crumbled

3 spring onions, finely sliced

3 tablespoons grated coconut or desiccated coconut

2 cloves of garlic, peeled and crushed

4cm fresh ginger, finely grated

1 large red chilli, seeds removed, very finely diced

a handful of cashews, finely chopped

juice and zest of ½ a lime

¼ teaspoon Chinese five-spice

a handful of finely chopped fresh coriander

½ teaspoon sea salt

To serve

75ml coconut vinegar (Pinakurat, optional)

DO IT

First make the dipping sauce. It's best made a little in advance, to allow for flavour mingling.

Put all the filling ingredients into a large bowl and combine well.

Soak your rice wrappers in warm water, following the packet instructions. Lay out the wrappers on a slightly damp chopping board and place 3 tablespoons of filling on each, closer to one edge than the other. Wrap 'em up into long spring rolls by folding both ends over the filling, then turning the roll over once and then again. This should make a nice tight, slightly translucent spring roll. You'll get the hang of this – it's a great life skill. Once a spring roller, always a spring roller!

You can serve them whole, or slice them diagonally down the middle, so you can see all the glorious innards. Serve with bowls of the dipping sauce and coconut vinegar, if you have it. Lumpia is also brilliant with good tamari or even some glorious sweet, sweet chilli sauce.

Masarap (tasty)!

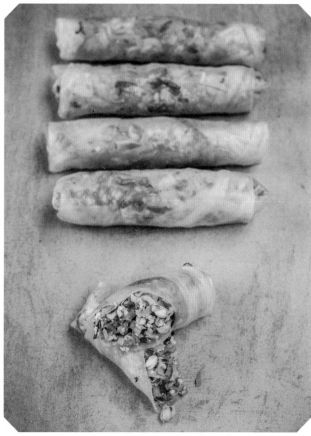

Olive, Artichoke & Pine Nut Pissaladière

FOR 4

This is a peach of a thin-style pizza from Provence. I don't like contending with a lot of soft dough when I munch a pizza – it has to be crispy and light. There are normally a few anchovies on top, but I think the olives, sweet peppers and artichokes more than make up for the lack of fishiness. My mate Mike (the meatiest geezer alive and proprietor of the Pot Kiln restaurant in Berkshire) makes the best pissaladière I have ever tasted. I am sure he'd be happy with this plant-inspired attempt. This dish works best with good-quality black olives and jarred, well-rinsed artichokes (unless you have time to prepare fresh ones).

THE BITS

3–4 tablespoons olive oil

3 large onions, peeled and chopped

2 cloves of garlic, peeled and crushed

½ teaspoon unrefined light brown sugar

1 tablespoon balsamic vinegar

2 red peppers, deseeded and cut into long, thick strips

4 tablespoons black olives, pitted and cut in half lengthways

2 tablespoons fresh thyme leaves

200g artichoke hearts, thinly sliced

sea salt and freshly ground black pepper

For the dough

1 teaspoon dried yeast

175ml water

250g unbleached strong bread flour

½ teaspoon salt

2 tablespoons olive oil

For the garnish

4 tablespoons pine nut Parmesan (see page 336)

DO IT

To make the dough, dissolve the yeast in 1 tablespoon of the water, then sift the flour and salt into a large bowl. Make a well in the centre, pour in the yeast and the rest of the water, along with the olive oil, and mix together with your hands to make a tacky dough. Knead on a lightly floured surface for 5–6 minutes, or until the dough is nicely elastic. Lightly oil the dough with your hands and pop it into a bowl. Cover it with a damp tea-towel and leave in a warm place for about an hour, until doubled in size.

Now heat 1 tablespoon of olive oil in a heavy-bottomed frying pan and add the onions. Cook for 45 minutes on a low heat, stirring regularly, until the onions are caramelized and very golden. Add a splash of water and lower the heat slightly if the onions are sticking. Add the garlic, turn up the heat, and cook for 3 minutes more, then add the sugar and balsamic vinegar. Stir and cook for a further 10 minutes. By this time you should have something resembling a lovely sweet and slightly sticky onion marmalade. Perfect. Heat 2 teaspoons of olive oil in a small frying pan and sauté your red peppers. Cook for 8–10 minutes, until they are caramelized all over. Preheat the oven to 200°C/gas mark 6.

Give your dough a quick knead, then roll it out very thinly on a lightly floured piece of baking paper into a roughly 30 x 25cm rectangle. Remember, it will rise a little in the oven. Using the baking paper, lift the base on to a baking tray and spread over a layer of onions, then sprinkle with the olives and thyme and add a good covering of artichokes and peppers. Drizzle lightly with olive oil and a sprinkle of sea salt and pepper. Brush the crust with olive oil and pop into the oven for 20–25 minutes, until the base is crisp and golden brown. Sprinkle over the pine nut Parmesan and serve.

Seitan & Sweet Potato Kebabs with Mango Barbecue Sauce

FOR 6 LARGE KEBABS

Full of tang and sweetness, these kebabs are the perfect skewer to whip out when you have friends and family coming over who are not part of the tofu brigade. Try to buy seitan in big chunks for these kebabs – it tastes like meat (which will confuse everybody!). Just slap these kebabs under the grill and you're well on your way to a vegan Tennessee hoedown!

THE BITS

240g seitan, well drained, cut into 5cm chunks

2 tablespoons tamari

2 sweet potatoes, scrubbed and cut into 2.5cm cubes

1 tablespoon vegetable oil

1 yellow pepper, cut into 5cm chunks

1 green pepper, cut into 5cm chunks

1 plantain, cut into 5cm chunks

1 red onion, cut into quarters, then halved

6 large red chillies (if you like chillies!)

3 tablespoons olive oil

sea salt and freshly ground black pepper

1 x of mango barbecue sauce (see page 325)

For the garnish
6 handfuls of watercress or spinach

DO IT

You will need 6 long wooden or metal skewers. If you are using wooden ones, soak them in water for 1 hour beforehand (this stops them burning).

Preheat the oven to 180°C/gas mark 4. Put the well-drained seitan into a bowl (squeezing out any excess liquid) and add the tamari. Mix together and leave to marinate for 30 minutes in the fridge. Toss the sweet potatoes in a little vegetable oil and roast in the oven for 20 minutes to soften them slightly before barbecuing.

Have all your ingredients handy. You don't have to be exact, just get a good spread of seitan and vegetables on each kebab, completing each one with a nice fat chilli. Place on a large tray or platter, brush well with olive oil and sprinkle with salt and pepper.

Make the mango barbecue sauce. Leave 6 tablespoons of the sauce in the food processor and blend until smooth. This will be your marinade for the kebabs. The rest will be your sauce.

The key here is to not burn the kebabs on the barbecue (it's a lot easier to control the temperature under a grill). The heat must be constant, but not blazing. Wait until the flames have died down and there is a white glow to the embers – about 30 minutes is good. Spread them out a little to form a good base of heat, then place your oiled kebabs on the griddle. We love crispy, slightly charred outer edges, but not a raw onion taste or crunchy sweet potato.

Barbecue the kebabs for 10 minutes, turning them regularly but not overdoing it (keep over-zealous fathers away!). Once they are well coloured, begin to brush on your marinade and continue turning and basting for 10 minutes.

If using a grill, set it on medium and turn the kebabs every few minutes. They should take 15–20 minutes – baste them regularly towards the end of cooking. This marinade can also be used over oven-roasted veggies. Serve the kebabs on some watercress, drizzled with the mango sauce.

Greek Filo Parcelettes with Creamy Pesto

MAKES 24

Greece made a huge impression on my palate when I was a younger fella. The main attractions on many Greek menus are of course the fresh seafood and hearty meat dishes, but like many great food cultures, once you scratch the surface, a whole host of vegan options pour in. I love dolmades, but struggled to locate vine leaves in rural Wales. I reached for the filo instead, and a very, very minor part of food history was made. This has all the flavours of dolmades, surrounded by crispy filo, and is served fresh from the oven. Best enjoyed with the sun on your back and your worries a distant memory.

THE BITS

125ml olive oil + 1 tablespoon for frying the onion

1 large red onion, finely sliced

175g long-grain brown rice (white is also cool, and millet is very cool indeed!)

1 teaspoon ground allspice

1 teaspoon sea salt

½ teaspoon freshly ground black pepper

3 tablespoons lemon juice

1 tablespoon lemon zest

3 tablespoons currants, roughly chopped

½ a handful of mint leaves, finely chopped

a handful of fresh dill, finely chopped

3 tablespoons toasted pine nuts

12 sheets of filo pastry

1 x creamy pesto (see page 333)

For the garnish
1 lemon, cut into wedges

DO IT

Heat 1 tablespoon of oil in a large pan and add the onion. Fry gently for 3–4 minutes, then stir in the rice, allspice, salt and pepper along with half the lemon juice. Pour in cold water to cover by 3cm and bring slowly to the boil. Cover tightly with a lid, and simmer gently for 35–40 minutes. Remove the lid and fluff the rice up with a fork, gently mixing in the remaining lemon juice and zest, currants, mint, dill and pine nuts. Season if needed and allow to cool. Meanwhile make your creamy pesto.

Now you need to make a bit of space, and the quicker and more organized you are, the easier the next bit will be. Be gentle with the filo, as it breaks very easily. On a well-oiled surface, lay out a sheet of filo and brush well with olive oil. Lay another sheet of filo on top, being as exact as possible (this is not easy!). Brush with olive oil, add one more sheet and – you guessed it! – brush more olive oil on it. This gives the filo its richness; otherwise it would be a bit of a dried-up affair.

Now cut the rectangle into 6 squares, using the tip of a sharp knife. Spoon 1 tablespoon of filling into the centre of each square and brush the outer edges with a little oil. Gather all the edges into the centre and nip them above the filling to form a small taut money-bag shape. Brush with olive oil, especially the random frilly edges that stick out. Continue with vigour and nimble fingers, making many tasty parcelettes.

Preheat the oven to 170°C/gas mark 3. Using a slice, gently place all the parcelettes on an oiled baking tray (you may need two). Bake for 10 minutes, then swap and turn the trays (so they are evenly browned) and bake for a further 10 minutes, until very golden and crisp. Serve the parcelettes with a bowl of the creamy pesto and a scattering of freshly cut lemon wedges.

Lazy Lahmacun

FOR 4

I tend to save bread-making for special occasions, and this lazy Lahmacun is a 'quickie', designed for almost instant satisfaction. Lahmacun is a thin Turkish pizza, normally served topped with minced meat and cooked in those hangar-like wood-fire ovens. You can of course make your own base for the lahmacun, but you can buy some great wholewheat pitta/flatbreads. The flatter and thinner the better – something like a khobez flatbread is perfect. Or you could try cutting a normal pitta in half. Nothing in the vegetable world comes closer to the texture and rich flavours of minced meat than roasted aubergine. When combined with roasted pepper, toasted pine nuts and fresh herbs, this quickly becomes an epic pizza.

THE BITS

1 large aubergine

1 red pepper

3 tablespoons olive oil

1 small onion

5 cloves of garlic, peeled and crushed

150g mushrooms, sliced

1 teaspoon ground coriander

a large pinch of ground cinnamon

½ teaspoon ground cumin

⅓ teaspoon chilli powder

½ teaspoon sea salt

½ teaspoon black pepper

1 teaspoon dried basil

2 tomatoes, grated

½ a handful of fresh flat-leaf parsley, chopped

4 wholewheat flatbreads

juice of ½ a lemon

For the topping

1 x lemon tofu feta (optional, see page 115)

5 tablespoons cashews, roughly chopped

DO IT

Preheat the oven to 200°C/gas mark 6. Pierce the aubergine many times with a fork, then put it on a baking tray with the red pepper and rub them both with olive oil. Bake in the oven – check the pepper after 15 minutes, then turn them both over with a spatula and bake for 15 minutes more. Take out the pepper and leave the aubergine in for another 10 minutes. They should both be soft and well coloured. Deseed the pepper, trim the aubergine, and roughly chop them both.

While that is going on, on a medium-high heat, warm 1 tablespoon of oil in a frying pan. Add the onions and fry for 6–8 minutes, then add the garlic, mushrooms, spices, salt and pepper, and continue cooking for 3–4 minutes. Add a splash more oil if needed. Now add the red pepper and aubergine, with the basil and tomatoes, and warm through on a low simmer for 6–7 minutes more. Stir in the parsley, cover and keep warm.

Your oven should still be rocking. Bring it back to 200°C/gas mark 6, lay out your flatbreads on baking trays and brush them with olive oil (especially the edges). Spread the vegetable mixture thinly over the bread – 4 tablespoons per lakmajun is normally cool. Top with cashews and tofu feta (if you're using it) and pop into the oven for 12–15 minutes.

Serve drizzled with a little more olive oil and even a little squeeze of lemon juice. Depending on the size of the flatbread, this dish makes a great little or big plate and can be cut into wedges to be served as an appetizer or rolled around some salad. Raw cashew hummus (see page 160) is a perfect accompaniment.

Big Plates

Big plates = big appetites. Here we have some hearty vegan fare, capable of sating even the most ferocious hunger.

I hear many non-vegans comment on the lack of richness in vegan food, something that I find surprising. With the addition of nuts and tofu, rich sauces and dishes can be devilishly satisfying, with the added benefit of being easily digestible. No after-dinner sloth is a real bonus for plant munchers!

I regularly cook with carnivores in mind – it's a wonderful challenge to sate a flesh-eater. Certainly this book has been written with meat consumers in mind. It's all part of my quest! Without coming across as a rampant zealot, I'm just chuffed to see a few more people down at the health food shop raiding the tempeh shelves and discovering the wonders of nutritional yeast flakes; realizing the vast potential of the humble bean in its multifarious forms and textures. 'I would eat more veggie food if it tasted like this!' is one of the highest compliments you could ever pay a vegan cook.

I feel a little sorry for friends and family when they come to visit and even worse when I visit them, especially on special occasions like birthdays or Christmas. When I told friends I was writing a vegan cookbook, most said the same thing: 'Thank God, we'll know what to cook for you next time!' I was surprised at their exasperation, but I understand only too well how much pressure can build around food and in the kitchen. Particularly when you're cooking for the people you love. You want to give them the best.

I hope this book will be helpful when you are on the receiving end of a vegan visit. Firstly, please don't panic; I assure you, we come in peace. I speak for all vegans when I say that we have very low expectations when 'eating out' (unfortunately).

The truth is, Vs are more than happy to nosh on a plate of tepid beans, maybe with a carrot thrown in there. Anything else is always a real bonus. The pressure is off – we know how complicated we are (you should try being us!).

Here I present some Big Plates, fit for special occasions and treat dinners, when the lovely vegan in your life is at the table. There are generally quite a few steps to preparation, but the methods are all simple and the delicious results are more than worth the extra effort.

Oven-baked Squash Gnocchi with Sun-dried Tomato, Fennel & Spinach Pistou

FOR 4–6

Making gnocchi with coloured vegetables makes brilliant sense. Any quite starchy root works well: parsnip, sweet potato, purple potatoes, cassava, pumpkin . . . But the vivid orange of squash really electrifies the plate (and the palate). With its vibrant oranges, reds and greens, this dish is a feast for the eyes as well as the belly!

Pistou is actually just a Provençal variation on pesto, without the hard cheese and pine nuts. It's lighter than pesto and allows the herbs more room to express themselves. I've thrown in a few hazelnuts for richness. This pistou is even better made the day before. Used in moderation, it brings herbal joy to soups, stews and of course, pasta. A nice variation, pistou-wise, is to use nettle leaves and wild garlic instead of the spinach and basil. This is best done in early spring, when you can forage your own.

Gluten-free option: use chickpea flour or potato flour instead of wheat flour.

THE BITS

1 large squash, about 1.5kg (the more starchy varieties of summer squash are best, such as butternut), peeled and cut into rough chunks

olive oil, for roasting

a little sea salt

1 large fennel bulb, thinly sliced lengthways

240g firm tofu, well drained

300g unbleached white flour, sifted

1 teaspoon sea salt

½ teaspoon white pepper

1½ teaspoons dried sage

2 big handfuls of sun-dried tomatoes, roughly chopped

1x spinach pistou (see page 332)

For the topping

2 tablespoons roasted hazelnuts, roughly chopped

DO IT

First make the spinach pistou (even better if you can make it the day before).

Preheat the oven to 200°C/gas mark 6.

Place the squash on an oiled baking tray. Rub a little oil and salt over it and bake for 30 minutes, turning the pieces gently over once. You're not looking for loads of colour here, just lovely soft, golden squash. Toss the fennel in olive oil, place on a separate baking tray and scatter with a pinch of sea salt. Bake for 30 minutes, turning once, until it's nicely golden and sweet. When the squash is ready, put it into a processor with the tofu and blend until smooth. Now, place in a large bowl and stir in the flour, salt, pepper and sage until a soft dough forms. Leave to cool down and firm up – it will be a lot easier to handle.

Using two teaspoons, make gnocchi shapes (lovely little flat oval dumplings) with the mixture and place on an oiled baking sheet, leaving about 5cm of space for each gnocchi to grow. Brush the gnocchi with a little more oil and bake for 20–25 minutes, until crisp and slightly golden.

Serve the gnocchi warm, on nice big plates, drizzled liberally with the pistou. Scatter the crispy fennel and sun-dried tomatoes on top with a little more pistou, and finish with some chopped roasted hazelnuts.

Black Kale, Leek & Pumpkin Farrotto with Pan-roasted Maple Chicory & Pecans

FOR 4–6

'Farrotto' is basically risotto without the rice, using spelt (or farro) instead, which is far more nutritious than your average white risotto rice (and wheat for that matter). It's low in gluten and has a magnificent nutty flavour that mingles nicely with the sweetness of the maple and roast pumpkin in this dish. Black kale, or cavolo nero, is one of the most nutritious and delicious leaves known to earthlings! It is a crop that actually thrives in our hillside north Welsh gardens, prospering in fog clouds and storms. We use it in everything, even smoothies and juices (see page 75–8). I love its contrast with pumpkin. You need big herb flavours when playing with spelt, and sage and rosemary are well up to the challenge. The pecans are an added luxury – not necessary, but with the maple syrup they add another killer combo to this dish.

Gluten-free option: use normal risotto rice or brown rice, altering the cooking time accordingly.

THE BITS

4 tablespoons olive oil

400g pumpkin, peeled and cut into 3cm dice

275g leeks, cleaned and finely sliced

4 cloves of garlic, crushed

4 sprigs of fresh thyme, leaves picked

6 fresh sage leaves, finely chopped

2 teaspoons finely chopped fresh rosemary leaves

300g farro

125ml white wine (veggie)

1.5 litres vegetable stock

200g black kale, woody stalks removed, finely sliced into fine ribbons

1 teaspoon sea salt

1 teaspoon black pepper

For the pan-roasted maple chicory

4 large chicory heads, halved lengthways

2 tablespoons maple syrup

1 tablespoon olive oil

a handful of pecans, very roughly chopped

juice and zest of ½ a lemon

150ml vegetable stock

a pinch of sea salt

For the garnish

a few sprigs of fresh thyme

DO IT

Warm 1 tablespoon of olive oil in a frying pan, then pan-fry the pumpkin on a high heat until it is nicely caramelized (around 5–7 minutes). Cover and set aside. You're looking for golden, slightly charred outsides and firm innards here – the pumpkin will cook through in the farrotto later.

In a large saucepan, warm 1 tablespoon of olive oil and begin to soften the leeks. Add the garlic and after 3 minutes pop the herbs in. Cook for 2 minutes, then add the farro, stir, and cook on a medium heat for a couple of minutes.

Now add the wine and bring to the boil, stirring. Cook until the wine has been almost completely absorbed, then add 2 ladlefuls of stock and stir. Allow all the stock to be absorbed and then proceed to add more, stirring regularly, one ladleful at a time.

Now's a good time to get your chicory started. Pick off any bashed or discoloured outer leaves and brush the face of the chicory pieces with a little of the maple syrup. In a large frying pan, warm ½ tablespoon of olive oil and add the chicory face down, on a medium-high heat. Cook for 5–7 minutes. Once the chicory has some good caramelization, flip it over, add the rest of the ingredients, and cover with a lid or a plate. Lower the heat and simmer for 20–25 minutes, until the chicory is nice and soft.

Once soft, take the chicory pieces out of the cooking liquid and cut them again (so they are now in quarters). Set aside and keep warm. The cooking liquid should be thick, but if not, continue cooking it with the lid off until it's nice and sticky.

After roughly 30 minutes of cooking the farrotto, add the pumpkin and kale. Continue until the farro is soft and chewy, which will take a while – maybe 40–50 minutes in total (roughly twice the length of time of a risotto). Make sure there is a decent amount of liquid left in the farrotto . . . there is nothing worse than dry spelt! When it's ready, stir in 2 tablespoons of olive oil, check the seasoning, pop a lid on and remove from the heat.

Ladle the farrotto into warmed shallow bowls and top with pieces of chicory, making sure everybody gets some of the pecans. Spoon over a little of the thick cooking sauce, garnish with a few sprigs of thyme, and serve.

Open-top Asparagus & Cashew Cream Pie, with Fig & Apple Compote

FOR 4-6

Asparagus always tells me that summer is around the corner. The little asparagus window is a joy each year, and in our Spanish house it grows wild and free in the dried-up river beds. This pie is perfect for a warm evening with a glass of something dry and crisp. I am drawn to this kind of topless pie – multi-layered, multi-coloured and brimming over with flavour. Although it sounds quite complex, this meal will take little preparation and cooking. It's one of those dishes that looks impressive without much effort. You can use sunflower seeds instead of the cashews, or half and half for an economical option. And if asparagus is out of season, try roasted courgettes or broccoli instead.

THE BITS

500g thin asparagus spears (if you have thick ones, cut them in half lengthways)

2 teaspoons olive oil

sea salt and black pepper

300g spinach leaves

500g puff pastry (from the freezer – stress-free option best)

a hanful of pinenuts (optional)

1 x fig & apple compote (see page 332)

For the cashew cream

150g cashew nuts, soaked in water for 2 hours

1 tablespoon cornflour

150ml almond milk (sugar-free)

½ teaspoon lemon juice

1 tablespoon nutritional yeast flakes (see page 30)

¼ teaspoon salt

1½ teaspoons Dijon mustard

DO IT

First make the compote then preheat the oven to 200°C/gas mark 6.

Bring a pan of water to the boil and trim your asparagus spears (just snap the woody ends off). Dunk the spears in the water and blanch quickly, then remove and immerse in cold water. Pat dry, toss in a little olive oil and a pinch of sea salt and set aside.

Now blanch your spinach in the same pan, cook for 1 minute and drain well. Place in the centre of a tea towel or muslin and gather in the edges, twisting and squeezing out as much excess liquid as you can (or press firmly in a colander).

With a rolling pin, roll the pastry out on a cold surface, quite thin, about 2.5mm thick. Make a shape that roughly fits a regular sized (40 x 20cm) baking tray. Push the pastry snugly into each corner and trim off any straggly edges (or leave them for a dishevelled look). Score a 1cm border around the edge, using a sharp knife, and prick the base of the pastry with a fork. Place in the fridge for 20 minutes.

Place the soaked cashews in a food processor and blend until creamy – you should have something resembling thin peanut butter. You will need to scrape the sides down of the food processor a few times. Add the rest of the ingredients, drizzling in the milk. Blend until a smooth sauce is formed, adding a little more water if needed, but remember – too thin and it will spill over the edge.

Now pop the pastry into the oven and blind bake for 12 minutes. Then turn the tray 90 degrees and bake for a further 12 minutes, until almost cooked. Check the base – it should be dark golden. Press down the base along the borders using a fish slice, making an indent in the centre for your filling.

With a palette knife, gently spread your cashew cream over the pastry to meet the borders. Break the spinach up and sprinkle over a good layer. Now place your asparagus spears on top, in neat rows widthways. Sprinkle with sea salt and black pepper (and pine nuts if you like). Lightly brush the borders with olive oil. Put back into the oven for roughly 10–12 minutes on a high shelf, until the pastry borders are a nice deep golden colour.

Serve the pie in big squares, with a spoonful of compote on the side. A crisp green salad is a great accompaniment.

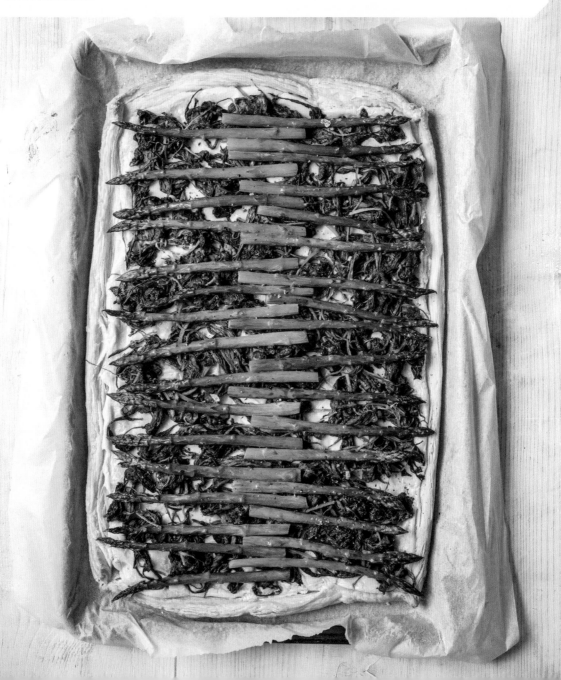

Roast Aubergine & Tomato Nut Roast with Macadamia Mustard Sauce

FOR 6

This is *the* nut roast, a heavenly, light slice of nuttiness, and the creamy macadamia sauce is the big fat cherry on top of the cake. I make this on Sundays – with a plate of saucy nut roast I feel connected with the veggie food pioneers of the 60s and 70s, and this is based loosely on a Cranks recipe I unearthed in an old dusty book. You use a lot of nuts here, but it's a treat dish, a Sunday special. You can use any combination of nuts; just steer clear of peanuts, as they can dominate. Good-quality rapeseed oil is a wonderful ingredient and adds a lovely butteriness to the dish, but vegetable oil is perfectly acceptable.

THE BITS

2 aubergines

rapeseed oil

2 teaspoons cumin seeds

2 teaspoons coriander seeds

1 large onion

4 cloves of garlic

½ teaspoon ground cinnamon

4 ripe tomatoes, roughly chopped

a handful of sun-dried tomatoes, finely chopped (including any oil)

½ teaspoon salt

¼ teaspoon black pepper

1 teaspoon dried mint

1 teaspoon dried thyme

2 handfuls each of walnuts, cashews, sunflower seeds, pumpkin seeds, hazelnuts, all soaked for 4 hours, plus a handful of unsoaked sunflower seeds for the tin

2 tablespoons sultanas, soaked for 2 hours

a handful of ground almonds

a big handful of chickpea flour or 2 handfuls of breadcrumbs (more if needed)

1 teaspoon sea salt

1 teaspoon black pepper

2 large handfuls of fresh parsley, finely chopped

1 x macadamia mustard sauce (see page 326)

For the garnish

2 tablespoons finely chopped fresh parsley

DO IT

Preheat the oven to 200°C/gas mark 6. Rub the whole aubergines with oil and place on a baking tray. Bake them for 40–45 minutes, turning them at least once, until they are very tender. Cover and set aside. When cooled, scoop out the soft insides and roughly chop. Discard the skins. Lower the oven temperature to 150°C/gas mark 2.

Roast the cumin and coriander seeds in a small skillet for 1 minute, until they pop and slightly brown. Grind together in a pestle and mortar or coffee grinder. Peel the onion and garlic and blend together in a food processor. Warm ½ a tablespoon of oil in a large frying pan on a medium heat, add the blended onion and garlic, and stir and fry for 4 minutes. Add the spices – the cumin, coriander and cinnamon – and fry for 1 minute. Add the aubergine, chopped tomatoes, sun-dried tomatoes, salt and pepper, followed by the dried herbs, and cook on a high simmer for 12–15 minutes, until the tomatoes have broken down and a thickish sauce has formed. Check the seasoning.

Blitz up the nuts and sultanas in a food processor until a rough crumb is formed. Put into a large bowl and mix in the rest of the ingredients, finally adding the warm tomato mixture. With your trusty wooden spoon or your hands, get it all well combined. It should be slightly dry, butdefinitely sticky to the touch. You should be able to form small balls with the mix. Add more flour or breadcrumbs if too wet.

(cont.) ➡

Sprinkle a layer of sunflower seeds in the bottom of an oiled and lined 450g loaf tin and pack in the nutty mix. Bake for 35–40 minutes, until the top is beginning to go brown and crisp. Check with a skewer – the middle should be piping hot. Once crisp, remove from the oven and allow to rest in the tin for about 5 minutes before turning out on to a wire rack.

While the nut roast is in the oven, make the macadamia mustard sauce.

Place the loaf on a warm serving platter and slice into hearty slabs. Serve with lashings of the macadamia mustard sauce, and sprinkle some fresh parsley over the top. A pile of roasted or steamed veggies rounds things off nicely (the winter roots braised in porter on page 138 would be perfect).

Persian Fava Bean, Seitan & Green Herb Stew

FOR 4-6

This is a version of gormeh sabzi, the national dish of Iran, and the Iraqis and Azerbaijanis are quite partial to it too. Iranian food is both distinct and diverse, and it has influenced all the countries around it, stretching as far as India and the Mediterranean. The name of the dish means 'green stew', and we use LOTS of herbs. Don't scrimp on them here; they're what makes this dish sing. Seitan can be picked up in select supermarkets or your local health food shop, or you can make it at home (see page 26). Dried limes are a popular ingredient in Iranian cooking and are easily found in the 'world food' aisles. You can use preserved lemons as a back-up. Traditionally red kidney beans are the way to go, but I tried it with fava beans (dried broad beans) once and have never looked back. Iranians would use fresh fenugreek leaves, but they can be hard to come by so I have opted for dried instead (also called methi leaves, used frequently in Indian cooking).

THE BITS

2 medium white onions, peeled and cut into thick wedges

3 tablespoons olive oil

50g gram (chickpea) flour, or unbleached white flour

salt and freshly ground black pepper

300g seitan (see page 26), or firm tofu, cut into 3cm cubes

1 teaspoon ground turmeric

1 tablespoon dried fenugreek (methi) leaves

5 sprigs of fresh thyme (leaves only)

1½ cinnamon sticks, or 1 teaspoon ground cinnamon

2 bay leaves

2 dried Iranian limes, well pricked

3 strips of lemon rind

3 medium carrots, quartered lengthways and cut into 2cm dice

2 celery stalks, halved lengthways and cut into 1cm pieces

a handful of small radishes, trimmed and halved

200ml white wine (veggie)

2 tablespoons tomato purée

4 portobello mushrooms (or any other meaty mushroom), cut into 5cm chunks

250g dried fava beans, soaked overnight and cooked (reserve the cooking juices)

300ml mushroom stock or bean cooking liquid

2 big handfuls of fresh parsley (reserve a little for garnish)

a big handful of fresh dill (reserve a little for garnish)

6 big handfuls of spinach, finely chopped

For the topping

a handful of pomegranate seeds

In a large casserole dish or sauté pan (one that has a lid), fry the onions in 1 tablespoon of olive oil for 10 minutes, until caramelized and soft. Scrape any stuck onions off the base. Set aside in a large bowl.

Put the gram flour into a flat bowl and stir in a teaspoon of salt and a generous grinding of pepper. Drain the seitan well and add to the bowl. Now toss together with your hands to give it a decent coating, shaking off any excess. The natural moisture of the seitan will make the flour stick.

Return the pan to a medium-high heat, pour in a tablespoon of olive oil, and fry the seitan until slightly charred. Tip into the onion bowl and cover again. Depending on the size of your pan, you may need to do this in batches. Scrape the bottom of the pan if the seitan is sticking.

Return the onions and seitan to the pan on a medium heat, along with the turmeric, fenugreek, thyme, cinnamon, bay leaves, dried limes and lemon rind. Cook for a minute and add the carrots, celery and radishes. Pour in the wine and add the tomato purée. Stir and cook on a high heat for around 2–3 minutes, until the sauce reduces and becomes thick.

Add the mushrooms, fava beans and the mushroom stock or bean cooking liquid and bring to the boil. Cover and simmer for 20–25 minutes on a low heat.

Remove the lid and check that the carrots are nice and soft. Stir in the fresh herbs and spinach, pop the lid back on and take the pan off the heat. Leave to sit for 5 minutes, to let the flavours mingle and the spinach wilt a little. The sauce should be nice and thick, not runny. Check for seasoning – if you've used bean cooking liquid, it may need a hit of saltiness. Stir in 1 tablespoon of olive oil just before serving to add a lovely shine.

Spoon the gormeh sabzi over some steamed white rice and top with a scattering of the reserved fresh herbs and the pomegranate seeds. Warm flatbread is also a treat with this dish.

 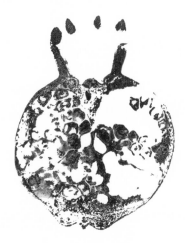 

Tofu Fillets in a Spicy Polenta Crust with Golden Beetroot & Blood Orange Salsa

FOR 4

I had my first taste of tofu in a Thai street – a blob of crispy, creamy gorgeousness that I could not believe wasn't some form of cream cheese. Since then, I have been a complete tofu convert and love its versatility. Use a firm tofu here – the firmer the better for frying. When pressed well it absorbs lots of the marinade and this means bags of flavour.

THE BITS

1 x 500g block of firm tofu, pressed and drained, then cut across into 1cm steaks

80g polenta

½ teaspoon chilli powder

½ teaspoon ground turmeric

½ teaspoon sea salt

4 tablespoons sunflower oil

For the marinade

3 tomatoes

juice of 1 lime

zest of ½ a lime

a handful of fresh coriander leaves

½ a handful of mint leaves

1 jalapeño chilli (or any hot chilli), finely chopped

2 cloves of garlic, peeled and finely chopped

3cm piece of fresh ginger, peeled and finely chopped

½ teaspoon ground cumin

½ teaspoon salt

For the blood orange salsa

1 large golden or regular beetroot, peeled and finely diced

1 green apple, cored and finely diced

1 blood orange or 1 small red grapefruit, peeled, de-pithed and finely chopped

1 small cucumber, deseeded, peeled and finely diced

a handful of roast peanuts, roughly chopped

½ a handful of fresh mint leaves, roughly chopped

a pinch of sea salt

juice of ½ a lemon

DO IT

Begin by pressing the tofu to remove excess moisture. Do this by wrapping it in a clean tea-towel and putting it on a plate. Place another plate over it and balance a few books on top. The weight should be enough to gently press the tofu without splitting it. Leave it for an hour, draining the liquid once or twice. Do this every time you use tofu and you'll have wonderful porous tofu that absorbs sauce and flavours. It also makes the texture of the tofu fuller.

Place all the marinade ingredients in a blender and blitz together; it should be nice and thick. Put the tofu fillets into a decent-size container and cover well with the marinade. Cover and pop into the fridge for an hour (overnight is even better). Toss the salsa ingredients together in a bowl then squeeze over the lemon juice.

On a large plate, combine the polenta, spices and salt. Remove the tofu fillets from the marinade and shake off the liquid (reserve the marinade). Lay the fillets on the polenta and turn them to cover all sides, top, bottom and the thinner edges. When you are happy that all sides have a decent coating of polenta, pop them on to another plate.

Heat the oil in a medium frying pan on a high heat and shallow-fry your tofu pieces in batches until they turn a wonderful reddish-gold colour – 1 or 2 minutes each side should do. Put them on a large plate covered with kitchen paper, and keep warm. Be careful not to dislodge the crust when handling. Serve the warm tofu fillets with the salsa and marinade in small serving bowls on the side.

Tempeh with a Maple & Orange Glaze, Bok Choi & Soba Noodles

FOR 2

Foods like tempeh, tofu and seitan have been eaten in the East for many, many years. Tempeh is not for the faint-hearted vegan as it is semi-fermented and ever so slightly meaty in texture. Drain it well and use it straight from the jar, or, if you buy it in large logs, steam it before using for best results. Prepping well is the key to this dish.

THE BITS

200g tempeh, seitan or firm tofu

1–2 tablespoons vegetable oil

250g bok choi, leaves halved lengthways

For the maple & orange glaze

1 teaspoon toasted sesame oil

2cm fresh ginger, finely grated

1 clove of garlic, peeled and crushed

½ red chilli, deseeded and finely diced

3 tablespoons tamari

2½ tablespoons maple syrup

zest and juice of ½ an orange

1 tablespoon rice wine vinegar

For the miso noodle broth

135g soba noodles

1 tablespoon tamari

1 star anise

3–4 tablespoons brown rice miso

For the topping

a handful of fresh coriander, finely chopped

2 spring onions, sliced thinly at an angle

DO IT

Drain the tempeh in a sieve and dry well with kitchen paper, pressing out excess liquid. To make the marinade, warm the sesame oil in a small pan and add the ginger and garlic. Fry for a minute, then add the rest of the ingredients. Bring slowly to a boil, then gently simmer for 5 minutes. Add the tempeh and cover. Set aside to marinate for 30 minutes to an hour.

Now drain your tempeh, keeping the lovely marinade. Heat 1 tablespoon of vegetable oil in a large frying pan on a medium-high heat, and when hot add the tempeh. Fry for 2–3 minutes, adding the marinade gradually along the way until the glaze becomes sticky – this should take around 10 minutes on a steady simmer. Set aside, cover and keep warm. Rinse out the pan for later.

To cook the noodles, half fill a large pan with water and bring to the boil. Cook your noodles according to the instructions on the pack. Drain in a colander, reserving about 500ml of the noodle water, then keep the noodles warm in a bowl, stirring in a little oil to prevent them from sticking.

Pour the reserved noodle cooking water back into the pan, put back on the heat and add the tamari and star anise. Put the miso into a small bowl and mix in a couple of tablespoons of the warm water until a runny paste is formed. Add this paste to the pan and keep covered, simmering the broth on a low heat. The flavour should be strong – add more tamari and miso if needed.

Heat ½ tablespoon of oil in your frying pan and add the bok choi. Cook for 2 minutes on a high heat, then add 3 tablespoons of the miso broth and continue cooking for 1 minute more. Bring the simmering broth to a slow boil. Divide your noodles between warm bowls, top with bok choi and ladle over some of the broth. Then stack on a decent pile of tempeh, topped with some sliced spring onions and a scattering of fresh coriander.

Parsnip & Walnut Rumbledethumps with Homemade Baked Beans

FOR 4

Scotland is a place where I misspent many of my formative years, and this is proper Scottish fare. This dish is a real rib-hugger – just the thought of it makes my hunger evaporate. Homemade baked beans are best; I don't care what it says on the tin. Give them a try – they're not quite as sweet as the famous tinned variety, but few things are. However, this is a quick dinner, so you are definitely forgiven if you reach for the tin opener on occasion. I normally cook double the quantity of the patties and beans, as they freeze brilliantly.

Gluten-free option: forget about the flour dusting – they're very tasty without!

THE BITS

2 large potatoes, scrubbed and cut into small chunks

2 carrots, scrubbed and cut into small chunks

3 parsnips, scrubbed and cut into small chunks

1–2 teaspoons sea salt

a large pinch of white pepper

100ml soya milk

3 tablespoons rapeseed oil

2 red onions, finely chopped

150g Brussels sprouts, trimmed and finely sliced

1 teaspoon dried sage

1 teaspoon dried thyme

3 tablespoon wholegrain flour, for dusting

½ teaspoon sea salt

For the homemade baked beans

1 tablespoon sunflower or rapeseed oil

1 onion, finely diced

2 cloves of garlic, peeled and crushed

1 apple, peeled, cored and finely diced

2 tablespoons tomato purée

4 large tomatoes, roughly chopped

2 teaspoons English mustard powder

a large pinch of allspice

2 tablespoons molasses or brown rice syrup (not blackstrap molasses)

1 teaspoon sea salt

50ml water

1 tablespoon sherry vinegar

2 bay leaves

175g dried haricot beans, soaked and cooked

For the mustard & walnut topping

3 tablespoons wholegrain mustard

2 handfuls of toasted walnuts, finely chopped

½ tablespoon good rapeseed oil

½ a handful of fresh parsley, finely chopped

DO IT

Put the potatoes, carrots and parsnips into a large pan of cold water, add a little salt, bring to the boil and simmer until very tender – 20 minutes should do. Drain well and allow the vegetables to steam dry for 2–3 minutes. Then put them all into a large bowl and mash with more salt, pepper and the soya milk, adding the milk in gradually until you get a good mash consistency that isn't too wet. Cover and set aside. Check for seasoning – mash loves salt!

Heat 1 tablespoon of rapeseed oil in a frying pan and add the onions. Fry gently for 15 minutes, until sweet and golden, then add the Brussels sprouts and dried herbs and continue cooking for 3–4 minutes. Once this mixture is nice and soft, stir it into the mash. Check the seasoning.

Form the potato mixture into four large cakes. Mix the flour and salt, and dust the cakes on both sides. Pop into the fridge for 1 hour.

To make the beans, heat the sunflower oil in a large heavy pan and cook the onions, stirring for 10 minutes until nicely caramelized. Well-cooked onions give the base for fuller flavour. Now add the garlic and cook for 2 more minutes, then add the apples, tomato purée, tomatoes, mustard powder, allspice, molasses, salt, water, sherry vinegar and bay leaves. Bring to the boil, then cover the pan and leave to cook for 30 minutes on a low heat, checking and stirring occasionally.

Give the mix a good stir to break down the apples, onions, etc. into a thick sauce, then mix in the cooked haricot beans and cover. Cook for 20 minutes more on a low heat. You should be left with a nice thick sauce. If this is not the case, cook further with the lid off.

Heat the remaining 2 tablespoons of rapeseed oil in a large frying pan and fry each rumbledethump for 5 minutes each side, until golden and nicely crisp. Mix the topping ingredients in a bowl, spoon over the rumbledethumps and serve warm, with the homemade beans.

Layered Filo Pie with Roast Cauliflower Mash & Carrot Purée

FOR 2 INDIVIDUAL PIES (2–4 PORTIONS)

This is the whole vegan hog . . . The layered technique can be used with any combination of ingredients your mind can conjure up – the filo pastry works as the perfect light crust for a whole host of puréed perfection. However, try not to use so many flavours it makes your tastebuds malfunction, which means you taste very little and the individual ingredients merge into one. You will need some small deep individual pie dishes here, the spring type with a trapdoor-like base. I can eat a whole pie, but most people only manage half. I have cooked these pies in deep bowls, but it is harder to get them out in one piece and you don't get to see all the lovely layers. Potato can be used instead of cauliflower for the mash, but I like the lightness that the cauliflower brings.

THE BITS

5 cloves of garlic, unpeeled

1 onion, roughly chopped

1 small cauliflower, roughly chopped

1½ teaspoons sea salt

2 tablespoons olive oil

75ml almond milk or soya milk

1 teaspoon lemon zest

2 tablespoons chopped parsley

3 large carrots, scrubbed and chopped

¼ teaspoon freshly ground nutmeg

2 teaspoon nutritional yeast flakes (see page 30)

6 sheets of filo pastry

2 tablespoons olive oil

For the topping

1 large red pepper, deseeded and finely diced

2 cloves of garlic, peeled and crushed

1 teaspoon fennel seeds

2 handfuls of black olives,

de-stoned and roughly chopped

2 tablespoons fine capers, well drained (if large, roughly chopped)

2 teaspoons lemon juice

½ teaspoon black pepper

4 tablespoons roasted almonds, roughly chopped

a large pinch of sea salt (if needed)

1 tablespoon olive oil

(cont.) ➡

Preheat the oven to 220°C/gas mark 7. Put the garlic, onion and cauliflower on to a baking tray, sprinkle with 1 teaspoon of sea salt and toss in 1 teaspoon of olive oil. Bake in the oven for 15 minutes, then check that the garlic is soft and remove it. Turn the onion and cauliflower over and put them back into the oven for 10–15 minutes more. All should be nicely cooked and slightly caramelized. Once they have cooled slightly, push the garlic out of the skins and put into a blender with the onions, cauliflower, almond milk, lemon zest and parsley. Blitz until creamy, then check the seasoning, cover and set aside.

Toss the carrots in 1 teaspoon olive oil and pop on a baking tray, cover with baking parchment or foil and bake in the oven for 30–35 minutes until they are soft. Place in the blender with the nutmeg and yeast flakes and pulse a few times, leaving some chunks. Cover and set aside.

On a lightly floured surface, lay 1 sheet of filo pastry, making sure to handle it gently. Brush well with olive oil, lay on another sheet, brush with oil once more, layer and brush. That's 3 sheets of filo per pie. Lay the filo over a small (20cm wide, 10cm deep) circular pie dish, press in and ease gently with your fingers, right down into the corners. Repeat the process with the other pie dish. Reduce the oven to 200°C/gas mark 6.

Your fillings should be cooled, but still warm. Using a spoon, form a good layer of carrot purée in each pie, again pressing it into the edges to form a nice distinct layer. Top with your cauliflower mash until it is 1cm below the rim of the pie dish. Trim the square edges of the filo, but leave a good 4cm overlap. The idea is that it gathers around the pie and looks vaguely like a flower with filo petals. Brush the pies gently with olive oil and place in the oven. Bake on the middle shelf for 15 minutes, checking that the filo is not cooking too quickly. Cover with foil if this happens.

Now, heat 1 tablespoon of olive oil in a frying pan. Add the peppers and sauté for 6–8 minutes, until beginning to caramelize. Add the garlic and fennel seeds, stir and sauté for 2 minutes, then pop in the olives, capers, lemon juice, pepper and almonds. Check if it is salty enough (the capers normally do the business). Cover and warm through on a low heat for 10 minutes. Set aside.

Serve the warm pies with a good layer of the peppers and almonds as a topping. Best with steamed greens of your choice. Pat on the back. Big well done and enjoy the fruits of your artistry.

Smoked Chocolate & Beetroot Beans with Baked Chilli Polenta & Avocado & Lime Salsa

FOR 6-8

The Mexicans have been using chocolate in savoury food for an age. The first time I tried mole poblano (a rich dark sauce made with chocolate, chilli, bananas and peanuts, among other things) my whole approach to food shifted, relaxed and heaved a sigh of relief. Chipotle chillies or paste are relatively easy to locate – try the 'world food' section of your local supermarket. If they still elude you, try smoked paprika to get that wonderful and essential smoky flavour. I recommend deseeding fresh chillies if they are really incendiary – but otherwise, leave the seeds in.

THE BITS

1 tablespoon sunflower oil

2 large beetroots, peeled and cut into 2cm cubes

2 red peppers, chopped into random 2cm chunks

1 tablespoon balsamic vinegar

2 onions, finely chopped

4 cloves of garlic, peeled and crushed

2 celery stalks, finely chopped

16 mushrooms (chestnut or similar), cleaned, stems trimmed and halved

2–3 large chipotle chillies, finely chopped, or 1 extra fresh red chilli plus 2 teaspoons smoked paprika

1–2 red chillies, deseeded and finely diced

2 teaspoons dried oregano

2 tablespoons tomato purée

1 teaspoon ground allspice

2 teaspoons ground cumin

225g black beans, soaked and cooked

400ml vegetable stock (or bean cooking liquid)

75g very dark vegan chocolate, finely chopped

1–2 teaspoons sea salt

For the baked chilli polenta

2 corn on the cobs (or 1 tin – roughly 200g drained weight)

2 tablespoons olive oil

2 cloves of garlic, peeled and crushed

200g coarse polenta

750ml very hot water

1 tablespoon nutritional yeast flakes (see page 30 – optional but tasty)

1 teaspoon dried oregano

1 large red chilli, finely diced, or ½ teaspoon chilli flakes

1 teaspoon salt

½ teaspoon bicarbonate of soda

For the avocado & lime salsa

1 avocado, peeled and cut into small chunks

a handful of fresh coriander, roughly sliced

juice and zest of ½ a lime

a pinch of sea salt

DO IT

In a large, heavy frying pan, add ½ tablespoon of oil and slowly fry the beetroots for 5 minutes, tossing them and stirring regularly. Add the peppers, turn the heat up and pan-fry for 5 minutes. Now add the balsamic vinegar and give it a minute to evaporate slightly, then add 2 tablespoons of water, cover, and allow to steam for 10 minutes on the lowest heat.

In a large pan, warm ½ tablespoon of oil on a medium heat and sauté the onions for 5 minutes. Add the garlic, celery, mushrooms, chillies, oregano, tomato purée and spices and cook for 5 minutes more. Ladle in the cooked beans and enough stock (or better still, bean liquid) to make a nice thick sauce. Allow it to come to a gentle boil. Add the beetroots and peppers, spoon in any cooking juices, then cover and simmer slowly for 15–20 minutes.

Now add the chocolate and allow to melt, then place a stick blender in the stew and pulse a couple of times, creating a creamy texture in the sauce. Check the seasoning.

To cook the polenta, first boil a kettle. Remove the corn from the cobs by holding them vertical and sawing a sharp knife downwards – the kernels should leap off. It takes a little practice, so watch your fingers!

Preheat the oven to 190°C/gas mark 5. Oil a baking dish (23 x 30cm sounds about right) and line the base with baking paper.

Heat the olive oil in a heavy-bottomed pan and sauté the sweetcorn for 2 minutes, until starting to caramelize. Add the garlic, stir for a minute, then pour in the polenta and heat for a minute, combining everything. Now add a quarter of the hot water, stirring and flattening out any lumps as you go.

With the heat on medium-low, keep giving it some elbow grease with your spatula, adding the water gradually, a quarter at a time, checking that the polenta doesn't stick to the bottom of the pan. Continue for 6–8 minutes – it will come together and absorb the water. Stir in the nutritional yeast flakes, oregano, chilli, salt and bicarbonate of soda. Have a taste – the polenta should be soft and not 'bitty'. If there are still lumps, get the stick blender out again and whiz it up. The lumps soon vanish.

Spoon into the prepared baking dish and flatten the surface with a spatula. The polenta should be a thickness of about 2.5cm all over. Bake in the oven for 30–35 minutes, until a dark golden crust is formed. Leave to rest in the dish for 5 minutes, then, using a flat spatula (two work best), loosen the edges of the polenta and ease it out on to a wire rack. Let it cool for 5–10 minutes – it will firm up nicely on the rack. Slide it on to a chopping board and cut into squares or triangles or whatever other cool shapes you like (you could use a pastry/cookie cutter, star shape . . .).

This seems like a lot of work, but I can think of few better ways of treating polenta. It is well worth the effort – crispy around the edges and soft inside.

Mix the salsa ingredients together in a bowl.

Ladle the stew over the polenta and serve the avocado and lime salsa on the side.

Pappardelle with Artichoke & Almond Sauce, Purple Kale & White Asparagus

FOR 4

This dish is a delight! So many shades of green, all bursting with flavour and nutrition. Artichokes have a unique flavour and they make a surprisingly creamy purée. Throw a few almonds into the mix and you're well on your way. In Spain, I buy fresh artichokes for pennies – kilos of the things are piled around our small kitchen and it can be difficult to know what to do with them. However, I recommend using good-quality jarred artichokes here. In this dish I tend to use white asparagus, but in autumn and winter I'd try to seek out some salsify. It's a creamy and rich root vegetable, perfect with this tangy sauce.

THE BITS

400g purple kale, stalks removed, thickly chopped

8–10 white asparagus spears

2 teaspoons olive oil

75ml nice white wine (veggie)

sea salt and black pepper

400g pappardelle (or similar egg-free pasta)

For the artichoke & almond sauce

5 tablespoons olive oil

a handful of almonds, soaked for 2 hours, skins removed if you have time

2 cloves of garlic, peeled and crushed

4 big handfuls of watercress leaves

1 x 390g jar of artichoke hearts

juice of ½ a lemon

For the topping

1 small handful of toasted almonds, finely chopped

1 big handful of fresh parsley, chopped

a handful of watercress

DO IT

To make the sauce, heat 1 tablespoon of oil in a frying pan and add the almonds. Sauté for 1 minute, then add the garlic and continue cooking for 2 minutes more. Add the watercress leaves, cover the pan, take off the heat and allow to cool.

Place the contents of the frying pan in a food processor with the artichokes, lemon juice and 4 tablespoons of olive oil, and blend to a smooth purée. The sauce should be thick and shiny. Add water to thin it out if necessary.

Heat 2 teaspoons of olive oil in a large heavy frying pan and add the asparagus. Pan-fry for 6–8 minutes, until nicely caramelized. Add a glug of white wine, and when the liquid has evaporated, season and cover. Leave to sit.

Bring a big pan of salted water to a boil and cook your pasta for roughly 8 minutes, until al dente. Add the kale halfway through the cooking time. Drain well, keeping aside a little of the pasta water. Add the drained pasta and kale to the artichoke sauce and toss together, adding some of the pasta water if it is looking a bit dry.

Spoon into warm shallow bowls and top with criss-crosses of asparagus and a sprinkling of toasted almonds and parsley. Finally top with the watercress and season with sea salt and black pepper.

In the Nantlle Valley, beneath Mount Snowdon

Curries

I remember the first time we went to a UK curry house. I was seven and we all ordered frazzled chicken chow mein and boiled soggy rice; Nana had pie, chips and mushy peas. It was the late 80s in Leicester and we hadn't got the hang of Indian food yet. Much has changed since then! I cringe at the thought of the incredible food we missed out on living in Leicester at that time, and I've been making up for the oversight ever since.

I've been round India a number of times, from peak to plain: I've hiked the Himalayas, I've woken up on a beach in Kerala, I've meditated for weeks in monasteries and eaten like a happy Buddha, I've lived with remote tribal communities and helped to milk yaks (which put me off milk for ever). I've even cooked fresh pasta in the back of a jeep during an avalanche (the pasta was slightly overcooked, but we survived!).

I am captivated by the bright lights and wonder of the ancient carousel of Indian culture and history, the ubiquitous spice markets, the fiery masala chai first thing in the morning. Curry (a very British term) encapsulates so much of the diversity and magic of this fascinating land. Travelling India is a constant adventure and teaches us much about life, the universe and everything . . . The food's pretty damn hot too!

Indian cuisine changes, sometimes drastically, from region to region, all heavily influenced by trade and conquerors, sometimes dating back thousands of years. The word 'curry' has no meaning in India; each dish has its own unique moniker and generally a long tradition, with stringent rules of preparation. I tend to adapt these rules and come up with something a little different, and my Indian friends normally like the results!

Curry is my favourite thing to cook; I love playing with spices and colours. Indian cuisine is so massive and diverse you need never cook the same dish twice. Dishes range from the simple tasty morsels offered by street vendors up to the lavish wedding banquets that last for days, where fine ghee is poured over food from silver teapots and the days of the Maharajahs are re-enacted via mountainous biryanis. India is an awe-inspiring land, with a culinary tradition to match.

Indian cooking can also be really healthy. Buying a few key spices – ground turmeric, cumin, coriander, paprika, maybe asafoetida – is a good idea (see page 31). Spices are always better freshly ground, so buy them in small batches and use often. When to add the spices to a dish depends on the dish and the spice. There is no right or wrong way, just don't burn them. If you are a spice connoisseur, there is no substitute for roasting your own spices (primarily cumin and coriander) and using others whole (cinnamon bark or sticks, star anise, cloves). At your local Indian food shop you may also pick up fresh turmeric, a magical ingredient.

Even better, go to Delhi, jump in an auto-rickshaw and do a restaurant crawl. Invade the sweet-shops for snacks, the dhabas for thalis and the finer restaurants for a whiff of the opulence of Mughal times. The only way to fully experience food is in the appropriate setting, the land from which it hails. Every plate and forkful is an expression of a culture; we learn so much about people by what they eat.

Most of the dishes here are highly untraditional. I have tampered with many – I have Indian friends whose eyes almost pop out when I go through the ingredients, muttering something along the lines of 'Insane!' or 'Mother would not be happy.' Still, cooking is about playing, expressing and most of all, enjoying.

Whenever possible, I like to veer away from tins and tubes and keep things natural, even sauces. I know it is much easier to use tinned tomatoes, but a freshly made sauce cannot be beaten and hardly takes any more time or effort. Buying good tomatoes makes all the difference – if the tomatoes are tasteless off the vine, they'll be tasteless in the bowl. Adding a large pinch of sugar and salt can bring the flavour out a little, but really, if you want to be in the good sauce gang, tasty toms are a must!

Om Namah Shivaya!

Kashmiri Turnip & Spinach Curry with Beetroot Raita

FOR 4

Kashmir! The name alone conjures up some epic, desolate, sublime corner of our world, swathed in beauty and crystal blue skies. Kashmir is famous for its turnip farming and you can see why, if you've ever tried one – they are in a league of their own. The secret to cooking turnips in Kashmir is to salt them, which draws any bitterness out, before roasting them until beautifully golden. Swedes are normally a good substitute if you can't get turnips, though they do take a little more cooking.

THE BITS

750g turnips, scrubbed and cut into 5cm wedges

sea salt

3 tablespoons vegetable oil

600g spinach leaves (the bigger the leaf, the better), sliced into 2cm ribbons

2 teaspoons cumin seeds

2 teaspoons coriander seeds

5 tablespoons soya yoghurt (unsweetened)

1 onion, sliced

2.5cm fresh ginger, grated

3 cloves of garlic, peeled and crushed

1 tablespoon methi (fenugreek) leaves

½ teaspoon ground fenugreek

1–2 teaspoons chilli powder

juice of ½ a lemon

1 x beetroot raita (see page 330)

DO IT

Place the turnips in a colander, sprinkle over 1 tablespoon of salt and mix it all around with your hands. Place the colander over a bowl or the sink and leave for 30 minutes. Warm a pan on a medium heat and add a slight splash of oil and half your spinach. Stir and the spinach will begin to wilt. Pop a lid on and lower the heat. Leave to cook for a few minutes, then drain well.

In a small skillet, toast the cumin and coriander seeds for about 1 minute, until they start to pop, then grind in a pestle and mortar. Mix the soya yoghurt into the cooked spinach. Place in a food processor and blend to a bright green sauce.

Rinse the turnips in cold water and dry with a clean tea towel. Heat half the oil in a large heavy frying pan and fry the turnips on a high heat until golden – 8–10 minutes will be fine. Remove, cover and set aside. Now add the rest of the oil to the frying pan and begin to fry your onions. Cook on a high heat for 6 minutes, until they are becoming caramelized. Add your ginger, garlic and methi leaves and sauté for 2 minutes, then add the ground fenugreek, cumin, coriander and chilli powder. Fry for a further 2 minutes and let the spices warm, mingle and infuse.

Now add the turnips to the pan and stir in the green sauce with 3 tablespoons of water and the rest of your spinach. Heat uncovered for 5 minutes – the sauce will thicken and the turnips will be nice and soft. Remove from the heat and cover. Make the beetroot raita.

After a couple of minutes sitting, the curry will be perfect! Thin the sauce with a little water if needed, then stir in the lemon juice and add salt to taste. Best enjoyed with lashings of your preferred rice and a hearty dollop of the vivid purple raita.

Spiced Chana Masala with
Brown Chickpeas, Tamarind & Kale

FOR 4

Straight from the Punjab, the green land of many rivers in the north-west of India, home to Sikhs and the Golden Temple. This is a very fecund area, where chana (chickpeas) thrive. Punjabi food is full-flavoured and sometimes quite rich – a Punjabi thali is a force to be reckoned with. Here's a simple and hearty curry for those times when you want maximum flavour for minimum effort. Brown chickpeas have a more robust texture, are slightly smaller and contain bags more fibre than your average chickpea. You can use normal chickpeas, but they are rather pale in comparison.

THE BITS

6 large kale leaves (any variety is fine), removed from the stems and finely sliced

240g dried brown chickpeas, soaked and cooked

200ml chickpea cooking broth, or vegetable stock

For the masala

2 tablespoons vegetable oil

1 teaspoon cumin seeds

2 bay leaves

1 small cinnamon stick (or 1½ teaspoons ground cinnamon)

6 cloves

1 large onion, finely diced

2 carrots, scrubbed and roughly grated

3 cloves of garlic, peeled

4cm of fresh ginger, peeled

1 hot red chilli, finely sliced

2 teaspoons garam masala

4 dates, soaked in water for 2 hours, then finely diced

a handful of cashews, soaked in water for 2 hours

6 ripe tomatoes, diced

2 teaspoons tamarind paste

¾ teaspoon sea salt, to taste

¾ teaspoon black pepper, to taste

For the garnish

2 tablespoons roasted cashew nuts, roughly chopped

½ a handful of fresh coriander leaves, roughly chopped

DO IT

Heat the oil in a large frying pan on a medium heat. Add the cumin seeds, bay leaves, cinnamon stick and cloves and fry for 30 seconds until they begin to pop, then add the onions and carrots, stirring well. Fry for 6–8 minutes, until the onions go soft and brown.

Now put the garlic, ginger and chilli into a food processor and blend until smooth, adding 50ml water to make a loose paste. Pour into the pan, and stir and cook for a minute. When you can really smell that garlic roasting, add the garam masala. Stir and fry for 2 minutes, making sure the spices don't stick (add 1 tablespoon of water if this happens).

Drain your dates and cashews, add them along with the tomatoes and tamarind paste to the food processor (no need to clean it out this time), and blend together until smooth (you can do this in advance). Add this tomato sauce to the pan and stir in, then set the heat to a decent simmer and cook slowly for 15 minutes. Add the kale and simmer for another 5 minutes. Add the chickpeas and thin out the sauce with the chickpea cooking stock (if needed – the sauce should be thick and concentrated). Now season (be heavy-handed with the black pepper). Stir and warm through for 5 minutes, then sprinkle with the chopped cashews and coriander.

Best served with lots of wholemeal chapattis (or brown rice chapattis, see page 237), or piles of steaming basmati rice.

Pakistani Pumpkin & Beetroot Bhuna with Banana & Lime Raita

FOR 6

Pakistani food has always seemed really intense and earthy to me when compared to that of its Indian neighbour, although they are really one and the same thing. I think it's because I always think of the Karakorum Highway and the Khyber Pass when my mind wanders towards northern Pakistan, a place that sounds so wild and desolate.

This style of bhuna is really easy – just spread it all out on a tray and roast until gorgeous and golden. The sauce should be shimmering and rich, the spices well toasted. This bhuna is a dry style curry, so don't expect loads of liquid here, that's where the raita comes in. The masala can be made the night before, which intensifies the flavours. Beetroot leaves are a magical ingredient with huge amounts of nutrients. If they look a little dodgy and past it, or if you cannot source beetroots with leaves on, use ruby chard or large spinach leaves instead.

THE BITS

2 large beetroots, scrubbed and cut into 5cm wedges, plus the beetroot leaves, roughly chopped, and stems, finely chopped

3 tablespoons rapeseed or vegetable oil

1½ teaspoons cumin seeds

1 teaspoon black mustard seeds

1 small pumpkin, scrubbed, deseeded and cut into 5cm wedges

5 banana shallots or 1 large onion, cut into wedges roughly the same size as the beetroot

½ teaspoon sea salt

½ teaspoon freshly cracked black pepper

10 large cloves of garlic

For the masala

½ tablespoon vegetable oil

1 large onion, finely sliced

4 cloves of garlic, peeled and crushed

2.5cm fresh ginger, peeled and chopped

½ teaspoon chilli powder

¼ teaspoon ground cardamom (or 4 cardamom pods, crushed)

½ teaspoon ground turmeric

⅓ teaspoon ground cinnamon

6 large tomatoes, chopped

1 tablespoon tomato purée

100ml water

2 teaspoons garam masala

½ teaspoon sea salt

For the banana & lime raita

400ml soya yoghurt (unsweetened)

2 just-ripe bananas, peeled, halved lengthways and cut into 1cm chunks

a handful of fresh coriander, finely chopped

juice of ½ a lime

1 teaspoon lime zest

½ teaspoon salt

For the garnish

1 tablespoon vegetable oil

1 large onion, finely sliced

1 yellow pepper, finely sliced

a handful of fresh coriander leaves

DO IT

Preheat the oven to 200°C/gas mark 6. To make the masala, heat the oil in a large frying pan, add the onion and sauté for 3 minutes. Bash the garlic and ginger in a pestle and mortar or a food processor and add to the onions, cook for 3 minutes, then add the chilli, cardamom, turmeric and cinnamon and warm through, stirring, for a minute.

(cont.) ➡

CURRIES 221

Now add the tomatoes, tomato purée and water to the pan and cook on a steady simmer with a lid on for 20 minutes. Stir in the garam masala and the chopped beetroot leaves and season with salt. Set aside and allow to cool. Pour into a food processor and blend until smooth (or blitz with a stick blender).

In a large ceramic baking dish, toss the chopped beetroots in oil. Cover and bake for 25 minutes. Add the cumin and mustard seeds, along with the pumpkin, shallots, salt and pepper. Toss all well together, making sure there is space between the veggies. If not, use a second baking tray. Put back into the oven and roast for 30–35 minutes, turning everything over halfway through cooking. When you turn them, add the garlic cloves and beetroot stems. The veg should be nicely caramelized and softened by now, but a mile away from mushy. Check the beetroots – they can be a little stubborn.

To make the banana and lime raita, mix all the ingredients together in a bowl. To make the garnish, put a heavy frying pan on a high heat, add the oil, and when hot, throw in the onions and peppers and stir-fry for 5–6 minutes, until all is sweet and a little charred round the edges. Season with a pinch of salt. Keep warm.

Drop the oven temp to 180°C/gas mark 4. Pour the masala over the roasting veggies and combine well (being careful not to break up the pumpkin). Warm through in the oven for 10 minutes. The sauce should be getting nice and concentrated by now, which is what we're looking for.

Sprinkle the bhuna with the warm onions and peppers, top with fresh coriander and place centre stage on the table. Big spoonfuls of the raita are a must, accompanied by your favourite fluffy rice.

Roasted Almond & Kohlrabi Koftas with a Tomato & Ginger Masala

MAKES 14 KOFTAS

Koftas are like saucy croquettes combining India's finest flavours. Wonderfully crisp on the outside and gooey in the middle, they're normally fried, but I have gone for an oven bake for healthier results. Koftas are normally cooked in a rich masala, but I like their crisp nature, so I just spoon over the sauce at the end, retaining their crunch. Koftas can be made with most combinations of vegetables – they are a great technique to have in your vegan repertoire and are a traditionally gluten-free option, using chickpea flour to bind the ingredients together. Ground coriander always adds a lovely nutty orange flavour and has the added benefit of acting as a thickener. Add as many almonds as you like here, the more the merrier!

THE BITS

750g potatoes, peeled and cut into small cubes

1 teaspoon sea salt

3 tablespoons sunflower oil

2 red onions, finely sliced

1 large carrot, scrubbed and coarsely grated

1 large kohlrabi, peeled and coarsely grated

2 red chillies, seeds removed, very finely diced, or 1 teaspoon chilli flakes

2 teaspoons coriander seeds

2 teaspoons cumin seeds

1 teaspoon ground turmeric

½ teaspoon ground cardamom

½ teaspoon ground cinnamon

1/8 teaspoon asafoetida

2 handfuls of fresh coriander (stems and leaves), finely chopped

2 big handfuls of roasted almonds, roughly chopped

3 tablespoons chickpea flour

3 heaped tablespoons cornflour, for dusting the kofta

For the tomato and ginger masala

6 cardamom pods or ½ teaspoon ground cardamom

a large pinch of sea salt

3 cloves of garlic, peeled and grated

5cm fresh ginger, peeled and grated

1 tablespoon vegetable oil

1 teaspoon cumin seeds

1 large onion, peeled and grated

a large pinch of asafoetida

1 teaspoon fennel seeds

1 red chilli, finely sliced, or ½ teaspoon chilli flakes

½ teaspoon ground coriander

5 large tomatoes, roughly chopped

225ml water

1 tablespoon gram (chickpea) flour or ground almonds

1 teaspoon unrefined brown sugar (depending on the sweetness of your tomatoes)

½ tablespoon lemon juice

olive oil

For the garnish

a handful of fresh coriander leaves, chopped

(cont.) ⇒

DO IT

Put the potatoes into a large pan and cover them with cold water. Add ½ teaspoon of sea salt and bring to the boil, then reduce the heat and simmer for 35 minutes, until tender. Press a knife tip into a potato – when they are ready it should pass through it with ease. Drain the potatoes and allow to cool. When cooled to warm, mash until smooth. (In an Indian kitchen you'd grate them, but this takes ages!) The potatoes are best cooked well in advance and refrigerated. The drier your potatoes, the firmer your koftas.

To make the tomato and ginger masala, first bash the cardamom pods in a pestle and mortar and pick out the cardamom husks, leaving the black seeds in the mortar. Add the salt, garlic and ginger and bash some more, to form a nice paste.

Heat the oil in a frying pan on a medium-high heat. Add the cumin seeds and sauté for 30 seconds until fragrant, then add your grated onion. Fry for 3 minutes, then add the ginger mix. Sprinkle in the asafoetida, fennel seeds, chilli and ground coriander and fry for 1 minute more, stirring all the time. Now add the tomatoes, water, chickpea flour and sugar. Simmer with a lid on for 10 minutes, then remove from the heat and check the seasoning.

Leave the sauce to cool slightly, then pour into a food processor (or use a stick blender) and pulse until smooth. It keeps for a day in the fridge and can even be served cold or used as a tasty dip. Whether serving warm or cold, add the lemon juice and a splash of olive oil just before serving.

To make the koftas, heat 1 tablespoon of oil in a frying pan on a medium-low heat. Add the onions and fry for 10 minutes, getting them well caramelized. Lower the heat if they are becoming charred. Now add the carrot and fry for 3 minutes more (turn the heat up), then the kohlrabi, chillies, spices and ½ teaspoon of salt. Continue to cook for 7 minutes, stirring regularly. We'd like the veggies to caramelize slightly, removing some of their water content.

Preheat the oven to 180°C/gas mark 4.

Put the potatoes into a large bowl and add the kohlrabi mix, fresh coriander, toasted almonds and chickpea flour. Blend it all together with a trusty spoon (or use your mitts) until everything is very well incorporated. Check the seasoning (you may need a tad more salt).

Pour 2 tablespoons of oil on to a large baking tray and put the cornflour on a large plate. Using your hands, form the kofta mixture into 10 fat sausage shapes (roughly 2 tablespoons of mix per kofta). Roll each kofta lightly in the cornflour, giving them a good dusting all over, then knock off any excess and place them on the oiled baking tray, rolling them over once to coat them in oil. Bake for 20 minutes, then turn them all over and bake for another 15 minutes. The koftas should be golden and crispy.

Serve the koftas on warm plates, with a few spoons of the tomato and ginger masala and a sprinkling of fresh coriander. Cauliflower rice (see page 144) would be an ideal accompaniment, and a mound of fresh green leaves.

Green Pea, Rose & Cauliflower Pulao with Coconut & Mint Chutney

SERVES 6–8

This is a light and fragrant rice dish, with the added wonder of coconut milk, saffron and a splash of rose water to bring luxury and a real sense of authenticity to a dish I've enjoyed countless times in India. Pulao comes in many forms – it basically translates as 'rice' and cooking it in this way takes humble rice to a whole extra level of loveliness. Adding a little rose water can bring a totally new and slightly floral dimension to veggie cooking. Too much rose water can kill a dish, though, and make it taste like a cheap boudoir, so err on the side of caution when using.

THE BITS

400g good-quality basmati rice

2 tablespoons coconut oil
(or vegetable oil)

1 big handful of cashew nuts
(halved lengthways is best, like
nutty half-moons)

½ a handful of curry leaves

1½ teaspoons cumin seeds

1½ teaspoons fennel seeds

3 onions, finely sliced

4cm fresh ginger, peeled and grated

4 cloves of garlic, peeled and crushed

1 cinnamon stick, broken in half

10 green cardamom pods, cracked

1 x 400ml tin of coconut milk

1½ teaspoons saffron, soaked in
1 tablespoon warm water (optional)

a handful of sultanas

½ a small cauliflower, roughly chopped into
small florets, using the stem as well

1 teaspoon sea salt

2 big handfuls of fresh green peas
(frozen will also do)

1–2 tablespoons rose water, to taste

For the garnish

½ a handful of toasted cashew nuts,
halved lengthways

a handful of fresh coriander, chopped

For the coconut & mint chutney

1.5cm fresh ginger, grated

1–2 small green chillies

1 large clove of garlic, peeled and grated

½ a fresh coconut, grated (or 120g desiccated
coconut, soaked for 2 hours)

1 tablespoon lemon juice

2 handfuls of fresh mint leaves, finely sliced

50g dried Bengal gram daal or 25g gram
(chickpea) flour

a large pinch of sea salt

125ml fresh water

DO IT

Wash your rice, covering it with fresh water and swooshing the rice around with your hand, then pouring the dirty water away. Rice has normally come a long way and it can get a little grubby. Repeat this swooshing motion until the water is running clear-ish. Drain again, then soak the rice in fresh water for 30 minutes. Drain well again.

Heat the coconut oil in a large frying pan on a medium heat and when hot, fry the cashews, curry leaves, cumin seeds and fennel seeds for 30 seconds. Now throw in your onions and ginger and cook, stirring well, until golden and becoming crispy – 10–12 minutes will do nicely. Remove 3 tablespoons of the onion mix and set aside for the garnish.

Now add the garlic, cinnamon sticks and cardamom pods and pan-fry this lot for 2 minutes – things will be getting really aromatic around about now.

Pour in the drained rice and stir well. Monitor the heat of your pan and take it off the heat if it's going crazy and starting to burn the rice. Set aside 2 tablespoons of the coconut milk and add the rest of the tin to the pan with the saffron, sultanas, cauliflower and salt. Then pour in enough water to cover the rice by 1cm. Stir and bring to a gentle boil. Cover tightly with a well-fitting lid and cook for 25 minutes on the lowest setting possible (without peeking!).

To make the coconut and mint chutney, put the ginger, chilli and garlic into a pestle and mortar or a food processor and blend together. Add the coconut, lemon juice, mint and the daal or gram flour and blend further, adding water gradually to make a thick paste. Add salt to taste. That's it! This chutney will thicken if kept in the fridge, so stir in a little more water if necessary to get a nice, creamy consistency.

Fluff up the pulao with a fork, add the peas, then cover and allow to cook for 5 minutes longer, adding a touch more water if needed. The pulao should be more moist than normal boiled rice, with a little sauce. Just before serving, stir in the rose water to taste, remembering that a little goes a long way. Mix in the reserved coconut milk for a final saucy flourish.

I like to serve rice dishes like this in one big pyramid on a large serving platter or plate. Garnish with the reserved caramelized onions and a scattering of cashews and fresh coriander. Serve the chutney on the side in small bowls, or drizzled around the base of the pulao for maximum 'eye candy' effect.

Keralan Coconut & Vegetable Curry with Pineapple & Watermelon Salad

FOR 4

This dish is called aviyal and comes from tropical Kerala, in south-western India. I've taken the liberty of adding some 'English vegetables' to the mix (this is what the older Keralans still call things like carrots and green beans), along with fistfuls of the lifeblood of this lovely part of the world: coconut. In Kerala they use a large vegetable called 'drumstick', which resembles an elongated okra and adds a lovely subtle flavour. When I'm cooking over there I normally pick them straight from the tree. They're a real star ingredient. The general rule with curry leaves is the fresher, the better. When pineapples and watermelons are out of season, try making the salad with fruit combinations like apple and peach, or pear and orange.

THE BITS

2–3 fresh green chillies

2 big handfuls of freshly grated or dessicated coconut

2 teaspoons cumin seeds

220ml coconut milk or unsweetened soya yoghurt

2 large carrots, scrubbed

2 large potatoes, scrubbed

1 large courgette

6 fat asparagus spears

2 green plantains, peeled

200ml water

1 heaped teaspoon ground turmeric

½ teaspoon sea salt

1 big handful of mangetout or green beans

2 tablespoons coconut oil

2 teaspoons mustard seeds

3 tablespoons curry leaves

For the pineapple & watermelon salad

½ a small pineapple

⅓ of a small watermelon (don't bother deseeding, just munch them)

1 large cucumber

1 small handful of fresh coriander, roughly chopped

a pinch of sea salt

a large pinch of chaat masala mix or black salt (optional)

DO IT

In a pestle and mortar or a food processor, blend together the chillies, coconut and cumin seeds (if you're using desiccated coconut, add 2 tablespoons of the coconut milk to make a thick paste). This is best done in advance and can be left overnight in the fridge to develop zing.

Cut the carrots, potatoes, courgette, asparagus and plantains into 2.5cm pieces. Heat the water in a large pan and add the turmeric, salt, carrots and potatoes. Bring to a steady boil, then lower the heat to a simmer and pop a lid on the pan. Cook for 10 minutes, then add the courgettes and plantains and cook for 10 minutes more, still with the lid on.

Add the coconut paste to the curry with the coconut milk or yoghurt and stir carefully to combine. Cook uncovered for 8–10 minutes on a gentle simmer. Check that the carrots and potatoes are tender, then add the asparagus and mangetout and remove the pan from the heat. Cover and set aside for a few minutes.

To make the salad, peel the pineapple, watermelon and cucumber and cut into 1cm chunks. Put into a bowl with the rest of the salad ingredients.

In a small frying pan, warm the coconut oil and roast the mustard seeds and curry leaves for 1 minute. Remove from the heat (you can leave them to sit a while – this intensifies the flavours). Stir the seasoned oil into the aviyal and serve with steaming piles of your preferred rice and a small bowl of the pineapple and watermelon salad on the side.

Tiger Mountain Beans with Red Pepper Masala, Peanut & Coriander Salad & Sesame Pancakes

FOR 4

I live on Tiger Mountain in North Wales, so called because of the vivid orange and black stripes that can sometimes be seen during autumn sunsets. This simple everyday curry is a staple at that time of year and combines two of my favourite things, curry and beans. It makes a wonderful base for all kinds of additions, my favourite being smoked tofu. I can be quite heavy-handed with my spices, but have realized that subtlety is the key, and a gently spiced dish can have as much effect as something highly spiced. This tomato and pepper masala sauce is softly spiced and the perfect accompaniment to the hearty kidney beans. The sesame pancakes are delicious, but the dish is equally wonderful just served with simply cooked rice.

Gluten-free option: opt for GF flatbreads instead of the pancakes.

THE BITS

4 teaspoons coriander seeds

4 teaspoons cumin seeds

1 tablespoon vegetable oil

1 large carrot, cut into 2cm chunks

1 celery stalk, cut into 2cm chunks

1 aubergine, cut into 2cm chunks

2 bay leaves

½ teaspoon ground cardamom or 6 cardamom pods, bashed and husks removed

¼ teaspoon ground cinnamon

½ teaspoon chilli powder

200g dried red kidney beans, soaked and cooked

about 75ml bean cooking liquid or water (as needed)

1½ teaspoons ajwain seeds or dried thyme

1 teaspoon sea salt

¼ teaspoon freshly cracked black pepper

2 handfuls of French beans, cut into 5cm pieces, or mangetout

1 teaspoon jaggery (or unrefined brown sugar)

200g smoked tofu or firm tofu, cut into 1cm cubes (optional, but awesome – my favourite brand is Taifun)

For the red pepper masala

2 red peppers

a little vegetable oil

3 cloves of garlic

4cm fresh ginger

1 large onion

5 large tomatoes

For the peanut & coriander salad

2 handfuls of raw unsalted peanuts

2 tablespoons vegetable oil

a pinch of sea salt

1–2 red chillies, deseeded and finely diced

½ a red onion or 3 spring onions, as finely diced as you can

1 tablespoon lemon juice

1 big handful of fresh coriander leaves, roughly chopped

1 x sesame & sweetcorn pancakes (see page 141), omitting the sweetcorn

To serve

soya yoghurt (optional)

DO IT

Preheat the oven to 200°C/gas mark 6. Rub the red peppers with a little oil and roast in the oven for 30 minutes, or chop and fry in a pan for 10 minutes on a medium heat. Either way, make 'em sweet and lovely.

Warm a large, heavy-bottomed frying pan (something like a traditional karai), add the coriander and cumin seeds and toast them gently for 1–2 minutes, keeping them moving all the time. They will be fragrant and popping. Then grind them in a pestle and mortar. Take out roughly 1½ teaspoons of the toasted spices and set aside, leaving the rest in the mortar.

Using the same pan, dry-roast the peanuts for your salad. Put them into the pan on a medium heat and stir until they are turning golden and slightly charred. Add half the peanuts and the salt to the spices in the pestle and mortar and pour in 2 tablespoons of oil (you could also use a food processor here), then crush the peanuts until a chunky crumb is formed. Add the rest of the nuts and do the same again. Put the peanuts into a bowl and mix with the chillies, onions, lemon juice and fresh coriander. Set aside.

Roughly chop all the ingredients for the red pepper masala, then turn on a food processor and, with the motor running, add the bits in this order: garlic, ginger, onion, peppers. Make a thick, smooth purée, remove from the processor and set aside. Now add the tomatoes to the processor and blend until smooth. Set aside.

To make the Tiger Mountain beans, heat 1 tablespoon of oil in your frying pan on a medium heat and add the carrots, celery and aubergine. Fry for 6 minutes, add the reserved 1½ teaspoons of toasted spices, the bay leaves, cardamom, cinnamon and chilli powder, stir for a minute and then pour in the red pepper mix. Cook on a high simmer for 5 minutes, stirring well, until the masala is getting sweet and fine!

Add the cooked kidney beans, with about 75ml of their lovely cooking juices, the blitzed tomatoes, thyme or ajwain seeds, salt and pepper and cook for 5 minutes more. Add the French beans, jaggery and smoked tofu, pop a lid on the pan and continue to cook for 2 minutes, warming things through. Take off the heat and keep warm. I like there to be a good amount of sauce with my Tiger Beans – add more kidney bean stock if needed. Check the seasoning.

Make your sesame pancakes at the last minute and keep them warm, wrapped in a tea-towel.

Serve the Tiger Mountain beans with the peanut and coriander salad on the side, and with piles of sesame pancakes nearby. Adding some soya yoghurt to the plate would not hurt at all, and you may even like to make a wrap out of it!

SPECIAL INDIA TEA
INDIA COFFEE BEAUTIFUL
KRISHNA POWER COLD TEA

Krishna's
Chai
best in Bundi

Travels in India.

Clay-baked Potato & Parsnip with Roasted Garlic & Date Masala

FOR 4–6

There is something ancient about clay baking and it is still popular in my Spanish neck of the woods, Murcia. It gives an intangible addition to the flavour, but if you don't have a clay dish, just use a large casserole instead. This is a sweet and warming cold-weather curry, using the wonderful roots that get us through those bleak chilly nights tempered by warm fires and mugs of spicy chai (see page 81). The flavour combination of dates and almonds is probably as old as cooking in clay pots. The dried chillies here are the large, flat Indian variety, not the very spicy squat ones. These chillies add a little piquant and smoky spice to the dish.

THE BITS

½ a small butternut squash

4 large waxy potatoes

4 parsnips

2 carrots

2 onions, skins on, halved (red ones look cooler)

10 cloves of garlic, unpeeled

4 large tomatoes, halved

3 tablespoons vegetable oil

sea salt

6 big dates, soaked for 2 hours in 4 tablespoons water, de-stoned

1 large handful of ground almonds

4cm fresh ginger roughly chopped

¼ teaspoon ground allspice

150ml water

zest and juice of ½ a lime

vegetable oil

½ teaspoon ground turmeric

1 teaspoon cumin seeds

½ teaspoon black mustard seeds

5 red chillies

a large pinch of freshly cracked black pepper

For the garnish

a handful of toasted flaked almonds

a handful of fresh coriander leaves, finely chopped

DO IT

If you have a couple of large clay dishes, submerge them in water for at least an hour. Alternatively, grab a few baking trays, or a combination of the two. You'll need three in total.

Preheat the oven to 180°C/gas mark 4. Deseed the squash, scrub the potatoes, parsnips and carrots, then cut them all into similar-size large wedges. Place the parsnips and squash on one dish or tray and the potatoes and carrots on another and set aside.

Toss the onions, garlic and tomatoes in the oil and place on a baking tray. Sprinkle with sea salt and place in the oven for 30–35 minutes, until the onions are well caramelized and the tomatoes have some colour. Turn the onion and garlic after 10 minutes using a fish slice. The smaller garlic cloves may be ready to remove from the oven at this point.

Put the dates, almonds and ginger into a food processor and blitz to a smooth paste. Add the roasted onion and garlic (pop them out of their skins), plus the tomatoes, allspice and water and pulse again until a nice thick sauce is formed. Pour into a pan and bring to a steady boil, cooking on a low simmer for 20 minutes. Stir in the lime zest and juice, check the seasoning, put a lid on the pan and keep warm.

Drizzle all the vegetables with oil and sprinkle over the turmeric, cumin seeds and mustard seeds, along with the red chillies, a sprinkling of black pepper and 1 teaspoon of sea salt. Mix all together using your hands. Now this is a proper bake-a-thon!

Pop the dishes or trays into the oven with the potatoes at the top. Bake for 25 minutes, turning everything over at least once with the fish slice. The parsnips will stick, so keep your eye on them. Remove the squash and leave the potatoes in for another 10 minutes (if needed). When the potatoes and carrots are gorgeously soft and golden, remove and turn the oven off.

Gently scrape the roast veggies into one dish and pour over the almond and date sauce. Combine gently with a spatula or wooden spoon (not a metal spoon). Cover and leave to mingle for 5 minutes in the still warm oven.

Serve sprinkled with toasted flaked almonds and fresh coriander, a nice Indian pickle (such as lime or garlic) and towers of wholewheat chapattis. A saucy little daal would be awesome too. An Indian feast!

Matar Daal with Watercress, Braised Red Cabbage Sabji & Brown Rice Chapatti

FOR 4

When you sit down to a bowl of daal, you are not alone – around a billion people are probably doing the exact same thing. Daal can only be second to rice in the global food-loving stakes and for me is the ultimate comfort food. It's the lifeblood of India and with a warm chapatti is one of my favourite foods. Matar daal is made with green split peas, which add a good colour and a nice richness and texture. This daal is much thicker than most that you are served in India, but you can add water to make it more soup-like.

THE BITS

For the matar daal with watercress

225g dried green split peas

1 litre water

2.5cm fresh ginger, grated or crushed

8 cardamom pods, crushed with the ginger

4 dried red chillies, cut into 2cm pieces

½ teaspoon ground cumin

1 teaspoon ground coriander

¼ teaspoon asafoetida

2 tablespoons curry leaves

3 handfuls of watercress, well washed, or spring greens/kale, very finely sliced

sea salt and black pepper

For the red cabbage sabji

1 tablespoon coconut or vegetable oil

½ a red cabbage, finely sliced, tough stalk removed

juice of ½ an orange

1 teaspoon orange zest

2 star anise

2 teaspoons cumin seeds

½ a handful of curry leaves

2.5cm fresh ginger, peeled and grated

4 cloves of garlic, peeled and grated

1 teaspoon garam masala

For the brown rice chapattis (makes 8–10)

350g brown rice, cooked

450ml water

¼ teaspoon salt

40g whole wheat flour

For the garnish

3 tablespoons grated carrot

1 tablespoon toasted sesame seeds

(cont.) ➡

DO IT

Rinse the split peas, put them into fresh water and leave to sit for 10 minutes, picking out anything dodgy that floats to the surface. Drain, then put the green split peas into a large, heavy saucepan with the water and bring to the boil. Drop in the ginger, cardamom pods, chillies, spices and curry leaves. Bring to a rolling boil, then lower the heat and simmer for 50 minutes to 1 hour, skimming off any white froth. Stir the daal regularly, ensuring that it doesn't stick on the bottom of the pan. Add the watercress and simmer for a further 5 minutes (10 minutes if using kale or spring greens). When the peas are cooked you should be left with a thick daal, the consistency of double cream. Season well and cover, removing from the heat.

To make the red cabbage sabji, heat ½ tablespoon of oil in a large frying pan on a medium-high heat and add the red cabbage. Fry for 5 minutes, stirring regularly, until the cabbage is beginning to get some nice colour. Add the orange juice, zest and star anise, cover the pan, drop the heat to lowest and allow to steam for 5 minutes. Set the cabbage aside and keep warm with a lid on.

Add another ½ tablespoon of oil to the pan and warm on a medium-high heat. Pop in the cumin seeds and curry leaves and sizzle for a minute. Quickly add the ginger and garlic and fry for another minute, then put the cabbage back into the pan with the garam masala and sauté for 2 minutes more. Keep stirring well to stop the spices sticking, adding small drizzles of water if needed. Cook until the cabbage is tender and has that beautiful, toasty, braised look about it.

To make the chapattis, put the rice, water, salt and flour into a food processor and blitz until smooth. On a well-floured surface, work the dough, sprinkling flour regularly to stop it sticking. It will come together a bit, but nothing like a normal bread dough. Don't worry, it will work itself out in the pan. Roll the dough into a ball and stick in the fridge for 30 minutes.

Heat a large, heavy-based frying pan (or tawa if you are the real deal chapatti aficionado) on a medium-high heat. Grab a squash-ball-size amount of dough and gently roll out into a circle, using a rolling pin, on a floured surface or board. Sprinkle well with flour and don't mind too much about it sticking. Sometimes just pressing it out with your fingers and the heel of your hand is easier than rolling. Using a flat spatula, pop the dough circle into the warm pan and sprinkle the top side with a little more flour. Cook for 2 minutes, then turn over and cook the second side for 1 minute. While this is going on, get your next chapatti ready, like a pleasant production line. Keep them warm, wrapped in a clean tea towel. I normally make 2 or 3 chapattis per person.

Serve the braised red cabbage in a shallow, wide bowl with the matar daal piled centrally on top. You might like to finish with a sprinkle of grated carrot to add even more colour to the bowl, and some lovely toasted sesame seeds. Don't forget the chapattis, which are warm and primed for action.

This dish is amazing with a spoonful of sweet mango pickle. You know the score, the classic, eye-wateringly sweet and fruity curry house classic (to make your own, see page 330).

Burgers, Bakes & Get Stuffed

These bombastic bakes will sing from your oven and fill the house with wafts of something very tasty; they're baked dishes that dance in the imagination and leave us all well-satisfied and ready for a nice sit down.

'Bake' conjures up an image of a tired pasta something-or-other, lathered with cheap Cheddar, the fat pooling on top, under hot lights, somewhere with plastic cutlery near a motorway (or is that just me?). But bakes need not be a greasy slab of slop, they can add a slice of colour and an incredible melding of flavours, compressed and carefully layered. The humble oven dish is suddenly transformed into a space for magnificent experiments in food.

To me, bakes chant of winter and darker, colder times. When the body needs a blazing fire on a freezing cold night.

Most of these bakes are quickly put together and not too vexing. Some, however, are more complex and feel as though they need a fortnight off work to prepare. We'll just call these special occasion dishes. Well worth the effort, I may add. Good food is rarely convenience food.

The stuffing here is done with bags of love and delicacy. 'Stuffed' has almost as bad a rap as 'bake' in the food vocabulary, but in many cultures stuffing things is the height of culinary excellence.

Here I hope to revive both of these misrepresented cooking techniques and give them all the green goodness of a full-on vegan makeover. Expect colourful and nutritious results that dance a jig all over your tastebuds.

Just when you thought you'd ventured to the far shores of the great burger sphere, in comes the vegan crew with a whole host of new and wild combos to try. I am sure normal burgers are very tasty, but they will struggle to compete with this colourful bunch for nutrition and sumptuous flavours.

Veggie burgers are hopelessly hit and miss. I have rarely had anything resembling a decent veggie burger. They need to be packed with flavours and have the right texture, otherwise you're left with a crumbling pile of bean matter or a dense and sloppy pattie.

Vegan burgers open so many doors in your foodie repertoire, an almost infinite palate of ingredients to play with and merge into delicious discs. The question is, how much can you handle in one bun? How far can we push this format until we reach the stage of a three-course burger? Something like the pasties my mining ancestors used to take down the pit, with meat in one corner and dessert in the other!

Vegan food in general requires a little thought and dedication, otherwise you end up living on crisps and bananas. I won't say these burgers and bangers are as easy to prepare as their meaty counterparts, but that's not the point! I know you all love cooking, so spending time in the kitchen is a pleasure, right? Elbow deep in vivid green bhaji mix or grappling with vibrant vegan chorizos, I can see you there, smiling and enjoying every minute well spent.

Here I give you burgers and bangers that are dressed to impress, with OTT trimmings and then some. Glorified sandwiches that demand complete tastebud attention and will no doubt prompt finger-licking happiness across the nation.

Portobello Pecan Burger with Roasted Pumpkin Wedges

MAKES 6–8 MAMMOTH BURGERS

Here we have a burger that is rich, with a deep flavour from the mushrooms, cumin and miso. It is packed with heavy umami flavours, with the seaweed, pecans and miso working their potent charms. Sun-blushed tomatoes can be found in most delis nowadays and ooze fragrant tomato all over this burger. If you are struggling to find them, I know some fantastic people on the Isle of Wight who can sort you out (see Suppliers, page 338). This burger mix will keep very well in the fridge, 5 days easy. Try making it into 'meatballs', with a tomato sauce and pasta.

Gluten-free option: just cook 25g more rice and omit the breadcrumbs.

THE BITS

4 tablespoons olive oil

350g Portobello mushrooms, cut into cubes

1 aubergine, chopped into 2cm pieces

a large pinch of sea salt and black pepper

3 tablespoons fresh oregano leaves or 1 teaspoon dried oregano

1 onion, sliced

2 celery stalks, finely diced

4 cloves of garlic, peeled and crushed

20g dried seaweed, cut into very fine ribbons

175g flageolet beans, soaked overnight, then cooked with ½ teaspoon bicarbonate of soda and cooled, or 1½ x 400g tins

120g toasted pecans

100g red or brown rice, cooked and cooled

2 heaped tablespoons brown miso

1 teaspoon bicarbonate of soda

100g fine wholewheat breadcrumbs

For the pumpkin wedges

750g pumpkin, scrubbed, seeded and cut into 5cm wedges

2 tablespoons vegetable oil

a large pinch of sea salt

1 x tarragon aioli (see page 328)

To serve

8 seeded wholewheat rolls, halved (for gluen-free aternative, use your favourite GF bread)

1 big handful sun-blushed tomatoes

buttery lettuce leaves (something like oak-leaf)

DO IT

To make the pumpkin wedges, preheat the oven to 180°C/gas mark 4. Put the pumpkin on a baking tray, toss with the oil and salt, and roast for 30 minutes, turning over once. The pumpkin should be tender and nicely coloured.

Heat 3 tablespoons of oil in a large, heavy frying pan on a medium-low heat and add the mushrooms and aubergines. Cook for 10 minutes, then add the salt and pepper. Cook for a further 5 minutes, until the aubergine is soft. Stir in the oregano leaves and set aside in a bowl.

In the same pan, heat 1 tablespoon of oil on a medium-high heat and cook the onion and celery for 5 minutes. Add the garlic and seaweed and cook for another 2 minutes, then remove from the heat and combine with the aubergines and mushrooms.

In a food processor, combine half the beans, pecans, aubergine mix and rice with the miso, sifting in the bicarbonate of soda. Blitz to a thick paste. Add the breadcrumbs and the rest of the beans, rice and aubergine mix, along with the rest of the pecans. Pulse until a chunky mix forms, coarse in texture but finely chopped. Check the seasoning – the miso is quite salty. Transfer the mix to a bowl, combining it all well with your hands. Form the mix into 6–8 fat burgers. Put them into the fridge for 30 minutes to firm up. Meanwhile, make the tarragon aioli.

Pop an ovenproof frying pan on a medium-high heat and lightly oil it. Cook each burger for 5 minutes per side, until beautifully light brown. If they lose shape and are unruly in the pan, press them down using the back of a spatula. Veggie burgers are sensitive and need to be handled with soft hands (and spatulas).

Put all the burgers into a warm oven, 150°C/gas mark 2, for 10 minutes to finish cooking.

Cut your bread rolls in half and put them into the warm oven for 5 minutes. On the base of each warm roll, scatter sun-blushed tomatoes (with a little of their oil) and top with a lettuce leaf, the burger and a good topping of tarragon aioli. Serve with the warm pumpkin wedges.

Beetroot Quarter-pounders with Butter Bean Purée, Pineapple & Chickpea Chips

MAKES 6–8, DEPENDING HOW CHUNKY YOU LIKE YOUR BURGERS!

This style of 'beet' burger is one of my all-time favourite things. You can play around with the accompaniments, but the burger itself is a legend in vegan circles far and wide. You can give the burgers a crunchy coating by patting them with polenta (the purple with the yellow looks very cool indeed), but I've left them naked here so we can see the charred outside and lovely pink middle.

Try to get your breadcrumbs really dry here – toast them slightly in the oven beforehand and they will be even better at binding everything together. Gluten-free folk, just use gluten-free bread or finely crushed gluten-free crackers.

Add Marmite or English mustard depending on which flavour you prefer. You can even use both. They will each dominate the 'pounder' if you take them too far, though. Marmite comes with added extras in the form of vitamin B12, which us vegans need and love. Brown rice is a brilliant substitute for buckwheat.

THE BITS

½ tablespoon vegetable oil

1 small onion, peeled and grated

3 cloves of garlic, peeled and grated

225g buckwheat, cooked and cooled, not too mushy

115g brown or green lentils, cooked and cooled, drained well

260g beetroot, grated

30g fine wholewheat breadcrumbs

1½ teaspoons ground cumin

1 teaspoon ground coriander

3 teaspoons Marmite or 1½ teaspoons English mustard

4 tablespoons cashew butter (or almond butter)

½ teaspoon salt

¼ teaspoon fresh black pepper

vegetable oil, for frying

For the butter bean purée

175g dried butter beans (soaked overnight)

½ teaspoon bicarbonate of soda

1 large clove of garlic, crushed

juice of ½ a lemon

a handful of fresh parsley, finely chopped

a large pinch of sea salt and black pepper

75ml olive oil

For the chickpea chips

250g gram (chickpea) flour

2 tablespoons nutritional yeast flakes (see page 30)

800ml water

1½ tablespoons olive oil

a large pinch of sea salt

vegetable oil, for frying

To serve

6–8 big seeded wholewheat bread rolls, halved (for a gluten-free alternative, use your favourite GF bread)

1 small mild red onion, finely sliced

Little Gem lettuce leaves

6–8 rounds of fresh pineapple, very thinly sliced

(cont.) ➡

The butter bean purée is best made in advance, even the day before, if you can. Drain the soaked butter beans and put them into a heavy saucepan with plenty of fresh water to cover. Add the bicarbonate of soda and bring to the boil, then cook on a fast simmer for 45 minutes, until the beans are nicely tender. Drain them and cool slightly. Put them into a food processor with the other ingredients, drizzling in the oil as the blades are running. Check the seasoning, allow to cool completely, then pop into the fridge.

Heat ½ tablespoon of vegetable oil in a small frying pan and cook the onion for 5 minutes. Add the garlic and cook for a further 2 minutes. You're just sweetening them a little.

In a food processor, pulse the cooked and then cooled buckwheat and lentils with the grated beets and the cooked onion and garlic. Blitz until the mixture comes together, but still has a slightly rough texture. Now transfer it to a mixing bowl and add the rest of the ingredients, apart from the frying oil. Use your hands to mix very well. Everything should be well incorporated. Place the mixture in the fridge for 30 minutes to chill and firm up.

To make the chickpea chips, sieve the gram flour into a heavy saucepan and add the yeast flakes, water, olive oil and salt. Cook over a medium-low heat until the paste becomes thick, stirring constantly. This usually takes about 10 minutes. When the mixture is thick and starts to pull away from the sides, remove from the heat and quickly spread the paste out on to a shallow baking tray or deep plate. Allow to cool, then place in the fridge for one hour until completely cold.

Cut into chip-like sticks (however you like them best). Heat 3cm of vegetable oil in a heavy saucepan and fry the chips in batches for a couple of minutes each side or until they they are golden and crisp. Remove with a slotted spoon and drain on kitchen paper. Sprinkle with sea salt and keep them warm in a low oven. If you prefer a healthier option, you can bake the chips in a preheated oven on a well-oiled baking tray for 20 minutes at 200°C/gas mark 6, turning them halfway through.

Heat a large frying pan (thick-bottomed, preferably) over a medium-high heat. Now form the chilled burger mixture into decent fat quarter-pounder shapes (each patty should be made with 125g or so of mixture). To get perfectly shaped burgers, use a large ring or other funky-shaped cutter (stars and animals work great with the kids).

Pour a very thin layer of oil into the pan and cook the burgers for about 10–12 minutes, flipping them occasionally and pressing down gently with a spatula. Drizzle in a little more oil as needed. The burgers should be charred at the edges and heated through – they should look medium rare!

Stack your pounders! Spoon some butter bean purée on to each bread roll, followed by a red onion slice and a lettuce leaf, then your burger, topped with 2 thin slices of pineapple and the top of the roll. Serve straight away, with piles of chickpea chips. Homemade ketchup (see page 328) is a welcome addition to the party.

Spinach Bhaji Burger with Homemade Mango Chutney, Mint Raita & Peanut Masala Chips

MAKES 8 BIG BURGER BHAJIS

Vivid green crispy bhajis and tangy sweet chutney . . . creamy, cooling raita and crunchy masala chips . . . what a thing! This is the best of Indian street food wrapped up in a very white bap, inspired by a delicious Mumbai street snack called pav bhaji. If you can find them, use unripe green mangoes, normally found in Caribbean and Asian food stores. Failing that, use as unripe a mango as you can find. Green tomatoes and pineapples will also work perfectly in a chutney like this. If your mango is a little sweet, add a touch of white wine vinegar to the chutney, to get that glorious balance of chutney sweet and sour. These burgers are definitely best served fresh from the stove, nice and crispy.

Gluten-free option: replace white flour with gram flour.

THE BITS

1 teaspoon vegetable or groundnut oil

250g spinach leaves

125g silken tofu

3 large cloves of garlic, peeled and crushed

200g gram (chickpea) flour

50g unbleached white flour

1 teaspoon bicarbonate of soda

1 teaspoon ground turmeric

1 teaspoon freshly ground cumin

½–1 teaspoon chilli powder

1½ teaspoons dried mint

150ml water

300g cauliflower, chopped into small florets

2 large red onions, finely sliced

1 teaspoon sea salt

vegetable oil, for deep frying

1 x homemade mango chutney (see page 330)

1 x mint raita (see page *330*)

For the peanut masala chips

vegetable or groundnut oil, for deep-frying

600g potatoes, peeled and cut into your favourite chip shape

½ teaspoon ground turmeric

½ teaspoon chilli powder

a large pinch of sea salt

1½ teaspoons unrefined brown sugar

½ teaspoon dried mango (amchur) powder

1½ teaspoon cumin seeds

1 big handful of raw peanuts (unsalted)

1 tablespoon sesame seeds

To serve

8 soft bread rolls, halved (for a gluten-free alternative, use your favourite GF bread)

1 small red onion, finely sliced

1 large tomato, thinly sliced

a handful of fresh coriander leaves

DO IT

Make the mango chutney and the mint raita.

To make the bhajis, heat 1 teaspoon of vegetable oil in a pan on a medium-low heat, then add the spinach and wilt down until any liquid has evaporated. Place in a food processor with the silken tofu and garlic, and blend together until smooth.

Put the flours, bicarbonate of soda, spices and mint into a bowl. Make a well in the centre and add the spinach mix, then gradually add the water until a thick batter is formed. Stir in the small cauliflower pieces and the onions and season with salt. Make sure everything is well mixed.

(cont.) ➡

Warm 1cm of oil in a large frying pan (we're shallow frying these bhajis) on a medium heat (drop a little of the mix into the oil and watch it sizzle – now you're ready). Spoon 4 heaped dessertspoons of mix per bhaji (nice big 'uns) into the pan, frying three or four bhajis at a time. Press down into a burger shape, and loosen the bases after a minute using a flat spatula or fish slice. This will stop them sticking. Splash a little oil over the bhajis to help them cook evenly, like you do when frying an egg. Fry until both sides are golden brown and the bhajis are cooked right through – this will take 10–15 minutes.

Remove the bhajis using the flat spatula or fish slice and drain well on kitchen paper. Now fry the rest, adding more oil as needed. When they are all done, put them into the oven for 10 minutes at 150°C/gas mark 2 to finish cooking. Check that the centre of the burgers is piping hot before serving.

To make the peanut masala chips, take a separate large saucepan and cover the base with 2.5cm of oil and place over a medium-high heat. It is hot enough when you can stick a chip into the oil and it sizzles frantically.

Pat the potatoes dry with kitchen paper and lower them into the oil in small batches. Fry for 6 minutes, jiggling them in the pan to make sure they're not sticking together. When they are turning golden and becoming tender, sprinkle the turmeric, red chilli powder, salt, sugar, dried mango powder and cumin seeds into the pan. Turn up the heat and continue to fry for 4–5 minutes, until the chips are nice and crisp. Remove from the pan using a slotted spoon and drain on well on kitchen paper.

While the chips are frying, heat a small frying pan on a medium heat. Add the peanuts and toast for 2–3 minutes. Keep them moving, otherwise one side will burn. Add the sesame seeds and warm for a minute more. Sprinkle the nuts and seeds over the drained chips and mix together well.

Spread a bun base with the raita and top with onion, tomato and coriander leaves. Pop the spinach bhaji on top and spoon over some mango chuntey, then place the bun lid on the top. Serve with hot peanut masala chips, small bowls of extra chutney and raita on hand, and a Ravi Shankar raga flowing in the background.

Smoked Tofu Sausage Sandwich with Red Onion Marmalade & Kale Crisps

MAKES 8 CHUNKY SAUSAGES (2 PER SANDWICH)

If I'm left in the kitchen for long enough, this is the kind of thing that happens. This is a souped-up banger sanger fit for vegan royalty. Smoked tofu is delicious, but if you can't get it, use firm tofu and add ½ teaspoon of smoked paprika to the mix. Making vegan sausages is not quite as easy as opening a packet and sticking them in a pan, but your efforts will be so worth it.

THE BITS

3 tablespoons rapeseed oil

1 large leek, finely chopped

1 green apple, cored, peeled
and finely chopped

3 tablespoons fresh thyme leaves or
1½ teaspoons dried thyme

275g smoked tofu, mashed with a fork, or
firm tofu (+ ½ teaspoon smoked paprika)

2 tablespoons apple juice concentrate
(see page 28)

125g toasted hazelnuts

200g silken tofu

200g fresh white breadcrumbs
or panko crumbs

½ a handful of fresh parsley,
finely chopped

4 teaspoons Dijon mustard

sea salt and black pepper

For the coating

40g unbleached white flour

75ml soya milk (unsweetened)

90g dry breadcrumbs (such as panko)

3 tablespoons vegetable oil, for baking

For the kale crisps

300g kale leaves, cut from the stems and
roughly torn into 5cm pieces

2 tablespoons vegetable oil

1 tablespoon nutritional yeast flakes (optional)

a large pinch of sea salt and black pepper

1 x red onion marmalade (see page 331)

DO IT

In a heavy frying pan, warm the oil on a medium heat. Add the leeks and apple and cook until soft and golden – about 10 minutes. Add the thyme, smoked tofu and apple juice concentrate, then set aside to cool.

In a food processor, pulse the hazelnuts until a rough crumb is formed. Add the silken tofu and blend to a thick paste.

In a large mixing bowl, combine the breadcrumbs, hazelnut mix, leek mix, parsley, mustard and season well with salt and pepper. Mix until all is well incorporated. The mix should have the texture of a classic stuffing.

With damp hands, shape into your average sausage shape. Dip the sausages first in flour to coat lightly, knock off any excess, then splash into the milk. Roll in the dry breadcrumbs, pressing down very gently, getting a good coating. Place on a plate, cover and whack in the fridge for 30 minutes to get together.

Preheat the oven to 180°C/gas mark 4. Place the sausages on a well-oiled baking tray, drizzling them all with a touch more oil (using a pastry brush here may help). Bake for 20–25 minutes, turning twice to colour evenly.

To make the kale crisps, wash and completely dry the kale leaves (any moisture at all will make them soggy and they'll not crisp up). Put the oil, yeast flakes (if using), pepper and salt into a large bowl. Toss the kale in the oil and salt, giving it all a good, shiny coating. Place the kale on a baking tray, or two trays if it's getting crowded. Bake for 10–15 minutes, checking regularly after 10 minutes, and turning them over. Slightly overcooking the kale leaves will make them burnt and bitter, while slightly underdone they are soft and un-crispy. When ready, sprinkle with more yeast flakes.

Serve the sausages in a soft bun, with a healthy spoonful of the red onion marmalade and a nice pile of kale crisps.

Chickpea, Squash & Apricot Burgers with a Red Onion, Orange & Black Olive Salad

MAKES 6-8 BULKY BURGERS

Like flat, elaborate falafels, these burgers transport us to somewhere towards the centre of the globe. The spice mix baharat is from the Middle East – it is so versatile, and whenever my cooking strays to that part of the world, baharat is never far behind. These burgers are not designed to be very thick and they cook quickly. Served in warm flatbreads with some creamy avocado cheese, they are a crunchy, fruity special. The onion really makes this salad. Some parts of the world have such mild, sweet red onions, but they can be hard to find here. If the onion is bitter, the salad just isn't quite the same, so get the sweetest onions you can.

Gluten-free option: use GF flatbreads.

THE BITS

1 teaspoon cumin seeds

2 teaspoons coriander seeds

1 tablespoon vegetable oil

250g butternut squash, finely diced

200g dried chickpeas, soaked overnight

3 spring onions, finely sliced

2 cloves of garlic, peeled and crushed

½ a handful of finely chopped fresh coriander

¼ teaspoon cayenne pepper

½ teaspoon ground cardamom

½ teaspoon ground turmeric

(or 2 teaspoons baharat spice mix instead of all the spices)

a handful of dried apricots, finely diced

¾ teaspoon baking powder

½ teaspoon salt

2 tablespoons light tahini

2 tablespoons gram (chickpea) flour

3 tablespoons water

vegetable oil, for shallow-frying

3 tablespoons gram (chickpea) flour, for dusting

For the avocado cheese

2 ripe avocados

150g firm tofu

2 tablespoons lemon juice

a pinch of sea salt and black pepper

½ tablespoon nutritional yeast flakes (optional, see page 30)

For the red onion, orange & black olive salad

1 teaspoon cumin seeds, toasted

4 medium oranges, peeled and sliced, bitter pith removed

1 large red onion, finely sliced

4 dates, finely sliced

½ a handful of pitted black olives, finely sliced

a pinch of sea salt and black pepper

2 tablespoons lemon juice

3 tablespoons olive oil

To serve

4 wholewheat pitta breads

a handful of pomegranate seeds (optional)

DO IT

In a large frying pan, warm the cumin and coriander seeds on a medium heat for 1 minute, moving them all the time in the pan. When popping and fragrant, pour into a pestle and mortar and grind.

Heat 1 tablespoon of oil in the same pan on a medium heat, and add the butternut squash. Stir and cook for 15 minutes until tender and cooked through.

Rinse and drain the soaked chickpeas and blitz in a food processor with the spring onions, garlic, half the squash and the fresh coriander. The mix should hold itself together, but not be mushy. Now add the rest of the squash, the spices, apricots, baking powder, salt, tahini, gram flour and water and

(cont.) ➡

mix together by hand. Cover the mixture and leave in the fridge for an hour or until ready to use. To make the salad, toast the cumin seeds in the small skillet for 1 minute. Arrange all the salad bits in a flat bowl and leave the flavours to mingle for half an hour.

To make the avocado cheese, place all the ingredients in a flat bowl and mash together well with a fork. The avocados must be ripe, otherwise you will not be able to mash them up. (Try placing unripe avos in a bowl with some bananas for a day or so. This normally does the trick.)

Heat 1cm of oil in a deep frying pan until a small piece of the burger mix sizzles when dropped in.

With damp hands, press 2 heaped tablespoons of mixture into the palm of your hand and make a slender burger-shaped pattie, roughly 10cm in diameter. Place the gram flour on a plate and give each burger a light dusting, then drop them into the hot oil and fry for 2–3 minutes on each side, until nicely golden. Drain and place on kitchen paper, flipping them to absorb excess oil.

Warm your pittas in the oven or under the grill (don't toast them) – they should still be nice and soft (place a plate over them). Make a slit in each pitta and form a pocket. Stuff the pocket with some of the salad, top with the chickpea burgers and spoon over the avocado cheese. You can even sprinkle with pomegranate seeds if you fancy. To make a real meal of these, try serving them with mujadarra (see page 142) and a lovely tangy green tomato chutney (page 331).

Puy Lentil & Walnut Burger with Roast Fennel & Jerusalem Artichoke Frites

MAKES 6-8 BURGERS

The nuttiness of Puy lentils makes them a perfect burger base. This is the kind of burger that's ideal for the colder months. Parsnip purée is one of my favourite wintertime treats, so simple and with a glorious sweet flavour. I've called it clotted cream because it reminds me of very heavy Cornish cream (and I imagine it would be amazing on a scone!) Flax seeds are outrageously good for us and are also very high in fibre. When soaked they form something like a seedy gel, which not only adds bags of nutrition, but also binds things together. These burgers need careful handling in the pan, but caramelize beautifully.

Gluten-free option: use GF oats.

THE BITS

150g Puy lentils

2 bay leaves

1 tablespoon vegetable oil

1 medium leek, finely sliced

4 cloves of garlic, peeled and crushed

8 fresh sage leaves, sliced into fine ribbons, or 1½ teaspoons dried sage

1 tablespoon fresh thyme leaves or ⅓ teaspoon dried thyme

2 teaspoons tamari

200g walnuts

225g firm tofu

4 tablespoons flax seeds (preferably ground), soaked in 4 tablespoons water for 1 hour

85g rolled oats

¼ teaspoon freshly ground black pepper

240ml vegetable stock

vegetable oil, for frying

For the roast fennel & Jerusalem artichoke frites
500g Jerusalem artichokes, scrubbed and cut into long thin 'frites'

1 large bulb of fennel, cut into 2cm slices lengthways

2 tablespoons olive oil

a large pinch of sea salt and black pepper

For the parsnip clotted cream
2 large parsnips, peeled and diced

500ml almond milk or oat milk

a pinch of grated nutmeg

a pinch of sea salt

To serve
6–8 your favourite burger buns, halved

2 handfuls of watercress

DO IT

Place the Puy lentils and bay leaves in a large pan and add 750ml of water. Bring to the boil, then reduce the heat and simmer for 25–30 minutes, until the lentils are tender. Drain well in a colander, removing the bay leaves. Set aside to cool in the colander, tossing the lentils regularly to remove excess liquid.

To make the parsnip clotted cream, simply put the parsnips, milk, nutmeg and salt into a small, heavy-bottomed sauce pan. Bring slowly to just below boiling, then simmer on a very low heat for 1 hour, stirring regularly, until the parsnips are very tender. The liquid should reduce by about half. Parsnips burn easily when cooked like this, so keep an eye on them and lower the heat if necessary. Rushing this will not end well – you can turn a seductive white purée into a beige blob quite easily! Pour into a food processor and blend into a thick cream. Check the seasoning and set aside.

Meanwhile, make the roast fennel and Jerusalem artichoke frites, preheat the oven to 190°C/gas mark 5. Toss the veggies in the oil and seasoning. Place them separately on lightly oiled baking trays and roast for 40 minutes, turning them twice. When they are all nicely coloured and tender, remove from the oven and keep warm.

Now to the serious business of burger making . . . Heat the oil in a frying pan, add the leeks, and cook for 6 minutes. Add the garlic, sage, thyme and tamari and cook for another 2 minutes. Pop the walnuts into a food processor and blitz to a rough crumb. Add the tofu, flax seeds, cooked lentils, oats, pepper and the leek mixture, and pulse together until a coarse paste is formed, adding the vegetable stock as needed. Remember that the oats will absorb a lot of liquid, so make it quite a sticky, loose mixture. It will firm up in the fridge. Place in the refrigerator for 30 minutes.

Form the mixture into thick burgers. Warm a large frying pan on a medium heat and lightly oil it. Brown the burgers on both sides, then cook them for 15 minutes, until heated through. They will firm up nicely in the pan, but be careful with your flipping!

Warm the parsnip cream in a small pan and spread a generous amount over each of your halved buns. Place a burger on top and crown with a couple of roast fennel slices. Finally, scatter over a little watercress and top with the bun lid. Toss the crispy artichoke frites in a little sea salt and serve on the side.

Chargrilled Chorizo Pinchos with Pistachio & Coriander Pesto

MAKES 8 FAT CHORIZOS

The tapas bars of San Sebastián are some of the best food emporiums anywhere in the world, and that's where you'll find the greatest pinchos. Going on a pub crawl in San Sebastián is gourmet heaven, and in the morning you can have a nice stroll along the beach and let the fresh sea air get to work on your appetite for breakfast (see tostada con tomate, page 67).

Pinchos are normally a one or two bite affair, but I've made them into something slightly more substantial, venturing into main course territory as opposed to a canapé. These pinchos are designed to be the shape of the small, dumpy variety that you get in Spain. Think a giant chipolata. They will be best cut in half lengthways and griddled like that. They will also work well cooked on a barbecue.

Panini-style bread is ideal for these pinchos, as it offers a good flat base for stacking, but you can use ciabatta or any nice flatbread.

Gluten-free option: use GF bread to replace the wheaty stuff.

THE BITS

1 handful of sun-dried tomatoes (in oil)

2 tablespoons olive oil

1 large onion, grated

300g tempeh, broken up with your fingers into a rough crumble

1 red chilli, finely diced, or ½ teaspoon chilli powder

3 large cloves of garlic, crushed

1½ teaspoons dried oregano

2 teaspoons smoked paprika

1 tablespoon sweet paprika

2 tablespoons sherry vinegar

150g silken tofu

100g fresh wholewheat breadcrumbs

½ teaspoon sea salt

½ teaspoon black pepper

extra olive oil, for brushing

1 x pistachio & coriander pesto (see page 333)

To serve

4 paninis, halved

3 handfuls of fresh rocket leaves

½ a handful of green olives, pitted

wooden skewers, cut in half

DO IT

Blend the sun-dried tomatoes in the food processor, until smooth. Heat the oil in a frying pan and sauté the onion until soft and slightly golden – at least 10 minutes. Add the tempeh, chilli, garlic, oregano and spices and cook for 2 minutes. Now stir in the sun-dried tomato purée and vinegar and allow to heat through. Add the silken tofu and let it warm through.

Place the breadcrumbs, salt and pepper in a food processor and blitz together with the tempeh mixture until nice and smooth. The mix should be firm, and should stick together when pressed between finger and thumb. Add more breadcrumbs if needed. Pop into the fridge to cool for 30 minutes while you can make the pistachio pesto.

Using your mitts (rub a little oil into them), form the mix into 6 fat and dumpy chorizos (if you have time, pop them into the fridge for a while to become even firmer). Warm a large, heavy, griddle pan. Brush generously with oil and cook each chorizo for 5 minutes each side. Don't mess with them too much, just gently flip them once. We'd like some cool-looking charred tramlines. For traditional-looking pinchos, cut the chorizo in half lengthways and griddle for slightly less time. Once the chorizos are crisp and warmed through, set aside and keep warm in a low oven.

Cut the paninis in half and brush them with olive oil on both sides. Toast on a griddle pan (or under a warm grill) for a couple of minutes, pressing them down firmly and often. Once toasted, cut each piece of panini into thirds.

Top each piece of warm panini with a scattering of rocket leaves, spoon over the pistachio pesto and place the chorizos on top, keeping things nicely in place with skewers. Pop an olive on the end of each skewer and serve on a large platter. Dive in with reckless abandon and smiles! Best served with small glasses of lively Basque Sagardoa cider.

The pinchos can also be embellished with chunks of roasted peppers, to make the stack even higher.

Asparagus Club Sandwich with Rainbow Chard & Pine Nut Cream

MAKES 2 SANDWICHES (ENOUGH FOR 4 TO SHARE)

The Trump Tower of sandwich construction, the Empire State Building of munch, the Shard of . . . you get the idea. This one is quite tall. Hopelessly green and healthy, with a touch of chard psychedelia among the layers. It's a light and quick sandwich to whip up and stack. Three tiers of tofu and pan-fried asparagus goodness here, with a smooth pine nut cream. Rainbow chard gives this sandwich a technicolor vibe that is unmistakable. Delicious served with homemade vegetable crisps (see page 153). And try it with tomato, ginger and orange chutney (see page 331). The trick here is to try to slice your bread as thinly as possible.

THE BITS

325g firm tofu or tempeh, well drained and cut widthways into 8 x 2cm slices

1 tablespoon unbleached white flour

sea salt and cracked black pepper

2 tablespoons olive oil

6 spring onions, trimmed and halved lengthways

6 asparagus spears, halved lengthways

1 teaspoon fennel seeds

2 cloves of garlic, peeled and crushed

6 large leaves of rainbow chard, cut into 2cm ribbons

50ml dry vermouth or dry sherry

a handful of basil leaves

For the pine nut cream

100g toasted pine nuts (hazelnuts will also be delicious)

125g silken tofu

1 small clove of garlic, peeled and crushed

½ tablespoon lemon juice

a large pinch of sea salt and black pepper

To serve

6 thin slices of sourdough bread

olive oil, for brushing

1 large ripe tomato, finely sliced

DO IT

Drain the tofu well (see page 200) and pat dry with kitchen paper. Season the flour with sea salt and cracked pepper and place on a plate. Dust the tofu slices with the seasoned flour – they have to be very dry to crisp up nicely. To make the pine nut cream, put the pine nuts into a food processor with the rest of the ingredients and blitz until smooth and creamy. Check the seasoning and set aside.

Heat 1½ tablespoons of oil in a large, heavy frying pan on a medium heat. Add the spring onions and sear for 5 minutes, until tender. Remove and keep warm, then add the tofu slices in the centre of the pan, arranging the asparagus around the edges. Fry the tofu and asparagus until nicely golden – this will only take 2 minutes on each side for both. The asparagus may need turning more than the tofu, but see how they get on. Remove everything from the pan and keep warm.

Add ½ tablespoon of oil to the same pan on a medium heat and add the fennel seeds and garlic. Heat through for a minute, then drop in the chard. Stir and sauté for 3 minutes. Drizzle in the vermouth and let it steam for a moment, then add the basil leaves, season, and cover tightly with a lid. Turn the heat down to low and allow to steam together for 5 minutes.

Heat a grill, then brush your sourdough bread with olive oil and lightly toast on both sides. Time to build your triple-decker! Grab 2 pieces of toasted bread, spread them with a thick layer of the pine nut cream, top each one with a couple of slices of tomato and 2 pieces each of tofu, asparagus and spring onion. Top with a second slice of bread and repeat for the next layer, but this time spoon over some of the chard and basil instead of the asparagus and onion. Press down firmly, then cut the sandwiches in half.

Jane's Magic Bread

MAKES ONE LARGE LOAF OR TWO SMALL

Jane loves the stuff and here we have the best toast loaf we know. Why is it magic, I hear you cry? Well, it goes with everything, from Marmite to marmalade; it loves to be toasted and is equally happy in a sandwich. This may sound like most breads, but that just makes all bread magic! The best way I've heard this bread described is 'like a crumpet, crossed with a loaf'.

The dough here is quite wet, but this leads to a nice dense loaf with a super-crispy crust. You can use any of the flour mixes below, but we normally make it with pure, unadulterated spelt. Spelt is lower in gluten than wheat-based flour and is a whole grain, so retains loads of its health-giving nutrients.

This is bread-making just like the Romans used to do it! Walnuts are great with spelt, so try adding a large handful, roughly chopped.

THE BITS

500g stoneground spelt flour (or halve the amount of spelt and add 250g unbleached white flour or wholemeal flour)

½ teaspoon salt

1 teaspoon quick yeast

1 tablespoon brown rice syrup or barley malt extract

400ml warm water

1 tablespoon olive oil

a large handful of sunflower seeds

½ a handful of golden linseeds

DO IT

Mix together the flour, salt and yeast in a large bowl. Dissolve the sweetener in the warm water and mix into gradually into the flour. The mix will be slightly wet and sticky – don't worry, this is very cool.

Add the oil and seeds and continue to mix. Knead for a few minutes, then place in a large (1kg) loaf tin or 2 smaller (500g) tins. Cover loosely and leave to rise for 30 minutes.

Preheat the oven to 200°C/gas mark 6.

Bake the bread for 40–45 minutes. Tap the bottom – if you're getting a nice hollow sound, it's done. The smaller loaves will take 5–10 minutes less to bake. Leave to cool on a wire rack for at least 20 minutes before slicing.

Poppy & Herb Rolls

MAKES 18 SMALL ROLLS

Making your own bread takes time, but for me, it's the only way to go. You just can't replicate the flavour and aroma of home-baked bread – it's food for the soul. This is a nice way to serve bread to a gathering of people. The rolls are baked together in a pan and your guests and loved ones can rip their own rolls off the steaming mass of bread loveliness. You can make these little rolls into a visual treat by making half with white flour and half with brown. It's a technique I use over and over and it never fails. Play around with whatever good herbs you have, dried or fresh, and you can use other seeds instead of the poppy seeds.

THE BITS

1 teaspoon dried yeast

1 teaspoon unrefined brown sugar

360ml warm water

300g unbleached plain white flour

145g wholewheat flour
(or spelt/rye flour)

¾ teaspoon sea salt

1½ teaspoons dried mixed herbs

3 teaspoons olive oil

2 tablespoons poppy seeds

For the topping

1 tablespoon olive oil

1 teaspoon poppy seeds

DO IT

In a small bowl, combine the yeast, sugar and a tablespoon of warm water. Set aside for 10 minutes and allow to go frothy. Put the flours and salt into a large mixing bowl and combine with a wooden spoon. Add your herbs to the yeast mixture. Make a well in the centre of the flour and pour in your yeast mixture and the oil, then gradually pour in the water with one hand, mixing all the time with the other. This is a little like rubbing your nose and patting your head at first, but you'll get the hang of it; it's an important bread-making technique, I find. Very slowly, pour in enough water so that the dough comes away from the bowl, but is still slightly tacky to the touch. You may not need to add all the water.

On an oiled surface, begin to work the dough. Knead it around 100 times or for 10 minutes, getting that gluten elasticity going and your arm muscles toned. Doing this to your favourite tunes helps loads. Place the dough in a lightly oiled bowl and cover with a tea towel, then leave in a warm place for an hour. Slightly warmer than room temperature is best (but no hotter) – near a warm radiator or fire is perfect. The dough should more or less double in volume. If it doesn't, leave for another 15 minutes. (You can even leave the dough overnight in a fridge to achieve the same results.)

Knead the risen dough a few more times, knocking it back, and cut it into 18 even-sized pieces. Roll them around in your cupped hands to form little balls and place them tightly together in an oiled 25cm quiche/pie dish (or any round, shallow baking pan). Cover very loosely with a tea towel (careful, they may stick) and allow to rise for another 30 minutes in a warm place.

Preheat the oven to 220°C/gas mark 7. When the dough has risen again, brush very lightly with some olive oil and sprinkle over the poppy seeds. Bake the rolls for 30 minutes, or until golden brown and hollow-sounding when tapped on their undercarriage. Once the rolls are in, do not open the oven. If you do, it may affect the bake and you will never forgive yourself! Allow to cool for 20 minutes on a wire rack.

Roasted Chestnut & Fennel Casserole with Oregano Crumble

FOR 4

I've adapted this from a recipe of my old pal Dan's – a brilliant dabbler in all things vegan. I have also tried this dish with rhubarb instead of fennel and it works a treat. No chestnuts? Use walnuts. To make it gluten free, just swap the breadcrumbs for your favourite gluten-free loaf or crackers.

THE BITS

200g roasted chestnuts (see method)

1 tablespoon rapeseed oil

2 carrots, quartered lengthways and cut into 1cm chunks

2 leeks, cut same size as the carrots

2 bay leaves

1 large bulb of fennel, fronds trimmed and chopped as above

4 cloves of garlic, peeled, crushed and chopped

5 fresh sage leaves, finely sliced, or ¾ teaspoon dried sage

2 sprigs of fresh rosemary or 1 teaspoon dried rosemary

· 4 tablespoons fresh oregano or 1 teaspoon dried oregano

125ml white wine (veggie)

150ml vegetable stock, or cooking juice from the beans

1 tablespoon cornflour

1 red chilli, deseeded and finely diced

4 ripe tomatoes, cut into eighths

1 tablespoon tamari

175g crab eye or rosecoco beans, soaked and cooked, or 2 x 400g tins of beans, drained

a large pinch of sea salt

¼ teaspoon cracked black pepper

For the oregano crumble

125g wholewheat breadcrumbs (nice and dry)

a large pinch of sea salt

2 tablespoons rapeseed oil

For the mash

1kg floury potatoes, scrubbed and cut into chunks

1 tablespoon rapeseed oil

75ml soya milk (unsweetened)

1–2 teaspoons sea salt

DO IT

Preheat the oven to 200°C/gas mark 6.

Using a razor-sharp knife, cut a small slit in the skin of each chestnut. Place them on a baking tray and bake for 25 minutes, turning them over once during cooking.

While this is going on, put your potatoes into a large pan of salted water. Bring to the boil, then reduce the heat and simmer for 30 minutes. Drain them in a colander and leave to cool for 10 minutes, then mash them in a large bowl with the rapeseed oil and milk, and salt to taste.

While the potatoes are cooking, warm 1 tablespoon of rapeseed oil in a large shallow casserole dish (hob-friendly) on a medium heat and sauté the carrots and leeks for 3 minutes. Add the bay leaves, fennel, garlic, sage, rosemary and half the oregano and cook, stirring, for 2 minutes. Glug in the white wine and allow it to bubble for a minute, then add the vegetable stock or bean juice and stir in the cornflour (mixed into a thick lump-free paste with 2 tablespoons of water). Toss in the chilli, tomatoes and tamari, bring to the boil and stir. Wearing a sturdy pair of oven gloves (the dish is going to be slightly volcanic), pop a well-fitting lid on the pan and place it in the oven for about 40 minutes.

The chestnuts are done when the skins open and become slightly blackened, and the insides are soft, sweet and delicious. Allow to cool for 10 minutes, then peel away the outer skin and the pithy inner skin and cut into quarters. Finely dice about a quarter of the chestnuts for the crumble, then cut the rest in half and put aside. Put the diced chestnuts into a bowl with your breadcrumbs, salt and oil. Combine well.

Check the casserole after 40 minutes to see if the carrots are getting there. Take out of the oven and stir in your crab eye beans and chunky chestnuts. Check for seasoning and remove the rosemary sprigs and bay leaves. Give the casserole a decent scattering of the breadcrumb mix and put it back into the oven without the lid for 12–15 minutes, or until all is nicely bubbling and the top has turned a wonderful shade of deep golden brown. Sprinkle with the rest of the oregano and serve with lashings of mash.

Potato, Aubergine & Basil Gratin with Crispy Onions

FOR 4–6

This is a variation on one of my mum's classic gratins. When you cut into them, they were full of cheese, onion and soft potatoes. Enough to make any hungry teenager weak at the knee. I've dropped the cheese, taken the onions up a level and made them delightfully crispy. I've also added some Mediterranean touches in the guise of basil and aubergine.

Salting aubergines is not always essential, though I have to say that it does make them more pliable and flexible when layering in this dish. Also, Mum swears by this practice and I couldn't even comteplate going against her advice!

The colder months are the time when comfort food really comes to the fore. At home we have a massive roaring fire, our only heat source come the Arctic times, and we eat in front of it every night, normally curled up around a bake like this one. It's real hardcore sustenance, not for waistline watchers.

THE BITS

2 large aubergines, stems removed, sliced thinly lengthways

2 tablespoons sea salt, plus ½ teaspoon

4 tablespoons olive oil

3 large onions, finely sliced

3 large potatoes, scrubbed, sliced thinly lengthways

1 celery stalk, finely diced

4 cloves of garlic, peeled and crushed

8 ripe tomatoes, roughly chopped

½ teaspoon unrefined brown sugar

4 tablespoons finely diced sun-dried tomatoes

¼ teaspoon cracked black pepper

2 handfuls of fresh basil leaves

400g firm tofu, drained and finely sliced (optional)

For the garnish

1 big handful of toasted pine nuts

½ a handful of fresh parsley, finely chopped

(cont.) ➡

DO IT

Place your aubergine slices into a colander above a sink or bowl and sprinkle over 2 tablespoons of salt. Rummage around until they're well covered and leave for 45 minutes to drain. (If you are in a hurry, don't worry too much about this stage.)

Heat the oil in a decent-sized heavy frying pan on a medium heat, and fry two-thirds of the onions until they are very crisp and golden. This will take around 10–12 minutes. Stir often and keep your eye on them, lowering the heat a little if they start to brown too much. Remove the onions with a slotted spoon, reserving as much oil as possible. Place them on a thick blanket of kitchen paper, to absorb the excess oil.

Preheat the oven to 220°C/gas mark 7.

Put the potatoes into a large, heavy baking dish and toss them with a good amount of your onion-infused oil and ½ teaspoon of sea salt. You may need a second baking dish. Cover and bake for 15–20 minutes, until the potatoes have softened a little, but are not fully cooked. This will depend on the variety of the potatoes. Set the potatoes aside and keep warm. Try not to break any of them up.

Now make a tomato sauce. Spoon 1 tablespoon of the onion oil into a large saucepan and add the rest of the onions and the diced celery. Fry on a steady heat for 4 minutes, add the garlic, give it a minute, then follow with the tomatoes, sugar and sun-dried tomatoes. Simmer gently with a lid on for 15 minutes. Season with salt and the black pepper. Finally, tear your basil leaves into the sauce and remove from the heat. Once cooled slightly, blitz the sauce with a stick blender until smooth, then pop a lid on the pan.

Cover the base of a warmed baking dish with a quarter of your tomato sauce. Top with a neat layer of potatoes, then a layer of aubergines (followed by the tofu, if using), pressing everything gently down. Spoon over another quarter of the sauce and repeat the layers twice more, finishing with a good covering of the tomato and basil sauce.

Cover with foil or baking parchment, then place in the oven and bake for 1 hour. Scatter the sweet crispy onions on top and bake for a further 10 minutes uncovered. Remove from the oven and leave to sit for 5 minutes to cool slightly before serving.

Serve topped with the toasted pine nuts and a sprinkling of fresh parsley.

Cauliflower Cashew Cheese
with Purple Sprouting Broccoli

FOR 6–8

This is a very healthy, nutrition-packed version of most people's childhood favourite, cauliflower cheese. We pull out all the vegan stops here to replicate a creamy cheese sauce and it works – your mouth enjoys the richness and 'cheesiness' of the dish, but your belly is light as a feather and your heart loves you. The cashew cheese sauce can be made well in advance and keeps nicely in the fridge – use it as you would any other cheesy sauce. It also makes a pleasant dip, especially when spiced up with some chipotle paste or sprinkled with pickled jalapeños. The almonds and sprouting broccoli make a fancy topping, but you can always be a purist and leave them out.

THE BITS

3 tablespoons olive oil

2 red onions, sliced

1 large head of cauliflower, cut into small florets, including most of the upper stem, finely chopped

500g purple sprouting broccoli, tough lower stems chopped off, larger stems halved lengthways

a large pinch of sea salt

1 x creamy cashew cheese sauce (see page 327)

For the topping

½ a handful of toasted flaked almonds

2 tablespoons nutritional yeast flakes (see page 30)

DO IT

Heat 2 tablespoons of olive oil in a frying pan on a medium heat and gently fry the onions until caramelized, about 10 minutes. Set aside and keep warm. Make the creamy cashew cheese sauce.

Put your cauliflower into a large pan of salted boiling water and cook for 8 minutes, until just becoming tender (it will cook more later in the sauce). Don't mess with the cauli too much, otherwise it will break up. We want nice fat florets, undiminished by metal spoon antics. Using a slotted spoon, gently remove the cauliflower and place in a colander over a sink.

Preheat the grill on a medium-high heat.

Blanch your broccoli in the cauliflower water for 3–4 minutes, until nicely tender. (Save this water – it's soup/stew gold dust in liquid form.) Add the cauliflower and onions to the simmering sauce and gently combine them with a wooden spoon or a spatula. You may need to thin the sauce out with a little more milk.

Get ready a large ovenproof dish. Toss your broccoli with 1 tablespoon of olive oil and a pinch of sea salt. Arrange the broccoli stems in the centre of the dish, in one green, neat line. Surround with a stacked border of cauliflower cashew cheese. Place under the grill until the broccoli is slightly charred and the cauliflower cheese is golden and bubbling.

The entire plate now gets a good scattering of almonds and lovely cheesy yeast flakes. Serve with smiles – no further embellishments required.

Stuffed Round Courgettes with Artichokes, Sun-dried Tomatoes & Tofu Ricotta

MAKES 8

I work in an idyllic little retreat centre called Trigonos, where I often serve stuffed courgettes like these. The centre has its own organic veg garden and I am spoilt for choice when it comes to glorious produce. Round courgettes are generally small and dumpy fellows, perfect for stuffing. If you can't get them, long courgettes work just as well – you just need to be a bit more careful when filling them. Yellow (or golden) courgettes are brilliant and can easily be tracked down by a good fruit and veg supplier. They really add an eye-catching element to this dish. Good-quality jarred artichokes don't always need rinsing. Artichokes normally come already cut into quarters, so here you'll need 12 pieces for the filling.

THE BITS

8 round courgettes

3 tablespoons fruity olive oil

1 onion, finely diced

1 carrot, finely diced

1 teaspoon dried mint

3 tablespoons sun-dried tomatoes, finely diced, plus a little of their oil

3 artichoke hearts, cut into quarters (tinned ones are fine, but rinse them well)

juice and zest of ½ a lemon

1 tablespoon fresh thyme leaves or 1 teaspoon dried thyme

2 tablespoons fresh oregano leaves or 1½ teaspoon dried oregano

a handful of toasted almonds or pistachios, roughly chopped

¼ teaspoon sea salt

cracked black pepper

For the tofu ricotta

300g firm tofu, pressed and roughly chopped

2 tablespoons lemon juice

1 tablespoon nutritional yeast flakes (see page 30)

a large pinch of sea salt

a handful of cashews, soaked for 2 hours (optional, for added creaminess)

For the garnish

2 handfuls of radishes, scrubbed and halved lengthways

8 cloves of garlic, in their skins

3 handfuls of rocket leaves

extra virgin olive oil

a handful of toasted almond or pistachios, finely chopped

DO IT

Preheat the oven to 180°C/gas mark 4.

Trim your radishes and tidy them up, leaving the stems on if they look in good condition. Cut the base off your round courgettes, just enough to make them stand up tall and steady. If you are using normal courgettes, cut them in half lengthways, leaving the stem attached.

Brush a baking tray with 2 teaspoons of olive oil. Arrange your courgettes, radishes and garlic on the tray and bake for 20 minutes, turning the the radishes and garlic once. The courgettes should still be firm and not squishy at all, otherwise they'll just fall apart when you try to handle them. The garlic should be soft and the radishes roasted – pop them back into the oven for 5 minutes longer if necessary. Set the courgettes aside, uncovered, to cool. Cover the radishes and garlic and keep warm.

(cont.) ➡

When the courgettes have cooled, lop the tops off, making little green hats (with the stems attached). Now use a teaspoon or melon baller to scoop out the watery innards and seeds. Use your hands to squeeze out any excess water from the innards, then roughly chop.

Heat 2 tablespoons of olive oil in a frying pan on a medium heat. Add the onions and carrot and sauté for 6–8 minutes, until the carrot is softened. Now add your courgette innards, dried mint, sun-dried tomatoes and artichokes and cook for a further 4 minutes. Add the lemon juice and zest, along with the fresh herbs and almonds, and season with sea salt and pepper. Cover and set aside.

To make the tofu ricotta, put all the ingredients into a food processor and blend until thick and creamy. If using the nuts, add them first and blend well, then add the other ingredients.

Spoon your artichoke mixture into the hollowed-out courgettes. Pack it down lightly with the base of your spoon, leaving a shallow indent for the tofu ricotta to sit in. Mound some of the ricotta into the courgettes and bake on a lightly oiled oven tray for 10 minutes, until warmed through. Remove from the oven and pop their little hats back on (at a jaunty angle preferably!).

On a large serving plate, arrange the courgettes with plenty of space between them. Scatter the rocket leaves in between, sprinkle the roasted radishes and garlic around, and top with a drizzle of olive oil, a scattering of nuts and a pinch of sea salt.

Mexican 'Pastor' Pie

FOR 4–6

I love Mexico and have spent many happy times there. *'Pastor'* means 'shepherd' *en español*, so you can see what I've done here – I've adapted many of the brilliant flavours of Mexico and whacked them into a vibrant and healthy version of the old-school shepherd's pie. This has more colour, more flavour and more nutrition than the original and it's a bit more-ish too. The sweet potato changes things totally, in colour as well as in nutrition. Firm tofu is a good substitute for the seitan if you can't find it. Lingham's sweet chilli sauce has been a faithful friend for many years and contains no nasties whatsoever. I rarely use factory-made flavourings in my cooking, but Lingham's is an exception. For the fresh chillies, use good, strong jalapeños if you can. There should be a little fiery Mexican twang to the sauce.

THE BITS

For the mash

600g sweet potatoes, peeled and roughly diced

400g floury potatoes, peeled and roughly diced

5 spring onions, finely sliced, green bits too

1–2 teaspoons salt

200ml soya milk or almond milk (unsweetened)

For the filling

1 tablespoon vegetable oil

1 teaspoon cumin seeds

1 onion, finely diced

1 celery stalk, finely diced

8 kale leaves, removed from stems and sliced into 5cm strips

2 corn on the cobs, kernels removed

2 chillies (jalapeño are best), finely diced

3 teaspoons chipotle chilli paste or 1½ teaspoons smoked paprika

1 teaspoon ground coriander

2 teaspoons dried oregano

¼ teaspoon ground cinnamon

1 large courgette, cut into 2cm cubes

6 tomatoes, roughly chopped

2 tablespoons tomato purée

175g red kidney beans or aduki beans, soaked in water and cooked

200g seitan or firm tofu, cut into 2cm cubes (optional but very good)

2 tablespoons Lingham's sweet chilli sauce

½ teaspoon sea salt

¼ teaspoon cracked black pepper

For the topping

2 teaspoons vegetable oil

2 red peppers, thinly sliced

a pinch of sea salt

½ a handful of fresh coriander leaves

DO IT

Put all the potatoes into a large pan and cover well with salted water. Bring to the boil, then reduce the heat and simmer for 35 minutes, until they are tender and a knife tip can be pressed into them without resistance. Drain well and leave to cool in the colander. (Keep the cooking water – it makes magnificent stock.)

Heat the oil in a large, heavy-bottomed frying pan on a medium heat. Sprinkle in the cumin seeds, followed by the onions and celery. Fry and stir for 5 minutes until soft. Add the kale, corn, chillies and all the herbs and spices. Warm through, stirring, for 3 minutes.

(cont.) ➡

Now add the courgette, tomatoes and tomato purée along with the cooked beans (plus about 300ml of their cooking juices), seitan and sweet chilli sauce. Simmer for 10 minutes, then remove from the heat. Season with salt and pepper, cover the pan and set aside.

Mash your potatoes, giving them a good pummelling. Stir in the spring onions, salt and milk (as needed). We're looking for a lovely smooth orange mash, but not runny.

Preheat the oven to 200°C/gas mark 6.

Ladle your sauce into the base of a large warmed baking dish. Cover with your mash. Using something like a cake slice or the back of a knife, spread the mash to meet every edge of the dish. Drizzle with a little oil and run a fork over the top, creating cool-looking spiral patterns in the mash. Place the dish on a large baking tray (to catch any overspill) and stick in the warm oven for 35 minutes.

Clean out the frying pan, put it back on a high heat and add 2 teaspoons of oil. Add the peppers and fry and stir for 10 minutes, until well caramelized and superbly sweet. Add a pinch of salt.

After 35 minutes, the mash should be slightly toasted and golden brown and the sauce will probably be bubbling all over the shop. This is perfect. Leave the pie to sit for 10 minutes out of the oven, then scatter over the red peppers and fresh coriander. Serve with big spoons and even bigger appetites. This is great with lots of green leaves and avocado with a nice citrus dressing. *Viva 'El Pastor'!*

Rainbow Chard with Swede, Dill & Dijon Mash

FOR 4–6

A gorgeously straightforward oven bake that takes your average week-night fare into the realms of a weekend treat, with little added effort and a few savvy vegan twists. You don't have to use rainbow chard, it just looks so cool on the plate, turning a mashed dinner into a psychedelic feast. Swiss chard, ruby chard ... whatever you can get your hands on is fine. Kale or bigger-leaved varieties of spinach would be lovely too. Try to buy unrefined, good-quality rapeseed oil to add to the mash, as it makes a big difference (see Suppliers, page 338).

THE BITS

For the swede mash

1 small swede, peeled and diced

5 large potatoes, scrubbed and diced

2 tablespoons rapeseed oil

½ tablespoon Dijon mustard

2 tablespoons fine capers, well rinsed

1–2 teaspoons sea salt

100ml almond milk (or other milk of your choice)

a handful of fresh dill, roughly chopped

For the chard

1 tablespoon vegetable oil

4 large shallots, cut into wedges, or 1 large onion

3 cloves of garlic, peeled and minced

4 sprigs of fresh thyme, leaves removed

a large pinch of sea salt

125ml white wine (veggie)

1 tablespoon tomato purée

500g rainbow chard, base of roots trimmed, leaves cut into 5cm ribbons

3 big handfuls of cherry tomatoes

cracked black pepper, to taste

For the garnish

a handful of toasted hazelnuts, roughly chopped

DO IT

Put your swede and potatoes into a large pan of salted cold water and bring to the boil, then reduce the heat and simmer for 35 minutes. When tender, drain well, put into a large bowl with the rest of the mash ingredients and mash until smooth. Check the seasoning, then cover and keep warm.

Preheat the oven to 200°C/gas mark 6.

Heat 1 tablespoon of vegetable oil in a large frying pan on a medium-high heat and sauté your shallots for 3 minutes, until slightly browned. Add the garlic, thyme, salt and pepper and fry for 2 minutes more. Add the white wine and tomato purée, followed by the chard, then cover the pan and cook for 3 minutes. Now lower the heat to minimum, drop in the cherry tomatoes, and check the seasoning. Pop the lid back on and turn off the heat.

Spread the chard and tomato mixture in a large warmed oven dish and spoon over the mash, making sure the chard is covered, though the mash doesn't need to touch the sides of the dish. Drizzle with a little more oil.

Place in the oven and bake for 20 minutes, until the mash is crispy on top. Remove from the oven and top with a smattering of toasted hazelnuts, if you're feeling decadent.

Ruby Chard Bundles Filled with Beetroot, Millet & Raisins, with a Brazil Nut & Rosemary Cream

This is a homage to one of my favourite Dennis Cotter recipes. Wrapping things in leaves is old hat – the Greeks have it perfected with vine leaves and rice (aka dolmades). We need to try something new, so I've reached out to the veg patch for these bright leaves and roots and decided to keep things indigenous with some wholesome millet.

I love the colour of ruby chard, it reminds me of Pinot Noir. Any type of chard can be used, but it may ruin your finely crafted colour scheme. If there are any leaves on your beetroot, you can either fry them and use them as a side dish, or chop them and mix them in with the rest of the filling, along with any smaller chard leaf siblings. Any leftover filling can be kept in the fridge, mixed with a few leaves and served as a mighty tasty salad. Brazil nut butter is increasingly easy to find, but you can also make your own using Brazil nuts, a pinch of salt and a blender. Just blitz until creamy and smooth.

THE BITS

160g millet

1 sprig of rosemary

1 bay leaf

2 bundles of ruby chard (roughly 16 decent-sized leaves), left whole, with the stems cut off and finely diced

½ tablespoon olive oil

1 large beetroot, scrubbed and finely diced

1 large carrot, scrubbed and finely diced

2 tablespoons balsamic vinegar

1 onion, finely diced

1 celery stalk, finely diced

4 cloves of garlic, peeled and crushed

a handful of toasted pumpkin seeds

½ a handful of raisins, roughly chopped

a handful of fresh parsley, finely chopped, plus extra for garnish

½ teaspoon sea salt

a large pinch of black pepper

For the Brazil nut & rosemary cream

3 tablespoons Brazil nut butter

150g silken tofu

1 teaspoons fresh rosemary, very finely chopped

1 clove of garlic, peeled and crushed

1 tablespoon lemon juice

a large pinch of sea salt

150ml almond milk or soya milk

1 tablespoon olive oil

DO IT

Warm a pan on a medium heat and add the millet. Dry-toast these little yellow seeds, continuously stirring them for 6 minutes. They should turn slightly darker in colour. Cover the millet with 1.5cm of water, drop in the rosemary sprig and bay leaf, and bring to a rolling boil. Place a lid on the pan and lower the heat to minimum. Leave to cook for 35 minutes without lifting the lid. You should have perfectly fluffy millet. Use a fork to fluff it up further. Cover and set aside.

Bring a pan of water to the boil and set a steamer on top. Steam the chard leaves for 5 minutes, until nicely tender and pliable, but not cooked through. Spread out on a large plate and allow to cool uncovered.

(cont.) ➡

Heat ½ tablespoon of oil in a large frying pan on a medium-high heat. Add the beetroot and carrots and pan-fry for 10 minutes, then add the balsamic vinegar and 2 tablespoons of water. Cook until all the liquid has evaporated, then add the onions, celery and chard stems and cook for a further 5 minutes. Then add the garlic, pumpkin seeds and raisins (plus any beetroot leaves or small chard leaves can also be thrown in here) and cook for another 5 minutes. Now add the cooked millet (removing the rosemary and bay leaf) and chopped parsley, season well with salt and pepper, stir and leave to cool slightly. (Note: if the millet is sticky, this is perfectly normal – just break the larger clumps up using your fingers.)

To make the Brazil nut and rosemary cream, put the Brazil nut butter, tofu, rosemary, garlic, lemon juice and salt into a food processor. Blend to a paste, gradually adding the milk until the texture resembles thick double cream. Warm in a small saucepan, without boiling, for 20 minutes. Just before serving, stir in the oil. This gives a nice sheen to the cream.

Preheat the oven to 180°C/gas mark 4.

Place a chard leaf on your work surface, with the widest end nearest you, and spoon in roughly 2–3 tablespoons of the millet filling (depending on the size of your leaves). Roll the leaf away from you once, then tuck in the outside edges and roll again, tucking the ends in again. Keep going until you have a nice neat parcel. Repeat with the other leaves.

Place the parcels on a lightly oiled large baking tray, well spaced out, and brush them with a tad more oil. Sprinkle them with 3 tablespoons of water (to stop them browning and becoming bitter) and bake for 12–15 minutes, until they are warmed through.

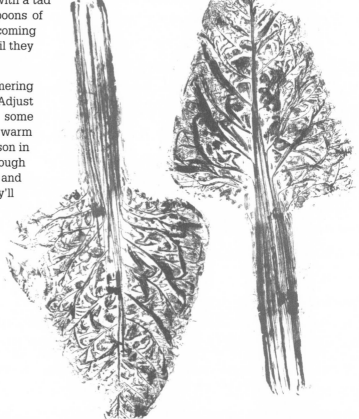

Check the consistency of your simmering sauce and add more milk if needed. Adjust the seasoning if needed. Now ladle some sauce into the centres of individual warm plates and arrange two parcels per person in the middle of each. You should have enough sauce left over to pour into a bowl and allow people to help themselves. They'll definitely be looking for more!

You can garnish with chopped parsley, or even some sprouts or finely chopped Brazil nuts. Although I think they look great just the way they are.

Tempeh Chorizo & Chickpea Wraps with Orange, Avocado & Coriander Salsa

FOR 4

Chargrilled chorizo was one of the hardest things to give up when I first became vegetarian. We used to eat it in little clay tapas bowls down at our local tavern in Spain. They cooked it in sherry and it was quite spectacular. So when I'd made my mind up that meat was no longer cool in my world, I set about creating a reasonable substitute for chorizo.

This is like the loose-style raw chorizo, much easier to get together when making a quick lunchtime wrap. You should get all the familiar spices of chorizo with a nice caramelized touch from the onions and tempeh. Sometimes I use cream sherry instead of sherry vinegar, to remind me of my former favourite tapas. If you are in quick-lunch territory, you can use shop-bought wraps instead of the pancakes. The raw cashew hummus on page 160 goes really well alongside.

Gluten-free option: use GF wraps instead of the pancakes.

THE BITS

For the tempeh chorizo

1 tablespoon vegetable oil

350g tempeh, well drained and crushed with a fork

1 teaspoon cumin seeds

1 bay leaf

½ an onion, grated

1 teaspoon smoked paprika

1 teaspoon sweet paprika

½ teaspoon ground coriander

½ teaspoon dried oregano

½ teaspoon dried thyme

a large pinch of ground cloves

a large pinch of ground cinnamon

¼ teaspoon chilli powder

½ teaspoon sea salt

⅓ teaspoon cracked black pepper

2 cloves of garlic, peeled and crushed

1½ tablespoons sherry vinegar

250ml vegetable stock

For the chickpea wraps (makes 4 big ones)

60g wholewheat flour

60g gram (chickpea) flour

½ teaspoon bicarbonate of soda

½ tablespoon vegetable oil

1 teaspoon tamari

100ml soya milk or almond milk

100ml water

3–4 tablespoons vegetable oil, for frying

For the orange, avocado & coriander salsa

1 orange

2 spring onions, trimmed and finely sliced

1 ripe avocado, peeled, de-stoned and finely diced

1 red chilli, deseeded and finely diced

½ a handful of cherry tomatoes, quartered

½ a handful of fresh coriander leaves, roughly chopped

a large pinch of sea salt

To serve

1 small head of oakleaf lettuce, or any soft lettuce

½ a beetroot, scrubbed and grated (optional)

DO IT

To make the salsa, peel the orange, removing the pith from the segments as best you can. Run a knife along the inner edge of each segment, trimming the pith off, and the rest of the skin should easily slip off with a little careful tugging. Pith is bitter and not welcome at this party. Finely dice the segments with a sharp knife. Combine in a bowl with the rest of the salsa ingredients and set aside.

To make the tempeh chorizo, heat the oil in a large frying pan on a high heat and pan-fry the tempeh, cumin seeds, bay leaf and onion for 3 minutes. Add the rest of the herbs and spices, salt and pepper along with the crushed garlic. Continue frying for 5 minutes, then add the sherry vinegar and stock. Cook on a fast simmer for 5 minutes, until all the liquid has been absorbed by the tempeh. Put the chorizo into a warmed bowl and cover.

To make the chickpea wraps, sift the flours and bicarbonate of soda into a large mixing bowl. In a separate, smaller bowl whisk together the oil, tamari, milk and water until well combined. Now mix the dry ingredients into the wet ingredients until a thin batter is formed. Cover the mixture and place in the fridge for 20 minutes to chill.

Wipe your frying pan with kitchen paper and then lightly oil the base and set over a medium-high heat. Spoon roughly 3 tablespoons of the mixture at a time on to the hot pan and spread it out in circular motions, using the back of the spoon. We're looking for thin wraps. Cook until one side is nicely golden brown, 2-ish minutes. Flip over and fry the other side for slightly less time. This should leave you with a perfectly cooked pancake to stuff with gorgeous fillings. Wrap the finished pancakes in a clean tea-towel to keep them warm.

Now get your wraps together. Place a pancake on a plate, layer a couple of lettuce leaves in the centre, and sprinkle with a line of grated beetroot. Spoon over 3 tablespoons of the chorizo and top with 2 tablespoons of salsa. Flip one edge over the filling and tuck it under with both hands, then roll it over gradually with both hands until tightly wrapped.

Aubergine Involtini with Creamy Spinach Stuffing & Roast Tomato & Olive Sauce

FOR 4

Involtini means 'wrapped', and in this case the wrap is slices of aubergine. A few simple steps and you have a dish that looks as good as it tastes – the contrast of colours on the plate sets things alight! The bigger the aubergines the better here – big fat involtini are best. Take your time when slicing them, as the more even and straight they are, the nicer the dish. Try laying them on their side and cutting slowly with a long sharp knife. Don't use the last slices of the aubergine on either side, maybe even the last two slices, as they will not be large enough to roll – save them for more aubergine antics at a later date.

THE BITS

4 tablespoons olive oil

2 large aubergines, cut into 1cm slices lengthways

½ teaspoon sea salt

¼ teaspoon black pepper

For the roast tomato & olive sauce

2 tablespoons olive oil

125ml red wine (veggie)

10 ripe tomatoes, quartered

1 onion, finely sliced

1 teaspoon dried oregano

4 cloves of garlic, peeled and crushed

1 tablespoon red wine vinegar

1 teaspoon unrefined brown sugar

a handful of green olives, pitted and finely sliced

a large pinch of sea salt

plenty of black pepper

For the creamy spinach stuffing

2 teaspoons olive oil

275g spinach leaves, washed

2 cloves of garlic, peeled and crushed

a large pinch of sea salt

200g firm tofu

3 tablespoons ground almonds

a small pinch of black pepper

½ tablespoon lemon juice

1 tablespoon nutritional yeast flakes (see page 30)

For the garnish

a handful of fresh parsley, finely chopped

DO IT

Preheat the oven to 190°C/gas mark 5. Put all the tomato sauce ingredients into a large baking dish, combining everything well, and place on the top shelf of your oven. Bake for 30 minutes, stirring once, then cover with a lid or foil and bake for a further 35 minutes. The tomatoes should have some nice colour.

Grab two baking trays and pour 1 tablespoon of olive oil on to each, spreading it out so that the trays are well covered. Place the aubergine slices on the baking trays, season and drizzle over the rest of the oil. Bake for 15 minutes on one side, then turn the slices over and bake for another 10 minutes, until softened and golden.

To make the creamy spinach filling, heat 2 teaspoons of olive oil in a large pan on a medium heat. Add your spinach, garlic and a large pinch of salt, and pan-fry for 5 minutes, until the spinach has wilted and most of the liquid has evaporated. Remove from the heat. Place the rest of the filling ingredients in a food processor, add the spinach, and blitz until thick and creamy – something like green clotted cream is great.

Your tomatoes should now be ready. Leave them to cool slightly, then wipe out the food processor and pour in the toms. Pulse a few times – we'd like a chunky sauce. Taste and season if needed.

Now let's roll! Lay the aubergine slices on your work surface, facing lengthways away from you with the narrow end nearest. Spread 2 tablespoons of the spinach filling on to each slice and gently roll them away from you. Continue rolling until all your aubergine slices are used up. Don't press them down too hard when rolling, otherwise the filling will spill out of the sides.

Pour the tomato and olive sauce back into the baking dish and place the Involtini face down on top of the sauce, well spaced. Bake uncovered for 15–20 minutes, until all is bubbling and warmed through.

Serve sprinkled with a little freshly chopped parsley. I like this dish with boiled pasta or new potatoes and watercress. Another nice idea is to add an additional topping of pine nut Parmesan (see page 336) before you bake the involtini.

Jacket Skins Stuffed with Leeks & Wild Mushrooms & a Chive & Lemon Yoghurt

FOR 4

This is really just a blinged-up jacket spud. Hardly any more trouble, but the simple flavours knock your socks clean off! You can use any mushrooms here, but the wilder and more intense in flavour, the better.

THE BITS

4 large baking potatoes

2–3 tablespoons olive oil

1 leek, finely sliced, green parts included

4 cloves of garlic, peeled and crushed

1 small head of broccoli, florets and stems finely diced

300g wild mushrooms of your choice, roughly chopped

½ teaspoon dried rosemary

½ teaspoon dried sage

1 teaspoon dried thyme (or 2 teaspoons mixed herbs instead of the above three)

1 teaspoon salt

¼ teaspoon black pepper

75ml almond milk or soya milk

1 big handful of toasted sunflower seeds

2 tablespoons nutritional yeast flakes (see page 30)

2 tablespoons wholegrain mustard

For the chive & lemon yoghurt

a handful of fresh chives, finely chopped

300ml soya yoghurt (unsweetened)

1 tablespoon lemon juice

½ tablespoon lemon zest

a large pinch of sea salt

DO IT

Preheat the oven to 180°C/gas mark 4.

Prick the potatoes all over with a fork and rub them with oil. Bake for 1¼ hours, until golden and soft, turning them over once during that time. Cut them in half and leave to cool.

Heat 1 tablespoon of olive oil in a large frying pan and fry your leeks for 6 minutes, until softened. Add the garlic, broccoli and mushrooms and fry for a further 5 minutes. Pop in the dried herbs, stir and season, then take off the heat and cover.

Now the potatoes are cool enough to handle, carefully scoop out the insides and put them into a bowl, leaving the crispy skins intact. These be our stuffing vessels! Mash the insides with the milk, then stir in the vegetables, seeds, nutritional yeast flakes and mustard, adding a little more salt as needed. Spoon the mash back into the waiting skins, packing them full to bursting, and place them on an oiled baking tray. Heat the oven to 180°C/gas mark 4 again and pop your posh pots in for 10–15 minutes, until piping hot.

To make the chive and lemon yoghurt, mix all the ingredients together in a bowl.

Serve the stuffed potato skins with a good dollop of chive and lemon yoghurt on the side.

Surfing on Dinas Dinlle Beach.

Dearest sweet teeth,

You have arrived in the plant-based Garden of Eden. Not so much the land of milk and honey, more the land of nut butters and dates. Not as poetic sounding, maybe, but equally sweet and rich.

Here you will find delicious sweeties that not only set the taste buds alight with wonderful flavours, but actually do the body good. You could call this a guilt-free dessert corner, if you approach dessert with your hips, heart and tummy-line in mind.

Vegan desserts are a BIG surprise (they are still surprising me!). I am regularly astounded by what can be done when the dessert staples are omitted (namely eggs, white flour and cream or milk). Creativity pours out of 'V' folk who crave their old favourites and imaginative substitutes are discovered.

Many vegan cakes do contain white flour and quite a lot of sugar; a vegan cake is not necessarily a healthy cake. I do not really buy into this über-sweet approach (although the Choc and Beet Brownies are quite something!); it's a little like vegetarians who slap loads of cheese on everything. We can do better than that! Much, much, much, better.

Bring on the sweet thangs!

Raw Blueberry &
Macadamia Cheesecake

FOR 8 WHOPPING SLICES

If you are yet to enter the magical world of raw desserts, this macadamia cheesecake is a sensational place to start. It's so very rich and surprisingly healthy. If you try one recipe in this book, this is the one. I have yet to meet anybody who can resist it! I like to use cashews in the filling purely because of the price difference – macadamias are expensive – but for a special occasion, go for it! Depending on the season, any berry can be used for this recipe. Blackberries are a personal favourite – I love their bitter edge with the sweet creaminess of the cheesecake – although blueberries are delicious too.

THE BITS

For the crust

300g raw macadamia nuts

a handful of pumpkin seeds

90g dates (soaked for 1 hour, then pitted)

20g freshly grated coconut (desiccated is fine)

For the filling

360g raw cashews or macadamias (soaked for at least 3 hours)

120ml lemon juice

120ml brown rice syrup (or other sweetener of your choice)

180ml coconut oil

a large pinch of sea salt

1 teaspoon vanilla extract

120ml water

For the sauce

400g blueberries

45g dates (soaked for 1 hour), pitted

DO IT

To make the crust, put the macadamias, pumpkin seeds and dates into a food processor and pulse together until a rough crumble is formed. Add more dates if it's a little dry or more nuts if it's wet. The mixture should be able to be rolled into balls and not be overly sticky.

Scatter a layer of coconut on the base of a cake tin (one of those with a pushy-out bottom). You can use a normal pie/quiche dish – it just makes it harder to extract the cake. Try lining your tins with a snug layer of clingfilm. Using your hands, press the macadamia crust on to the coconut covering the base. Press the edges down with your fingers, forming an even layer.

To make the filling, blitz all the ingredients in the now magically clean food processor (bless those kitchen elves) until you have a smooth cream-like texture. You may need a few goes to get it all incorporated, scraping the sides down with a spatula. Scrape out your filling mixture into the pie dish, bang it gently a few times on a work surface (to get rid of air bubbles) and smooth the filling down using a spatula.

Place in the freezer and freeze – for best results, eat on the day of freezing, or soon after. Remove from the pie dish using a thin cake slice around the edge and gently pushing the base out. Take it easy and slowly. Pop it into the fridge and allow it to defrost – a couple of hours will do.

Place the blueberries and dates into your food processor (now miraculously clean again) and blitz well. Add a little water to thin the sauce out if needed. Pour over the cheesecake before serving, and if there is any excess sauce, serve it in a bowl as a berry bonus.

Chestnut Cream with Gin-soaked Damsons

FOR 4

This super-tasty little dessert can be whipped up in double quick time. It can be eaten as it is, or thinned down slightly and served with pies and cakes. Chestnuts are lower in fat than all other nuts and are quite starchy, making them perfect for a purée. If you are lucky enough to have a damson tree in your garden, you'll be fully versed in the wonders of these tangy little plums. Any plum will work well here, but I have a particular fondness for damsons.

THE BITS

For the chestnut cream

300g chestnuts, peeled, brown skin taken off

2–3 tablespoons brown rice syrup (or other sweetener of your choice)

a small pinch of sea salt

100ml soya milk or almond milk

For the damsons

4 handfuls of damsons, cut in half lengthways and de-stoned

50ml of your favourite gin

2 tablespoons unrefined brown sugar

4 long ribbons of orange peel (use a peeler)

For the garnish

3 tablespoons chopped toasted almonds

DO IT

Put the damsons into a large bowl with the gin, sugar and orange peel. Make sure all the sugar has dissolved, then place in the fridge for at least 2 hours (overnight is very cool, and drinking the leftover damson gin is even cooler).

In a small pan, cook the chestnuts with 500ml of water, until soft – about 20 minutes will do. Drain, then place in a food processor with the syrup, salt and milk and blitz together until smooth and creamy.

Carefully spoon your chestnut cream into small, wide glasses – they should be one-third full. Top with your damsons and a sprinkling of toasted chopped almonds.

Charred Pineapple Wedges with Spiced Caramel & Lime Yoghurt

FOR 4–6

This sounds complicated, but is actually a cinch. Roasted pineapple is something that transports me directly to the Caribbean. I have added a couple of fancy accompaniments, but the star here is the caramelized fruit. I like to get my pineapple charred before the main barbecue session gets under way, while the grill is still clean, and this dish gets better when doused in the spiced caramel and kept warm in the oven. The pineapple is delightfully sweet, so the lime yoghurt makes the perfect companion. For a boozy touch, add a glug of dark rum to the caramel.

THE BITS

1 large ripe pineapple, peeled and all brown eyes removed

For the spiced caramel

250ml water

4 tablespoons unrefined brown sugar

2 star anise

4 cloves

1 cinnamon stick

For the lime yoghurt

juice of ½ a lime

zest of 1 lime

½ tablespoon brown rice syrup or other sweetner

300g unsweetened soya yoghurt

DO IT

In a small pan, bring the water to just about boiling and stir in your sugar and spices. Leave to simmer vigorously and uncovered, stirring and reducing the liquid by half or until it forms a syrup. Cover the pan and keep warm on the stove.

Cut your pineapple in half lengthways, then, with your knife at a 45 degree angle, cut out the tough central stem (you don't have to do this, but the slightly pithy texture bothers some). Cut the pineapple into 1cm thick half-moon shaped slices.

Get a barbecue or griddle pan to a high heat. Press a pineapple steak on to the grill – it should sizzle and smoke immediately. Place your pineapple pieces in rows and do not move them – this will make sure you get the desired charred-stripe look. Don't overfill the grill; leave enough space between slices to turn them over easily.

Leave to cook for 2 minutes on each side. It's best to have some long-handled tongs available here, as the wedges may stick. Use a metal slice to quickly scrape them loose with a jabbing motion and then, quick as a flash, turn with the tongs. It's a technique that's easily grasped. You'll be a master flipper in no time.

Place the charred pineapple in a large warmed ovenproof dish. Cover with foil and continue with a fresh batch of wedges. When all the slices are cooked, drizzle over some of your spiced caramel and place the dish in the oven on a low heat (just to keep warm).

Mix the lime juice, zest and syrup into the yoghurt, tasting and adjusting until it is to your liking. Serve the pineapple with extra caramel spooned over and a nice blob of lime yoghurt.

Coconut & Vanilla Rice Pudding with Mango & Basil Compote

FOR 4

This is a heady combination of flavours and richness, finished off with the sweetest and most fragrant of toppings. Ripe mangoes can be hard to come by here and must be savoured when they do appear. Organic coconut milk and vanilla extract are available now, and the extra pennies spent are very much worth it. Cheaper versions of these products taste really poor once you have tried the good stuff.

THE BITS

1 x 400ml tin of coconut milk

200g pudding (short-grain) rice

400ml unsweetened almond milk or soya milk

3 tablespoons brown rice syrup (or other sweetener of your choice)

1 vanilla pod or 2 teaspoons vanilla extract

1 tablespoon coconut oil

finely grated zest of ½ a lime

For the mango & basil compote

1 large, ripe mango

1 big handful of basil leaves

1 teaspoon lime juice

½ teaspoon brown rice syrup (or other sweetener, if needed)

DO IT

Set aside 3 tablespoons of the coconut milk and put the rest into a pan with the rice, almond milk and syrup. Bring slowly to the boil, keeping your eye on it, as it will boil over quite easily. Get a gentle simmer going, then add the vanilla (split the pod lengthways and scrape the pulp into the pan). Stir, pop a lid on the pan, and leave on a low heat for 20–25 minutes. The rice should be slightly more cooked than normal rice: nice and fat and soft: stir it often.

Now stir in your coconut oil, the reserved coconut milk and the lime zest, and leave to rest with the lid on for 10 minutes. The coconut oil will give the rice a nice shine and richness. Thin with warm water if necessary.

Serve the lovely unctuous coconut rice in warmed shallow bowls or on dessert plates and cover liberally with your gorgeous fruity compote.

Peel your mango. Destone it and slice into thin batons. Set aside half of it, plus the bits from around the seed (if you haven't munched them already). Take the rest of the mango, pop it into a food processor with the basil and lime and blend until smooth.. Check the flavour – if it needs a little sweetness, add ½ teaspoon of syrup. Transfer to a bowl.

Add the rest of the sliced mango to the compote. The fragrant basil will infuse with the already fragrant mango.

Brazil Nut & Chocolate Spelt Cookies

MAKES 16

We all need a standby cookie, something you can whip up almost with your eyes closed. Here is my chunky cookie of choice. Gillian is a wonderful friend and baker who lives over in the next valley. The concept of cooking without eggs, white sugar and white flour is daunting to many a baker, but Gillian came up trumps with this recipe, one of the finest vegan cookies I've munched on. The best thing that can be done with these cookies is to make them into an ice cream sandwich with the chocolate and maple ice cream (see page 314). While the cookies are still warm, this is a heavenly proposition. These sandwiches can also be made and frozen for future enjoyment. Sometimes, when feeling daring, I go for 100% spelt action here. It's full-on wholemeal, but I find its toasted flavour amazing.

THE BITS

120g unbleached white flour

140g spelt flour (or wholewheat flour)

1 teaspoon bicarbonate of soda

1½ teaspoons baking powder

¼ teaspoon salt

1 teaspoon ground cinnamon

200g unrefined brown sugar

180ml vegetable oil

1 teaspoon vanilla extract

60g vegan dark chocolate, chopped or broken into very small chunks

a handful of raisins, roughly chopped

a handful of Brazil nuts, roughly chopped

30ml water

DO IT

Preheat the oven to 180°C/gas mark 4.

Sift the white flour, spelt flour, bicarbonate of soda, baking powder, salt and cinnamon into a mixing bowl.

In a separate bowl blend together the brown sugar and oil, adding the vanilla. Add to the mixing bowl and stir gently, then add the chocolate chunks, raisins, Brazil nuts and water. Stir a little more until just combined, making sure everything is moist. The mixture should be clumpy. Add more water if it's still powdery and dry.

Spoon out the mixture, using one heaped dessertspoon per cookie (roughly squash-ball size), forming them into small balls with your hands. Line three large baking trays with parchment (or cook in batches) and place the balls on the trays, pressing them down into fat cookie shapes with your fingertips. Leave at least a 5cm gap between cookies, as they expand quite nicely in the oven!

Pop into the oven and bake, rotating the trays at least once, for 10–12 minutes. Cookies are quite sensitive and every oven is different, so keep an eye on your precious bics – they will highlight any oven hot spots for you! Take the cookies out when they have just about firmed up; they will continue cooking as they cool and crisp up nicely.

You should now be looking at a form of chewy cookie-based nirvana. They are supposed to be soft when they leave the oven – let them cool on the trays for a few minutes. When firm, transfer to a wire rack and allow to cool for 10 minutes before diving in (or until cool enough to scoff).

Carrot, Orange & Pistachio Halwa

FOR 4-6

Halwa seems to be one of those global dishes, claimed by so many countries, from Greece to India. It's a brilliantly simple dessert, loved by cooks across the world. Normally it's made with semolina, but I have opted for carrots here (you can also use beetroot). There are no compromises with flavour or texture at all, and you will not believe this dish is vegan, it is so creamy and rich. The orange blossom water is optional, but if you have it, pop some in and enjoy the insane fragrance that it emits when steaming away in your bowl. It adds a touch of citrus perfume to proceedings like no other ingredient. For a special occasion, I will add a large pinch of saffron to the simmering milk for that extra touch of luxury.

THE BITS

600g carrots, finely grated

700ml unsweetened almond milk

10 cardamom pods (seeds removed and ground in a pestle and mortar)

4 tablespoons unrefined brown sugar (or jaggery for the full-on Indian feel)

a big handful of pistachios, roughly chopped

a handful of dried apricots, roughly chopped

2 tablespoons almond butter

1–2 teaspoons orange blossom water (to taste)

For the garnish

a handful of pistachios or pomegranate seeds (optional)

DO IT

Put the carrots and almond milk into a heavy-bottomed saucepan. Bring to a boil, then lower the heat and set to a slow, steady simmer, stirring regularly. After 45 minutes add the cardamom, cook for a further 10 minutes, then stir in the sugar. Once most of the milk has evaporated, add the chopped pistachios, chopped apricots, almond butter and orange blossom water. Stir well and simmer for 5 minutes prior to serving.

I like halwa to be served warm, in small bowls (it's quite rich), sprinkled with pistachios or pomegranate seeds as an added extra. But it can also be eaten from the fridge. You may like to spread it into a square baking tray, pop it into the fridge for a couple of hours (once fully cooled) and serve it cut into slices, Indian sweet-shop style!

Rustic Apple & Whisky Marmalade Tart

FOR ONE BIG TART

This is the easiest and lightest tart I know, which is why I'm sharing it with you. It's the perfect answer to the old dinner party conundrum of desserts that look great, but are dead easy to make. The old British apples are my heroes – Golden Noble, Orange Pippin, Keswick Codlin, Grenadier, Peasgood Nonsuch, Dummlers Seedling. It is said that 1,500 varieties of apples once grew in the UK, and I love the comeback the indigenous apple is making. You'll want a firm and slightly acidic variety for this tart, so it doesn't turn to mush when baked.

THE BITS

1 sheet of puff pastry (frozen is easiest)

3 tablespoons rindless marmalade

1–2 tablespoons whisky (not malt whisky – never malt in cooking!)

4–5 apples (roughly 600–800g), cored

1 tablespoon unbleached white flour, plus a little more for dusting

70g unrefined brown sugar

a small pinch of sea salt

DO IT

Defrost the pastry in the fridge overnight, or leave it at room temperature, on a plate, for a couple of hours.

Put the marmalade into a small pan with the whisky and heat gently until it forms a thick syrup. Do not cook further.

Roll out the pastry on a lightly floured surface to a rectangle about 30 x 35cm. Cut off any unsightly straggly bits and place the pastry on a baking tray lined with baking paper. With a small sharp knife, score a 2cm border around the pastry and press down gently with a fork inside the edge, creating a slightly raised border. Prick the base with a fork. Pop into the fridge for 10–20 minutes.

Preheat the oven to 220°C/gas mark 7 and bake the pastry for 12 minutes, until just risen and becoming golden.

Halve your apples lengthways, leaving the skins on, and chop them into 5mm slices (so they look like little half-moons). Toss the apples with 1 tablespoon of flour and the sugar and salt.

Press the inside area of the pastry down with a fork, to form a level base. Arrange your apples in neat little rows along the pastry. Brush the border with some of the whisky marmalade glaze, then cover with foil and put back into the oven until the apples are softened – another 15–20 minutes will do it (depending on the apples you are using).

Brush the finished tart with plenty more of your whisky marmalade glaze and allow to cool for 15 minutes.

Best served with scoops of good-quality vegan vanilla ice cream (it actually exists!).

Choc & Beet Brownies

FOR 6–8

This is a super-rich brownie recipe, quite dense and with extra chocolate for good measure. I also love adding finely chopped prunes to really bump up the sticky richness stakes, and these brownies also taste great with other dried fruits, such as cherries, blueberries or raisins. Brownies are a funny bake: they don't look done, but they are. You'll need a little brownie experience to get it just right, but generally, they are much stickier than your average cake when probed with a chopstick or toothpick. I recommend a gentle press test – if the brownie has formed a decent crust and is slightly springy, you're there.

THE BITS

300g very dark vegan chocolate (check the packet)

150ml light vegetable oil

200g silken tofu

200g unrefined brown sugar

125g beetroot, finely grated

60g dried prunes, soaked until soft and finely chopped

100g walnuts, roughly chopped

125g unbleached white flour

DO IT

Bring a pan half-full of water to the boil (or just use the kettle), then remove from the heat and cover with a bowl (making sure the bottom of the bowl is out of the water). Put the chocolate and oil into the bowl, stir and let them melt. Once completely melted, set aside and allow to cool to room temperature.

Preheat the oven to 190°C/gas mark 5. Oil a 27 x 17cm baking tray well and line with baking paper.

With a whisk, beat the tofu and sugar together in a bowl, then grab a spatula and stir in the chocolate and add the grated beetroot, prunes and walnuts. Now slowly mix in the flour, folding it in a few times until just combined.

Pour the mixture into the oiled and lined baking tray, and level out with a spatula.

Pop into the oven and bake for 25–30 minutes on the middle shelf.

Leave to cool in the tray, then lift out on to a wire rack and cut into squares. Brownies should be nice and moist in the middle, more so than other cakes, as they'll firm up when outside the oven. The middle of the brownie should have formed a slight crust and the outer edges will be slightly crispy. This is bang on!

Best served warm, with vegan vanilla ice cream and a berry compote.

Chocolate & Maple Ice Cream

FOR 4-6

I have never owned an ice cream maker and can never see myself buying one, so I needed a method for making a decent ice cream without the hardware. Frances, our recipe tester, really helped us out here. Vegan ice cream wildly goes beyond any expectations and you can achieve excellent results with just a couple of stirs and a nice thick dish. This is not a low-fat ice cream, it's a good-fat ice cream. The kind of fat that makes you shine with well-being and which the body loves (and really needs). Decent maple syrup and coconut oil are not inexpensive, but they are well worth the moderate investment.

THE BITS

480ml almond milk

140g pecans, soaked for 2 hours

120ml maple syrup

100ml brown rice syrup

2 teaspoons vanilla extract (or scrape out 1 vanilla pod)

80g cacao powder

3 tablespoons coconut oil

For the topping

3 tablespoons toasted almonds, crushed

a handful of sliced seasonal fruits

DO IT

Place all the ingredients in a blender except the coconut oil and blitz together until very smooth. Warm the coconut oil in a small pan until it just melts, and drizzle it into the blender while the blades are running. Check that the mixture is sweet enough and blend for a couple of minutes until light and smooth.

Sieve the ice cream mix into a thick glass baking dish and cover with clingfilm. Pop it into the freezer. Once it is frozen, take the ice cream out of the freezer and leave it for 20 minutes until it is just starting to soften. Then place it in the large bowl of a food processor and whiz until the mixture becomes smooth and light. Don't whiz for too long, though, otherwise it will turn back to liquid. Put the ice cream back into the freezer immediately and leave for 3 to 4 hours.

This ice cream will be very hard straight from the freezer, so take it out at least 20 minutes before serving.

Serve topped with crushed nuts and/or sliced fruits. Drizzling over some almond cream (see page 320) makes a real sundae of it.

Raw Spiced Apple & Date Pie

MAKES 8–10 BIG SLICES

Each summer, Jane and I embark on a month-long raw food adventure, which we call 'Raw Earth Month'. This pie is completely raw and brilliantly healthy. It is also easy to get together and only takes some intermediate blender skills and a little spreading to create. No ovens or pastry-making required. It has all the glorious flavours of traditional apple pie, just in a different, more wholesome wrapping. There is more nutritional value tucked away in a small slice of this apple pie than in most main course plates. We have also enjoyed this pie with pears instead of apples. Macadamia and pecans make a great crust combination, as do cashews and walnuts, so use whatever is easiest to source.

THE BITS

For the crust
200g macadamia or cashew nuts
150g pecans or walnuts
50g dates
a large pinch of sea salt

For the filling
150g dried apples, roughly chopped
480ml apple juice
375g apples (about 3 or 4)
1 tablespoon lemon juice
8 big fat dates (medjool are ace), soaked until soft

½ teaspoon cinnamon
a large pinch of nutmeg
1 teaspoon vanilla extract
1 tablespoon maple syrup
a small pinch of sea salt

For the topping
90g pecans or walnuts, finely chopped
4 big fat dates, finely chopped
½ teaspoon vanilla extract
a large pinch of ground cinnamon

DO IT

Soak the dried apples in the apple juice for an hour.

To make the crust, pulse all the ingredients in a blender until a rough crumble is formed. You will need to scrape down the sides with a spatula at least a couple of times. The crust is ready when it is sticky between your fingers – the fats will slowly be released as you blend the nuts. Gently press the crust down with your fingers into a shallow pie dish or plate roughly 23cm in diameter, with a loose bottom or springform action. Press down around the edge with a spoon to make it look neat and tidy, then pop into the fridge for 1 hour to firm up.

To make the filling, drain the dried apples, which should now be soft and plump. Core and chop the fresh apples, leaving the peel on, and toss them in the lemon juice to stop them going brown. Put half the fresh apples into a blender with the dates, cinnamon, nutmeg, vanilla extract, maple syrup and salt, and pulse until well combined. Pour in a little of the apple juice from the dried apples if the filling is too thick. Add the rest of the fresh apples and dried apples, then spoon on to the pie crust and smooth out.

To make the topping, mix together the pecans, dates and vanilla in a bowl and spread over the top of the pie to form a nice crust. Sprinkle with the cinnamon.

Cover and place in the fridge for an hour to chill. Carefully slice and serve at room temperature.

Rosé-poached Rhubarb with Strawberries & Toasted Almond Buckwheat Crumble

FOR 4–6

A delicious vegan twist on the summer standard of 'crumble'. Buckwheat crumble is a new kid on the block, but I much prefer it to its old-time predecessor. This dessert is light as a feather and brazenly healthy. Buckwheat's full, nutty flavour is perfect for crumbles. I prefer warming it in a frying pan, where you can keep your eye on it and it's easier to stir. I use rosé wine here, but the recipe works just fine with white or even red wine. The glasses you use should be tall and not too wide, allowing us to ogle the careful layering and precision spooning. Any leftover crumble keeps very well in a sealed container and makes a wonderful granola substitute in the morning.

THE BITS

For the rhubarb

700g rhubarb, cut into 2.5cm cubes

200g unrefined brown sugar

1 star anise

4 green cardamom pods, crushed in a pestle and mortar

300ml rosé wine (veggie)

220g strawberries

For the crumble

2 tablespoons vegetable oil

200g buckwheat

1½ tablespoons buckwheat or wholewheat flour

75g unrefined brown sugar

¼ teaspoon ground cinnamon

3 tablespoons flaked almonds

For the vanilla cream

300g silken tofu

2 big handfuls of cashews, soaked for 2 hours

1–2 tablespoons brown rice syrup (or other sweetener of your choice)

1 teaspoon vanilla extract

For the garnish

sprigs of fresh mint (optional)

DO IT

To make the crumble, heat the oil in a large frying pan on a medium-high heat and add the buckwheat. Cook for 15–20 minutes, stirring regularly – the buckwheat will get nicely toasted. The darker the colour, the deeper the flavour.

Add the rest of the crumble ingredients to the pan and continue to cook for another 15 minutes. The sugar will stick to the flour, which will stick to the buckwheat, which is then stuck to by almonds, and all is toasted and happy. If it's a little dry, add a tad more oil. If it's a little oily, add a smidgen more flour. Try the buckwheat – it should be crisp, caramelized and light. Pour it out on to a big plate and allow to cool.

To make the rosé-poached rhubarb, put the rhubarb into a small pan with 180g of sugar, the star anise, cardamom and rosé wine. Bring to a gentle boil, cover, and simmer for 8–10 minutes, until the rhubarb is soft but not mushy. Check the sweet to tart ratio of the rhubarb; you may need a little more sugar.

Remove the rhubarb with a slotted spoon. Cook the liquid down until a syrup forms (reducing the volume by more than half). Spoon out the cardamom pods and star anise. Allow the syrup to cool and place the rhubarb back in the saucepan.

To make the vanilla cream, blend the tofu in a food processor with the cashews, brown rice syrup and vanilla until smooth and creamy. Taste and adjust the sweetness if needed.

Now for the assembly job. Slice the strawberries thinly. Place some rhubarb chunks in the base of a glass with a decent spoon of rosé rhubarb syrup and cover with some of the vanilla cream. Top with a decent layer of crumble and a scattering of strawberries. I would go for at least two layers if you have enough ingredients.

If it's a warm day, you may like to pop the glasses into the fridge and serve the crumble chilled and topped with fresh mint sprigs.

Double Chocolate Cake with Almond Cream & Raspberries

MAKES 8 BIG SLICES

This is light and chewy, just how I like my chocolate cake. I like to use olive oil, a light style, in my chocolate cakes. I think the bitterness of the cocoa and the acidity of the olives go together well. Fair enough, it is probably the last thing you'd expect in a chocolate cake, but for the record, olives can work in desserts! Use any seasonal berries on this cake. My favourites are raspberries – they just look so striking. Blackberries are also very good. Don't chop the chocolate too small, as it is always lovely to discover a lump of chocolate.

THE BITS

150g unrefined brown sugar

220g unbleached white flour

50g cacao powder

80g very dark vegan chocolate, chopped into small chunks

1 heaped teaspoon baking powder

1 teaspoon sea salt

75ml light olive oil

1 tablespoon apple cider vinegar

250ml water

For the almond cream

80g raw almonds, soaked in water overnight and brown skins peeled

75ml unsweetened almond milk or soya milk

100ml light olive oil

2 teaspoons almond extract

2 tablespoons brown rice syrup (or other sweetener of your choice)

For the topping

2 handfuls of fresh raspberries (or other berries)

2 tablespoons crushed pistachio nuts

DO IT

Preheat the oven to 180°C/gas mark 4. Place the sugar, flour, cacao powder, chocolate, baking powder and salt in a mixing bowl and mix together with a wooden spoon. Add the olive oil, vinegar and water gradually, and continue to slowly whisk until a batter has formed – don't overwork it.

Pour the mixture into an oiled and lined cake tin (I use a round tin, 24cm wide and 9cm deep, with a loose bottom or a springform action) and bake for 25–30 minutes. Leave to cool on a wire rack. A skewer thrust into the centre should have very little wet cake clinging to it when retracted.

To make the almond cream, put the skinned almonds into a food processor and blend, scraping down the sides, until nice and smooth. Drizzle in the milk and when this has fully combined to make a very smooth cream, begin to drizzle in the oil and the mix will thicken. Stir in the almond extract and sweetener. Check the flavour, adding more sweetener if required, and the texture – it should be the texture of whipped double cream. Thick enough to spread all over the top of your cake.

When the cake has just about cooled, spread a thick layer of the almond cream over it – if the cream drizzles over the edges, this is fine. It adds to the look. Arrange the berries on top. I like to put them in a circular shape just inside the edge. Why not try a mosaic of mixed berries for a really colourful look? For a final and completely OTT flourish, garnish with crushed pistachio nuts.

Sauces, Dressings, & Toppers & Other Stories

Something creamy, something sweet. Something tangy, all full-on unique! Here we slip into the dark art of sauce-making and realize that it's actually straightforward when you have a few techniques up your green sleeves. I have always been amazed at the secrecy surrounding sauce-making – what's the big deal? The wonderful asset of vegan sauces is no messing around with large quantities of butter or white flour to make a simple sauce; as usual, we stay close to the trusty food processor and tofu or nuts, to fantastic effect.

Having a decent high-powered food processor will mean much smoother sauces and purées. If you don't have one, maybe add it to your Christmas list!

Looking at this plethora of condiment-based goodness, if vegan food is not the future of tastiness, I have no idea what is! Here we have the opportunity to accessorize our dishes with the most vibrant colours and flavours around, like a colourful scarf in a hailstorm, that you can eat.

This chapter sees us spooning, dolloping and sprinkling our way to shining plates of plant goodness. After all, little embellishments can light up your life.

Mango Barbecue Sauce
MAKES A LARGE BOWLFUL

Sticky, fragrant and unctious, like the finest barbecue sauces. The addition of fresh mango really ups the ante on this one. This sauce will cling lovingly to tofu, seitan or tempeh when stir-fried and is a wonder with barbecued food. This tangy tastebud-tantalizer will just get thicker and stickier the longer it is cooked.

½ tablespoon vegetable oil

1 small onion, finely diced

2 cloves of garlic, peeled and crushed

1cm fresh ginger, grated

½ teaspoon ground coriander

½ teaspoon smoked paprika

100ml vegetable stock

1 star anise

1 large fragrant mango, peeled and chopped into chunks

1½ tablespoons tamari

1½ tablespoons tomato purée

1½ tablespoons light molasses or maple syrup

zest of 1 lime

Put the oil into a small pan on a medium heat and fry the onion for 10–12 minutes, until well caramelized. Add the garlic and ginger, cook for 2 minutes more, then add the coriander, paprika and stock and stir. Now add the star anise, mango, tamari, tomato purée and molasses. Bring to the boil and cover, then lower the heat and cook for 10 minutes, stir, cook for 10 minutes, stir, 10 minutes more, stir. It gets nice and sticky. Taste for sweetness and saltiness – there should be a nice balance of the two.

Allow the sauce to cool slightly and remove the star anise. Place in the small bowl of a food processor (or use a stick blender) and pulse a few times, allowing for some nice chunks of mango. Stir in the lime zest.

Smoky Chipotle & Cauliflower Cheese Sauce
FOR 4

I lived in the highlands of central Mexico for a short while, where the little town market was crammed with piles of chillies, all shades and sizes, and I tried them all! The chipotle, however, stands out. Chipotle is now increasingly popular in the condiment shelves of our shops and adds a truly unmistakable dose of Mexican flair to all it graces. That delicious and unique flavour that you get in Mexican food can normally be attributed to these smoked chilli delights.

This sauce is almost a meal in itself (just toss some steamed greens in its general direction and you're set!). All the best things about cauliflower cheese, condensed down and given a sultry, smoky Mexican makeover. It's thick enough to dip, or can be poured over roasted veggies or used in a gratin. I pop any leftovers in the fridge and spread it on bread and grill it until bubbling and golden. Think pasta sauce too. I like to use potatoes to thicken things up here, but you can use a tablespoon of cornflour for a lighter sauce.

650ml vegetable stock

½ a large cauliflower, cut into small chunks, stems included

1 large potato, peeled and diced

3 cloves of garlic, peeled and crushed

1 onion, finely diced

2 celery stalks, finely diced

2 large dried chipotle chillies or ½ teaspoon smoked paprika

½ teaspoon ground turmeric

½ teaspoon English mustard powder

2 tablespoons nutritional yeast flakes (see page 30)

½ tablespoon lemon juice

sea salt, to taste

1 tablespoon olive oil (or cashew butter for optional richness)

(cont.) ➡

Put the stock into a pan, bring to the boil, and add your cauliflower, potato, garlic, onion, celery, chipotle (or paprika) and turmeric. Cover with a lid and reduce the heat to medium-low. Simmer for 30 minutes, until the potato is very tender.

Pop the contents of the saucepan into a food processor (or use a stick blender) and add the mustard and yeast flakes. Blitz to a thick sauce.

Pour the sauce back into the saucepan, add the lemon juice and salt to taste, and heat until it begins to slowly bubble, stirring occasionally. Allow it to cook and thicken for 10 minutes.

Stir in the oil (or cashew butter) and serve warm.

Macadamia Mustard Sauce
MAKES ONE SMALL BOWLFUL

A decadent creamy sauce with a mustard twang. The key here is to blend the macadamias for a while – this makes them extra creamy and smooth. Ideal with the roast aubergine and tomato nut roast (see page 197).

2 teaspoons good rapeseed oil or olive oil

½ a white onion, finely sliced

2 big handfuls of macadamia nuts,
soaked for 4 hours

2½ teaspoons apple cider vinegar or
white wine vinegar

½–1 tablespoon English mustard powder (to taste)

1½ teaspoons brown rice syrup
(or other sweetener of your choice)

½ teaspoon sea salt

125ml vegetable stock or water

Warm the oil on a medium heat. Add the onions and cook for 6–8 minutes, until they are soft and sweet. Place in a food processor with the macadamias, vinegar, mustard, brown rice syrup and salt and blitz until smooth. Now drizzle in the stock, little by little, until

(cont.) ➡

you have a thick sauce. Keep blending until very smooth. Pour the sauce back into the pan and warm through, without boiling. It should have the consistency of double cream.

Sun-dried Tomato
& Marjoram Sauce
MAKES ONE SMALL BOWLFUL

I love marjoram – it abounds where other herbs wilt. In Wales it grows like herbaceous wildfire and works perfectly in sauces with a hint of the Med about them. This sauce is ideal for stirring into pasta and spreading on ciabatta or bruschetta. You can sun-dry your own tomatoes by just leaving them in the oven overnight on the lowest setting, with the door open. This does seem a complete waste of energy, but it works and the more the tomatoes shrivel, the tastier they get. I own a dehydrator (like a big hairdryer), which means I can dry the late summer glut of tomatoes into jars upon jars of sun-dried tomatoes, allowing me to experiment with oil marinades. It takes a little time, but as with most cooking processes you reap the gorgeous benefits at a later date.

50ml extra virgin olive oil

4 cloves of garlic, peeled and crushed

½ teaspoon fennel seeds

40g sunflower seeds, soaked in water overnight

2 ripe tomatoes, roughly chopped

125g sun-dried tomatoes, roughly chopped,
plus any oil

½ a handful of fresh marjoram leaves,
or 1 teaspoon dried marjoram

freshly cracked black pepper and
sea salt, to taste

Warm the oil in a pan on a low heat and add the garlic. Allow to gently poach for a minute, without colouring, then add the fennel and sunflower seeds along with the tomato and sun-dried tomatoes.

(cont.) ➡

Warm through for 2 minutes more, then add the marjoram, pop a lid on the pan and set aside to infuse. Once cooled, place in a blender, add the seasoning and blend until smooth. The sauce should be a silky, shiny affair and can be served hot or cold.

Creamy Cashew Cheese Sauce
FOR 4-6

A wonderfully versatile dairy- and gluten-free substitute for cheese sauce. So, so creamy, and not lacking in glorious richness. Use liberally on the cashew cauliflower cheese (page 277). I'm a mustard freak! I'd probably opt for a full teaspoon in my sauce, but see how you go with half to start with.

120g raw cashews, soaked and drained

2 tablespoons cornflour

1 tablespoon lemon juice

3 tablespoons nutritional yeast flakes
(see page 30)

a large pinch of ground turmeric (or enough
to get a nice shade of 'cheesy' yellow)

a large pinch of sea salt

½ teaspoon English mustard powder
(or to taste)

240ml almond milk or soya milk (unsweetened)

Drain the soaked cashews and pop them into a food processor. Blend until creamy – the texture should resemble smooth peanut butter. You will need to scrape the sides of the food processor down a few times to get things nicely smooth.

Add the cornflour and pulse a few times, then add the rest of the ingredients, drizzling the milk in gradually. Blend until a smooth and thick sauce is formed, adding drizzles of water as needed. This sauce can be enjoyed as it is or can be warmed gently – avoid boiling it.

Super Hero Dressing
FOR 4-6

Great with super hero raw sprouting salad (see page 122). Every one of these ingredients is a super hero in its own right, so whisking them all together can only lead to happy salads of death-defying tastiness.

2.5cm fresh ginger, finely grated

1 clove of garlic, peeled and crushed

4 tablespoons olive oil

½ tablespoon toasted sesame oil

1–2 tablespoons apple cider vinegar, or
white wine vinegar

1 tablespoon white or yellow miso

½ tablespoon brown rice syrup

tamari, to taste

Blend all the ingredients, except the tamari, in a food processor, putting the ginger and garlic in first. Thin out with a splash of water if needed. Add tamari to taste (your miso may be quite salty) and balance the acidity – more vinegar may be needed.

Fey's Parsley & Lemon Dressing
FOR 4-6

Fey is a massive and lovely star. When I sent her some recipes to try out, with her gang of Chicas (mates – Fey lives in Murcia, Spain), she loved them all except for the 'naff' dressing and came up with this one, which is ace with the Red Med tofu tostada with Murcian salad (see page 110).

1 clove of garlic

a large pinch of sea salt

a handful of flat-leaf parsley, chopped

juice of 1 lemon

1 teaspoon Dijon mustard

½ tablespoon brown rice syrup
(or other sweetener of your choice)

150ml extra virgin olive oil

sea salt and black pepper, to taste

(cont.) ➡

Crush the garlic in a mortar with the salt and parsley until it becomes a paste. Add the lemon juice and mustard and stir in, along with the brown rice syrup. Little by little add the olive oil until you get the right consistency and taste, adding salt and pepper as necessary.

Raspberry Dressing
FOR 4–6

It's worth buying raspberry vinegar just for this dressing. It finishes the beetroot, apple and raspberry salad (see page 125) perfectly.

2 tablespoons raspberry vinegar

1–2 tablespoons apple juice concentrate (see page 28)

4 tablespoons olive oil

1 teaspoon sea salt

Simply mix all the ingredients together in a bowl.

Pomegranate Dressing
FOR 4–6

Great with braised cauliflower and puy lentil tabouleh (see page 112). Pomegranate molasses is quite versatile and well worth having handy, especially to jazz up dressings and salads.

4 tablespoons olive oil

2 tablespoons pomegranate molasses or juice of 1 large lemon

zest of ½ a lemon

1 clove of garlic, peeled and well crushed

a small pinch of dried mint

a small pinch of sea salt

½ teaspoon cracked black pepper

Simply whisk all the ingredients together in a bowl.

Homemade Raw Ketchup
MAKES ONE SMALL BOWLFUL

This is much better than bottled ketchup and infinitely more healthy. I feel a tingling sense of smug satisfaction when making substitutes for generic household favourites, especially when they are filled with so many good things (instead of bad). The body loves it, the tastebuds love it and sweet potato chips probably quite like it too. Normal ketchup is a vehicle for sugar, which is why little nippers love it so. This homemade ketchup uses natural sugars and beautiful nuts to add richness. It's the kind of recipe that makes perfect sense all around. Blend well for best results.

1 big handful of cashews or macadamias, soaked for 2 hours or overnight

2 handfuls of sun-dried tomatoes, roughly chopped

2 tablespoons apple cider vinegar or white wine vinegar

1 clove of garlic, peeled and chopped

1 ripe tomato, roughly chopped

1 teaspoon sweet paprika

4 tablespoons olive oil

1–2 teaspoons tamari (to taste)

3 large dates (medjool are best, soaked in water until soft), or 4–5 dried apricots

100ml water (use the soaking water from the dates)

Place all the ingredients apart from the water in a blender. With the machine running, gradually add the water until you have a thick, smooth ketchup. Will keep, refrigerated in a jar, for a week or two.

Tarragon Aioli
MAKES ONE BIG BOWLFUL

Great with Portobello pecan burgers (see page 244). Sunflower seeds are a good replacement for the macadamias in this aioli. Unmistakably French, tarragon brings a taste of sweet, herbaceous anise.

(cont.) ➡

140g raw macadamias,
soaked overnight

60ml water

a handful of fresh tarragon leaves

½ tablespoon olive oil

2 tablespoons lemon juice

2 cloves of garlic, peeled and crushed

a large pinch of sea salt

Put all the ingredients into a food processor and purée until smooth, adding water to thin it out, if needed.

Mushroom, Leek & Thyme Gravy
FOR 4-6

I normally make this at Sunday lunchtime, when the oven is filled with roasting goodies. It goes perfectly with a nut roast (see page 197), and is equally at home poured over roasted or steamed veggies and with some perfectly roasted potatoes on the side. After a Sunday lunch like that, the real deliciousness of a vegan diet becomes clear. Tofu converts are never far behind.

1 tablespoon olive oil

1 leek, finely sliced

2 cloves of garlic, peeled and crushed

14 mushrooms, finely diced
(I normally opt for chestnut, but
your favourite variety will be fine)

300g silken tofu

5 fresh sage leaves, finely sliced,
or ½ teaspoon dried sage

1 large sprig of fresh rosemary,
or 1 teaspoon dried rosemary

leaves from 2 sprigs of fresh thyme,
or ½ teaspoon dried thyme

2 tablespoons nutritional yeast flakes
(see page 30)

2 tablespoons cornflour (or gluten-free
thickener of your choice)

480ml warm vegetable stock

150ml soya milk (unsweetened)

sea salt and black pepper, to taste

(cont.) ➡

Warm the olive oil in a frying pan on a medium heat and add the leek. Cook for 5 minutes, then pop in the garlic and mushrooms. Cook and stir for 5 more minutes, then add the silken tofu and the herbs and cook for 2 minutes more, stirring regularly.

Add the nutritional yeast flakes and sprinkle in the cornflour (making sure it's well broken up, no lumps). Cook for 1–2 minutes, then gradually pour in your stock, stirring quickly as you go, and add enough soya milk to make a thick gravy. Warm through gently for 20 minutes, uncovered. Check that there is no 'floury' taste to the gravy – if there is, cook for 5 minutes more and re-taste.

Pick out the rosemary sprig, then blend the sauce using a stick blender or in a food processor until a good gravy is formed, adding more milk if needed. Check the seasoning and serve with great pride to happy folk.

Homemade Teriyaki Sauce
MAKES ONE SMALL JARFUL

Japanese cooking at home is becoming increasingly popular and is ideal for us vegans, as dairy rarely crops up on the Japanese menu. Teriyaki sauce is my favourite Japanese condiment, the perfect balance of sweet and salty that brings the fresh and clean flavours of sushi to life. This sauce keeps perfectly in the fridge for months. I like mine a little sweet – but give it a quick taste as you may prefer a dash more tamari. If you like a sweet teriyaki sauce, just add 1–2 teaspoons of unrefined brown sugar to the mix. Mirin is readily available nowadays in supermarkets.

10 tablespoons tamari

15 tablespoons mirin

Put the tamari and mirin into a small pan over a medium heat and simmer gently. Remove from the heat when a third of the sauce has evaporated.

Easy Dipping Sauce
MAKES ONE SMALL BOWLFUL

You know this sauce. You've probably dipped thousands of spring rolls and sushi chunks into something like this over the years. A classic dipping sauce – also makes a good Asian-style dressing. Great with raw lumpia (see page 178).

3 tablespoons rice vinegar

2 tablespoons tamari

1 teaspoon toasted sesame oil

1 teaspoon brown rice syrup

1 spring onion, finely sliced at an angle

3 small dried chillies, or ¼ teaspoon chilli flakes (optional)

Simply whisk all the ingredients together in a bowl.

Mint Raita
FOR 4

Soothing raita, an essential condiment when faced with the mind-bending flavours and fiery chilli heat of Indian cuisine. Great with spinach bhaji burgers (see page 252).

450ml soya yoghurt

juice of ½ a lemon

1 big handful of fresh mint leaves, very finely chopped

a large pinch of sea salt and black pepper

Mix all the ingredients together in a bowl and serve at room temperature.

Beetroot Raita
FOR 4

Freakin' pink! Brightens up any feast. Eating food this colour makes you feel alive! Good with Kashmiri turnip and spinach curry (page 219).

(cont.) ➡

450g soya yoghurt (unsweetened)

1 beetroot, peeled and grated

1 teaspoons fennel seeds

½ tablespoon lemon juice

a large pinch of sea salt

Mix all the ingredients in a bowl and serve at room temperature.

Horseradish & Dill Yoghurt
MAKES ONE SMALL BOWLFUL

Horseradish and dill are a fine fit. I like to have a horseradish root in the freezer, ready to grate, 24/7. Lovely with beetroot and cumin fritters (see page 168).

350ml thick unsweetened soya yoghurt

1 tablespoon lemon juice

3 tablespoons finely grated horseradish or 1½ tablespoons horseradish purée

a handful of fresh dill, finely chopped

a pinch of sea salt

freshly ground black pepper, to taste

extra virgin olive oil, for drizzling

Stir all the ingredients together in a small bowl. Season and drizzle with olive oil.

Homemade Mango Chutney
MAKES ONE SMALL JARFUL

Yes, you can buy it but it just ain't the same. Give it a try – it's like making jam only much, much better. The real chutney deal! Great with the spinach bhaji burger (see page 252) or matar daal (see page 238).

500g unripe green mangoes (or mangoes that are as unripe as possible), washed

1 tablespoon vegetable oil

1 large red chilli, finely diced

5cm cinnamon stick

2 teaspoons coriander seeds

(cont.) ➡

8 green cardamom pods, cracked

5 cloves

2 star anise

250ml water

½ teaspoon garam masala

160g unrefined brown sugar

½ teaspoon sea salt

2–3 tablespoons apple cider vinegar
(if the mangoes are sweet)

Cut the mango flesh into 2cm cubes. Heat the oil on a medium heat in a heavy-bottomed saucepan. Add the chilli, cinnamon, coriander seeds, cardamom, cloves and star anise, cook for 30 seconds, then add the mango chunks. Cover with the water and add the garam masala, sugar and salt. Add the vinegar if needed. Bring to the boil and gently cook, uncovered, for 45 minutes to 1 hour, or until nice and thick. Stir regularly to ensure that the chutney doesn't stick – this is especially important towards the end of cooking.

Spoon the chutney into a clean jar straight away. It will keep for several weeks in the refrigerator.

Green Tomato, Ginger &
Orange Chutney
FOR ABOUT 1.5KG (FOUR LARGE JARS)

I first made this chutney one baking hot day in Spain, when oranges and local green tomatoes were abundant in the fruit bowl. It was while eyeing piles of tantalizing tomatoes that this refreshing chutney sprang to mind. Something to complement the sweetness and ripeness of Spain's summer produce, and a receptacle for wonderfully fruity green tomatoes, which is the preferred shade for many of the local varieties like Raf, Kumato, Pata Negra and Mucho Miel. If you can't go green, try red (tomato-wise). This chutney is sweet and tangy, a one-pot wonder to be reckoned with.

(cont.) ➡

2.5kg green tomatoes, deseeded and quartered

2 large oranges (zest of one and both cut into
segments, with no white pith)

1 large onion, finely chopped

4 cloves of garlic, peeled and crushed

50g sultanas

1 tablespoon yellow mustard seeds

1 tablespoon cumin seeds

½ tablespoon coriander seeds
(smaller ones are best)

1 teaspoon ground turmeric

8 cloves

5cm fresh ginger, grated

400ml white wine vinegar

100g unrefined brown sugar

75ml apple juice concentrate
(see page 28), or apple juice

3 red chillies, deseeded and finely sliced

50ml olive oil

Place everything in a large, heavy pan and heat until the sugar is completely dissolved. Bring to the boil, then simmer, stirring regularly, for 1 hour, or until it thickens to a sticky chutney. Remember it will thicken even more as it cools.

Spoon the chutney into clean glass jars and seal well, or use Kilner jars (I find them a lot easier). Store in a cool dark place for a fortnight, ideally, before you tuck into it. Once opened, keep in the fridge, where it will last for weeks.

Red Onion Marmalade
MAKES ONE LARGE JARFUL

A bit of onion marmalade brings things to life. Vastly less sugar here than in most shop-bought varieties. Lovely with a smoked tofu sausage sandwich (see page 254).

1 tablespoon vegetable oil

2 bay leaves

5 large red onions, finely sliced

a large pinch of sea salt

a large pinch of black pepper

(cont.) ➡

½ teaspoon red chilli flakes

2 tablespoons balsamic vinegar

2 teaspoons unrefined brown sugar

Put a heavy-bottomed saucepan on a medium-low heat and add your oil, bay leaves and sliced onions. Fry for 20 minutes, stirring, then season with salt. Drop the heat, pop a lid on and cook for 1 hour, stirring occasionally, until the onions are very soft and caramelized. Take the lid off, turn the heat back up, then add the pepper, chilli, balsamic vinegar and sugar. Stir well and cook until all the vinegar has evaporated. Make sure the onions don't stick to the bottom. They should be very sweet and sticky by now; if not, continue cooking – they will just get sweeter and sweeter! Set aside to cool.

Fig & Apple Compote
MAKES ONE SMALL BOWLFUL

Thick and sticky! Figs are such a treat: fleshy centre, smooth skin, crunchy seeds. Paired with a bit of tart and zest, they are really at home in this compote, which is good with the open-top asparagus and cashew cream pie (see page 194).

8 dried figs, stems trimmed, cut into quarters and soaked for 4 hours

3 green apples, cored, peeled and roughly chopped

2 teaspoons lemon zest

½ teaspoon lemon juice

1 star anise

Put the figs (with 4 tablespoons of their soaking juice) into a small pan and add the rest of the ingredients. Bring to a gentle boil and slowly simmer uncovered for 20–25 minutes, until the apples are soft but still retain their shape. Remove the star anise and cinnamon stick.

Roasted Red Pepper & Black Olive Tapenade
MAKES ONE REASONABLE BOWLFUL

Like hummus and babaganoush, tapenade is part of the bedrock of any great picnic or summer spread, the beating heart of any canapé-based event. Tapenade adds a fruity intensity and saltiness, whether stirred into pasta or spread thinly over a cracker or crudité of your choice. It has the kind of potent flavour that we don't expect from 'just' plants, but I think few things can pack a punch like a nicely piquant tapenade.

90ml extra virgin olive oil

2 red peppers, deseeded and roughly sliced

80g black olives, pitted

½ a handful of fresh oregano or 1 teaspoon dried oregano

2 tablespoons fine capers, well drained and rinsed

½ a handful of fresh parsley, chopped

zest of ½ a lemon

1 large clove of garlic, peeled

50g sun-dried tomatoes

1 tablespoon lemon juice

sea salt, if needed

a large pinch freshly cracked black pepper

In a small frying pan on a high heat, warm ½ a tablespoon of olive oil and add the red peppers. Allow to sizzle, sweeten and soften for 10 minutes, then remove and allow to cool. Reserve any leftover oil.

Put the olives, peppers, oregano, capers, parsley, lemon zest, garlic and sun-dried tomatoes into a food processor and pulse together, gradually drizzling in the lemon juice and the rest of the oil. All should be well combined and shiny to the eye. Check for seasoning and add sea salt, black pepper and lemon juice accordingly.

The tapenade will keep in a sterilized jar in the fridge for weeks, but make sure you bring it to room temperature before using.

Spinach Pistou
MAKES ONE DECENT BOWLFUL

Great with oven-baked squash gnocchi (see page 190). Hazelnuts bring their sweet and mellow flavour to this classic pistou. Try this with nettles and wild garlic if you can (instead of spinach and basil).

100g hazelnuts
100g spinach or watercress leaves
2 big handfuls of fresh basil leaves
3 cloves of garlic, crushed
juice of 1 lemon
zest of ½ a lemon
a large pinch of sea salt
2 large pinches of black pepper
75ml extra virgin olive oil

Place the hazelnuts in a small skillet and warm on a medium heat. Keep them moving for 5–7 minutes – they will become roasted and smell so very sweet! Put them into a food processor and blitz for 30 seconds. The nuts should begin to break down into lumps and chunks, which is what we want. Add the rest of the pistou ingredients (except the oil) and blitz, drizzling the oil in gradually until you get a nice runny texture, like a thick sauce. You will need to scrape the sides of the food processor down a few times. Add more oil if the pistou needs thinning. Check your seasoning and set aside.

Pistachio & Coriander Pesto
MAKES ONE SMALL BOWLFUL

It's a bit of a cheek calling this a pesto without the cheese, but you will hopefully be pleasantly surprised by the non-traditional outcome. It's a meal in itself – spread it on toast! Or stir it into noodles or mashed sweet potato. Lovely with chargrilled chorizo pinchos (see page 260).

(cont.) ➡

3 handfuls of fresh coriander leaves
1 large clove of garlic, peeled and crushed
115g pistachios, soaked for 1 hour and drained
½ teaspoon dried mint
juice of 1 lime
2 teaspoons lime zest
100ml extra virgin olive oil
a handful of sun-dried tomatoes, roughly chopped
a large pinch of sea salt
and black pepper

Put the coriander leaves and garlic into a blender with the pistachios, dried mint and lime juice and zest, and blitz to a purée, drizzling the oil in while the mixture is blending. You should be left with a thick, chunky paste. Stir in the chopped sun-dried tomatoes and season to taste.

Creamy Pesto
MAKES ONE LARGE JARFUL

If you live in a warm part of the UK or you have a greenhouse, growing your own basil is a must. It's a sacred herb, so fragrant, easy to grow from seed and thrives come summertime. Pick a handful of leaves from a decent-size plant and be amazed at how it springs back after a short time. Even the pots that you can buy in supermarkets will last for a while if sensitively raided for leaves and watered on occasion. This pesto is ideally made the day before use and can simply be stirred into pasta and steamed vegetables or even lathered over a jacket spud. When times are tight, I turn to peanuts. They are a decent substitute for pine nuts (use a few more quantity wise) and they don't break the piggy bank. Try it on your pals – they won't be able to tell the difference!

150g silken tofu
2 big handfuls of fresh basil leaves
½ a handful of fresh chives, finely sliced
85g pine nuts (or 100g blanched/skinless peanuts)
2 cloves of garlic, peeled and crushed

(cont.) ➡

2 tablespoons nutritional yeast flakes
(see page 30)

75ml extra virgin olive oil

Pop all your bits into a food processor and blitz until it has a nice chunky pesto texture, adding the oil gradually and regularly scraping down the sides of your processor. Store in a clean jar – it keeps well in the fridge for 5 days.

Pumpkin & Olive Butter
MAKES A LARGE BOWLFUL

You might think vegans miss butter, but you'd be slightly off the mark. Being a vegan pushes you into some pretty creative corners, and that's when things like butter recipes arise. This is not butter, it's better. It's bright orange for a start! It also contains no bad fats and is vastly higher in nutritional value. It will keep well in the fridge or freezer and will firm up when cooled. Enjoy it spread over most edible things. If you prefer your butter unsalted, leave out the olives.

1 small pumpkin, peeled, seeded and diced

2 tablespoons fruity olive oil

1 small onion, finely diced

1 large clove of garlic, crushed

3 tablespoons almond, cashew or
sunflower seed butter

2 tablespoons finely chopped green olives

1 tablespoon white miso

1 teaspoon sea salt

Steam the pumpkin over boiling water for 25–30 minutes, until tender. Drain well and leave uncovered until cool. This will dry it out slightly.

Warm the olive oil in a pan and gently cook the onions for 5 minutes, then add the garlic and continue to cook until nice and soft. Now pop all the bits into a blender and blitz until smooth. Check the seasoning.

Nice served warm or cold on fresh bread, or makes a hearty dip.

Coriander & Pumpkin Seed Topper
MAKES ONE SMALL BOWLFUL

A potent topping for soups and salads, this can also be mixed into stews to add a nice richness. If you are making a soup or stew which hints at a Mediterranean origin, I would highly recommend this. It can even lighten up a curry. Mix liberally with a little oil and you have the makings of an ace dressing. This topper keeps well in the fridge in a sealed container. It's a lively little number – use sparingly.

3 tablespoons coriander seeds, toasted

½ teaspoon sea salt

1 large clove of garlic, peeled and crushed

5 tablespoons pumpkin seeds, toasted

2 tablespoons fruity olive oil

Grind the coriander seeds and salt in a pestle and mortar or a food processor, followed by the garlic. When a paste is formed, add the pumpkin seeds and grind well. Pound until some of the oil is released from the seeds, then gradually add the olive oil and grind until a glistening chunky paste is formed.

Pine Nut Parmesan
MAKES ENOUGH FOR ONE GOOD TOPPING

This is as close to Parmesan as you can get for the vegan palate. Toasted pine nuts are so precious: fatty and oily, when mashed up they morph into something very special. It's a good recipe to make in a large batch – just multiply the recipe a few times – as it keeps well for a couple of days, getting better with age. Sprinkle liberally and joyfully over anything that takes your fancy.

4 tablespoons toasted pine nuts

1 tablespoon toasted sesame seeds

a large pinch of finely grated lemon zest

(cont.) ➡

1 tablespoon nutritional yeast flakes (optional)
(see page 30)
a pinch of sea salt

Combine all the ingredients in a food processor, or use a pestle and mortar, and pulse or bash a few times until fine and crumbly, just like finely grated Parmesan.

Tofu & Herb Feta
FOR 4

Massively versatile and packed full of protein and nutrients, the only thing tofu lacks is lots of flavour. However, this gives us the perfect opportunity to show our creativity in flavouring this wonder bean block. This recipe is so simple, and transforms tofu into something delicious – a staple in the repertoire of most vegans. It makes a basic feta to accompany salads and much more. If you don't fancy any of the herbs, just leave them out.

240g firm tofu block, well drained
1 tablespoon lemon juice
½ teaspoon sea salt
1 clove of garlic, peeled and crushed
2 teaspoons fruity olive oil
1 tablespoon very finely chopped fresh chives
½ tablespoon very finely chopped fresh dill
1 tablespoon very finely chopped fresh parsley

Place a third of the tofu in a blender with all the other ingredients and blitz until smooth. Break the rest of the tofu up into feta-like chunks with your hands, then add them to the smooth mixture with the fresh herbs and stir to combine.

Taste and season, then leave to marinate overnight for the finest flavour.

Suppliers

We get most of our ingredients close to home, but when we buy online, where we choose to spend our money is highly important: who are we giving it to, and how will they use it? I believe it's one of the easiest and most effective methods of bettering the world we live in. Give your hard-earned money to the good ones. Here are a few suppliers we use regularly:

Suma (*www.suma.coop*)

The wholefoods collective for all your vegan/ organic/Fairtrade needs. Run as a cooperative since 1975 (the workers run the show). Get some like-minded people together and order in bulk every few months – it works a treat and is cheaper that way.

Yr Ardd Fadarch *(The Mushroom Garden)* *(www.snowdoniamushrooms.co.uk)*

Based in a little Snowdonia valley, this family business specializes in growing the most fantastic range of fresh, dried (and powdered!) mushrooms. Raised on fresh Snowdonia air and lashings of Welsh rain and mist. Small scale and wonderful 'shrooms.

Halen Mon Salt (*www.halenmon.com*)

Anglesey sea salt, made from the Irish sea water just opposite the Beach House in North Wales. The best salt I've ever tasted, it even has a protected designation of origin (like Champagne and Stilton). Try the vanilla salt with dark chocolate. Yum!

The Tomato Stall (*www.thetomatostall.com*)

For great tomatoes, incredible range, mind-blowing flavours. Try the dried tomatoes – wow!

Sojade (*www.sojade.co.uk*)

Our favourite soya yoghurt available in the shops. Can be found in many health-food shops. Family owned, always organic.

Source Foods (*www.miso.co.uk*)

Welsh miso never tasted so good! An extensive range of organic misos made with passion and a 99.99% recycling policy. Great folk!

Blodyn Aur Rapeseed Oil (buy at *www.gourmetwales.co.uk*)

The best rapeseed oil ever! Half the saturated fat of olive oil and eleven times the omega 3. Made like the finest olive oils by Welsh farmers.

Biona (*www.biona.co.uk*)

Ethically sourced and made organic supplier. A good brand for vegan margarine, which is not so easy to find non-hydrogenated and dairy-free.

Last but not least, the two most important food providers for any aspiring/casual/once in a while/hardcore vegan:

Your local organic farmer/gardener

Befriend your local organic vegetable farmers – there will be some around. Support them and revel in the fruits (and veggies) of their toil. Local organic fruits and vegetables are the cornerstone of any healthy, vibrant, ethical diet. So they are some of the most important people in our society! Even better, become your own local organic vegetable farmer by growing your own gorgeous fruits and veggies. Seasonal veggies will keep body and mind singing throughout the year; as Hippocrates said, 'Let thy food be thy medicine and medicine be thy food.'

Your local health-food shop

Normally a place of sanctuary and nourishment for vegans, the hub of all things ethical/organic/ vegan in your area. A fount of information and support (hopefully!) if you're a new vegan, and full of the ingredients you will find mentioned in this book, from cheap wholefoods to funny-sounding Asian condiments.

I also highly recommend good and regular foraging of hedgerows, coastlines, fields and forests, our free and natural supermarkets.

Index

Page references for photographs are in **bold**

Recipes marked ∗ are gluten-free, or offer a gluten-free alternative.

Big Love!

Most people have a novel in them, but it appears I had a cookbook! The birthing process of this wedge of veganity has been riddled with chaos and many surprises along the way. The opportunity came out of the big blue like a flash of bright green vegetal lightning. The story goes something like this: boozy New Year 2011 at my cousin's house in Durham, her husband Mick (who is directly responsible and a driving force in my baffling career in media circles) films me cooking and generally waffling on about lentils and the like, and next thing I'm in London cooking a blasphemous version of kitchuri for some lovely TV folk (cheers, Jo). Then I'm suddenly making a TV programme called *Meat vs Veg* with meaty Mike Robinson (which was a load of fun), leading to me meeting the big man Rob Allison (a top, top geezer and chef), who mentioned me to the Penguin gang at the Strand and BAM! I'm writing a massive vegan cookbook and fulfilling a lifetime ambition that I didn't even know I had! How cool!

Getting this book together has been a real trip, like the largest and most vibrant homework assignment ever. It has developed into a proper labour of love and I must firstly and foremostly thank and offer my undying gratitude and love for the complete support, patience, inspiration and constant giggles of my partner in life and travels, Miss Jane Legge. Without you, honeypie, I'd still be on that Filipino beach munching coconuts and reading Jung (in fact, let's get back there soon!). Jane built the Beach House, where we now live together with the coolest animal in the world, Buster, the feral Russian Blue (aka Punk Boy, Little Man, Roonie, Raja, Punkawallah, Bustusmaximus, Buzzywoooo, Buzzman, Funky Monkey . . .)

I've been on the road in India while writing this and have dealt with constant lack of internet, electricity or even a kitchen in which to create these recipes that reflect my life and mirror the richness of experience I have found by travelling the road less trodden. The recipes encapsulate my past and my present; old favourites and things I just ate for lunch have all made it into these pages. The process was all new to me and a big shout must go to Jonathan (my literary agent and a lovely bloke) for his sage advice at every juncture; to Lindsey, for embracing the idea of this cookbook and making it happen (while having a baby!); and to Tamsin (editor supreme and one of the Penguin gang), a hugely bright and positive energy who has managed to cajole and tweak *Peace and Parsnips* out of my untamed enthusiasm.

Thanks must go to Paul Gayler and Denis Cotter, who have always inspired me and pushed me forward in creating brighter and tastier food with veggies. To all the vegan cooks around the world: you are a creative, shining force! Thanks also to all the good, the bad and the largely ugly chefs whom I have worked with over the years. If you abused me, thank you; if you showed me how to make a sloppy roux, thank you also; both have made me the hairy hippy cook that I am today.

Two awesome cooks in particular, Frances and Sophie, worked tirelessly to make this food shine. Frances (recipe tester extraordinaire) offered a considered non-vegan perspective on things as well as managing to locate smoked tofu in Wiltshire. Sophie (home economist and